HIGH
CONFLICT
PEOPLE
in legal disputes

HIGH
CONFLICT
PEOPLE
in legal disputes

Bill Eddy, LCSW, ESQ.
Attorney, Mediator and Clinical Social Worker

JANIS
PUBLICATIONS

HIGH CONFLICT PEOPLE in legal disputes

Bill Eddy, LCSW, ESQ.
Attorney, Mediator and Clinical Social Worker

This publication is designed to provide accurate and authoritative information about the subject matters covered. It is sold with the understanding that the publisher is not rendering legal, mental health, or other professional services in this book. If expert assistance, legal services or counseling is needed, the services of a competent professional should be sought.

Names and information identifying private individuals have been changed to preserve anonymity. Many quotations have been modified to protect confidentiality and to demonstrate the principles of the book. Some examples are slight alterations of real cases, while other examples were inspired by real cases but are completely fictional. Quotes from Court cases and news publications are accurate and names are real. Appellate case citations are provided for interested readers who wish to review the original published opinions.

Library and Archives Canada Cataloguing in Publication

Eddy, Bill, 1948-
High conflict people in legal disputes / by Bill Eddy.
Includes bibliographical references.
ISBN 0-9734396-4-5
1. Attorney and client--Psychological aspects. 2. Personality
disorders. 3. Law--Psychological aspects. I. Title.
K126.E34 2005   347'.0504019
C2005-906716-0

Editor: Rod Chapman
Book design: CleanPix Corp.
Printing: Marquis Book Printing Ltd.

 Publisher:
Published by Janis Publications Inc.
www.janispublications.com

JANIS
PUBLICATIONS

Printed in Canada

TABLE OF CONTENTS

A Note to the Reader

This book is designed for professionals working with legal disputes: attorneys, mediators, therapists, judges, ombudspersons, administrators and others. It is written in a style to make it easy to read and also accessible to non-professionals. This book provides readers with an area of knowledge—personality disorders—that is usually kept private among mental health professionals. Knowledge is power. With the information provided in this book, you will have more power to effectively help people, or to hurt them. However, this book does not train you to accurately diagnose personality disorders. You should not use this knowledge to make public judgments of private people, nor use it as a weapon in interpersonal relationships. Instead, before you read this book, I ask that you make a commitment to use this knowledge with compassion and respect.

INTRODUCTION

In 1992, after a dozen years as a mental health professional, I became an attorney. I went to law school to become a full-service mediator: to be able to write binding agreements, inform clients about the law and have the credibility of being an attorney.

While I enjoyed counseling, I was particularly drawn to mediation, a method of resolving interpersonal disputes out of court in a counseling-like process. I had been involved in mediation since I heard about it in 1975, mostly as an unpaid volunteer handling a wide variety of disputes in schools, communities, businesses and families. By the late 1980s, the courts were promoting mediation and I realized that I could make it a paying career if I became an attorney.

The Beeper

When I opened my law and mediation office in 1993, I decided to keep my beeper. I still had a dozen counseling clients and still occasionally received a crisis call. "I'm in the kitchen. I have a knife and I feel like hurting myself," one of my clients with Borderline Personality Disorder[1] cried one Saturday night after beeping me as I waited in line outside a movie theater.

I was familiar with her case. "Put the knife away," I insisted. "Go to your room and write out two cognitive therapy worksheets. Bring them in when we meet next week. Remember what we talked about." And she did.

But such calls were rare from my counseling clients. It was my law clients in various states of crisis who beeped me the most.

"We have to file a new declaration. It's absolutely urgent," said one new client.

"But it's the weekend," I explained. "I can't file anything until Monday."

"It's so important I called you right away, so you could think about it."

---

[1] As will be explained throughout this book, a personality disorder diagnosis does not define a person. However, as with a diabetic or an alcoholic, it is a helpful shorthand for those seeking to understand and treat a specific identifiable problem.

The most common beeper calls were always about visitation crises. "He's twenty minutes late. He always does this to me. I can't wait all day. You have to do something about this!"

Most of my law clients handled these problems just fine on their own, or we addressed them during office hours and took appropriate legal action. But some of my attorney clients were frequently overwhelmed by emotions, suddenly and intensely angered, and constantly demanded that someone else solve their problems for them. After a decade as a psychotherapist, the pattern was familiar. I could handle a few personality disorders in my attorney caseload. But this wasn't why I went to law school. I wondered if many other attorneys had clients with personality disorders—and by the end of 1993 I got rid of my beeper.

"I Want My Day in Court"

When I set up my law and mediation office, I was also approved to be a superior court mediator for civil disputes filed with the court that were headed for trial. I mediated and settled business contract disputes, personal injury lawsuits, probate cases, partnership dissolutions and sexual abuse settlements. Many of the cases were car accidents with minor injuries that were hard to verify. But I particularly remember one case that did not settle.

We were sitting around a conference table with the plaintiff, Mrs. Payne, in a neck brace, as was common in these cases. Also present were her attorney, the defendant car insurance representative, and the attorney for the car insurance company. After a couple of hours there was no agreement. I had met with everyone together, separately with each party, and separately with each attorney, all to no avail. The insurance company said it could not pay for a claim for which it had no corroborating evidence. No bones were broken, no bruises were evident and the car was minimally damaged—plus, the repairs had already been paid for by the company. But Mrs. Payne was adamant about getting paid something for her pain and suffering.

"I don't care if I don't have any evidence to prove that I was injured. I know I was hurt and I still feel the pain. I've been taken advantage of all my life and somebody has to pay for it. I don't care what anybody here says, I'm going to have my day in court."

Mediation is not binding and it is completely confidential. Nothing said in the mediation process could be repeated in court. I am sure she had her trial–her day in court. However, with the burden on her to prove she was injured, it was extremely unlikely that she would obtain a favorable judgement without any supporting evidence. Legal cases are lost all the time for insufficient evidence.

But what struck me most about this particular case was her statement, which seemed all too familiar: "I've been taken advantage of all my life and somebody has to pay for it." She seemed completely stuck and rigid in her thinking, and nothing that was said or done in two hours had any impact on her. I had other car cases that didn't settle, but this one stood out. The reason that Mrs. Payne wanted to go to court seemed to have little to do with the legal issues in her case–but a lot to do with her personality.

"It's All Your Fault"

Only a small portion of my practice has been civil mediations. My primary focus has been family law, about half as a divorce mediator and the other half as a divorce attorney. The vast majority of these divorce cases settled without a court hearing or trial, using the guidelines and laws established over the past thirty years of no-fault divorce law, plus a little give and take.

Of the cases that went to court, I started to see a pattern. It was rare that the parties couldn't agree on the law. More often, they couldn't agree on the facts. One or both parties was misbehaving or misperceiving. Substance abuse, child abuse, domestic violence and lying about money were the primary issues, but in the cases that went to court one or both parties were stuck in the belief that "it's all your fault." Since the vast majority of my cases resolved out of court, it became clear to me that this rigid "it's all your fault" position didn't come from the divorce, but from within. It had more to do with the personalities of these parties.

Writing This Book

From the above experiences and many others like them, I have become convinced that undiagnosed and untreated personality disorders are driving much of today's litigation—and that this trend is rapidly increasing. Yet few people recognize this. Judges express concern about "vexatious litigants" and "frequent filers," attorneys complain about "difficult clients," and mental health professionals talk about "high-conflict families." But few of these legal professionals recognize the significance of personality disorders in these disputes.

During the 1990s I found this lack of shared knowledge frustrating, so I decided to teach others about personality disorders in court cases. In 1998 I wrote an article entitled "How Personality Disorders Drive Family Court Litigation." I sent the article to therapists, attorneys, mediators and judges in San Diego, I put it on my website, it was published in the magazine of the Solano County Bar Association, and a shorter version appeared in early 1999 in *California Lawyer*, the state bar association magazine.

This led to a few seminars for attorneys and mediators, who were very responsive and asked for books on this subject. I could find none. Then I taught a law school course in the summer of 2000 called "Interviewing and Counseling (With an Emphasis on Difficult Personalities)" at the University of San Diego, where as an adjunct faculty member I also taught courses on negotiation and mediation. The students were fascinated to learn about personality disorders and potentially difficult clients. They consistently asked for more case examples, and this feedback encouraged me to expand the course materials into a book. However, my information remained focused on legal professionals. I sent a book proposal to several publishers, but was told that the subject was too narrow to be commercially viable. So I decided to publish it myself.

Events of 2002

In 2002 I discovered a rapidly growing interest from several new directions. I offered a seminar on high-conflict personalities (HCPs) at the Association of Conflict Resolution annual conference in 2002 and delivered it to an overflow audience. I expected attorneys and mental health professionals, but surprisingly the majority of attendees worked for government agencies and educational institutions, with several from other countries.

Also in 2002, the Judicial Council of California asked me to co-present a seminar on parental psychopathology for family court services counselors in southern California. While they were well-trained in issues of substance abuse, child abuse and domestic violence, they were eager for training in personality disorders from clinicians who had been directly involved in mental health diagnosis and treatment.

As I was finishing this book, the subject of HCPs came up in discussions with friends in many different fields. They told me that the practical tools I was offering would be useful to anyone, as HCPs were increasingly showing up in schools, health-care facilities, businesses and various other professions.

Most surprising of all, I began receiving email letters in response to my 1998 website article on personality disorders. Apparently, it has become linked to various sites on the web. I heard from individuals embroiled in court cases with personality disorders from around the country and overseas—including restraining order cases, probate cases, divorces and abuse allegations. They were desperate to understand what was happening to them—why the person with all the signs of a personality disorder prevailed so often in court. They wanted books and referrals to attorneys and mental health professionals who understood these court cases.

Events of 2003-2005

After self-publishing this book in 2003, interest in HCPs has grown dramatically. I received orders from all over the United States, Canada and Europe. While I expected therapists to buy it, I have been pleasantly surprised at the large amount of interest and orders from attorneys, mediators and judges. In September 2004, I gave another seminar at the Association for Conflict Resolution and had nearly 200 attendees. In the first half of 2005 I was invited to provide seminars in six states as well as in Canada and France, without any solicitation on my part. The audiences for these seminars ranged from collaborative law attorneys, therapists and financial advisors to mediators and judges, along with ombudspersons for large corporations and universities.

Finally, to my great satisfaction, I was approached by members of Janis Publications—a new publisher specializing in high-quality conflict resolution books—who wanted me to allow them to publish this book. I feel confident that Janis Publications, whose principals have backgrounds in law, mediation and business, will expand the reach of this needed information to a much larger population of dispute resolution professionals—and eventually to the general public.

Format of This Book

The problem of HCPs has become much more far-reaching than I had ever imagined. As a consequence, while the information in this book is primarily designed for legal professionals—attorneys, therapists, mediators, judges, ombudspersons and other dispute resolvers—it may also be useful for the non-professional who is stuck in a dispute with a HCP, or who cares about someone who fits that description. For that reason, it may seem more conversational than most professionals would expect, and more technical than non-professionals are used to reading.

Many of the case examples in this book are taken from Court of Appeals cases, some come directly from real cases with only names and identifying information changed, and some are inspired by real cases but made up to demonstrate a point.

The book is divided into two parts. The first two chapters explain the basic dynamics of personality disorders—especially the types that often end up in legal disputes. Chapters Three through Six describe in depth the dynamics of the four most common HCPs, using numerous case examples. Chapter Seven focuses on the problem of enablers: how we inadvertently can make things worse if we are not careful, or if we misunderstand these personalities. If everyone were to stop enabling HCPs the number of disputes, and the harm caused by these disputes, would be greatly reduced.

Part II of the book emphasizes what to do. In Chapters Eight through Eleven I have reduced numerous tools and techniques to a basic four-step method that anyone can use—especially under pressure. In each step I include simple skills that you can adapt to your own situation. Finally, Chapter Twelve addresses the need to work together. The more people who have this knowledge, the easier it will be for all of us who deal with problem personalities.

For the sake of practical explanation, I often refer to a person with a HCP as a client, recognizing that most readers of this book are professional advocates and dispute resolvers. As an advocate and dispute resolver, I often advise family members and friends to also consider HCPs as clients, because HCPs are often seeking that type of relationship with those who are close to them. Thinking of the high-conflict person as a client may actually help family members or friends manage the upset emotions, and help keep the relationship from being overwhelmed by the disputes the HCP creates. Similarly, targets of blame can also be advised to think of the HCP as a client. This may help them in managing the relationship.

Abbreviations

ASP	Antisocial Personality
ASPD	Antisocial Personality Disorder
BP	Borderline Personality
BPD	Borderline Personality Disorder
HCP	High-conflict Personality
HP	Histrionic Personality
HPD	Histrionic Personality Disorder
NP	Narcissistic Personality
NPD	Narcissistic Personality Disorder

ACKNOWLEDGMENTS

In writing and publishing this book, I have relied heavily on the critical feedback, insights and experiences of friends and colleagues in numerous professions. Without them, this book would not exist.

First and foremost, I owe several debts of gratitude to my wife, Alice Fichandler, LCSW. She has provided me with unlimited encouragement, a therapist's wisdom, an editor's insights and a tremendous tolerance for my discussions of this topic.

I am indebted to my mentor and colleague, William M. Benjamin, a Certified Family Law Specialist and the most skilled, respected and ethical attorney I have ever known.

I want to thank the attorneys, therapists and judges who participated in our Attorney-Therapist Interface Luncheons at the San Diego County Bar Association over the last several years, coordinated by Betty Jackson, MFT, of the California Association of Marriage and Family Therapists. Many of the ideas in this book were inspired by our discussions about the increasingly difficult mental health issues arising in family court cases. The bench in San Diego is particularly dedicated to addressing these issues, and I especially want to thank those who have participated: Judges Ashworth, Bostwick, Clements, Denton, Lewis, Milliken, Powazek and Stern.

My formative years were as a clinical social worker, and several mental health professionals and close friends have continually educated and sustained me over the years. I am particularly grateful to the following for reading the entire manuscript, making corrections and giving me numerous suggestions for making it more useful to a wide audience: Therese Adair, LCSW; Ray Adair; Georgi DiStefano, LCSW; Doris Mellman, LCSW; Linda Maggio, Ph.D.; Matt Maggio; Joanne Mason, MFT; A.J. Mason; David Bright; Diane Wade and Stephen Sparta, Ph.D.

Since 1984, the National Conflict Resolution Center (formerly the San Diego Mediation Center) has been my primary source of dispute resolution inspiration and collaboration. Two of the people I met there have remained my closest allies in mediation and training: Barbara Filner and Robin Seigle, Esq. Their willingness to read the entire manuscript and give me feedback for this as a training tool has improved it immensely.

Other court-related mediators who have been kindred spirits and always encouraging include: Sharon Peterson, Esq.; Genell Greenberg, MSW, Esq.; Robert Macfarlane, Esq.; Janet Allen, Esq.; Elizabeth Allen, Esq.; Bleema Moss, MFT; Penny Angel-Levy, MFT; Ellen Waldman, Professor of Law; Allen Snyder, Professor of Law; Dennis Sharp, Attorney, Arbitrator and Mediator; Ellen Miller, Director of the San Diego Superior Court pilot project on court mediation; Patti Chavez-Fallon, MSW; Ruth Hatcher, MS; and Russell Gold, Ph.D.

I have a special appreciation for my good friend Dennis Doyle, Ph.D., an assistant superintendent in education. Since 1975, Dennis has assisted me with planning and accountability for accomplishing our career goals through thirty annual "year-in-review" walks and talks. For years he has encouraged my writing, and he helped define my career as a "counselor" at law.

A big thank-you to Tia Wallach for editing and proof-reading my first self-published book; to Debbie Gosch for obtaining copyright permissions, ISBNs, and for sticking with me for twelve years; to Ana Campos for typing forever and for being so positive; and to Sally Roberts, Jennifer Berger, Esq., and Mathoupany Srioudom. In addition to making our shared office an enjoyable place to work, they have been role models of patience in handling high-conflict legal cases, and a constant source of input in refining these ideas. Jenna Buchman gets credit for her enthusiasm and procedures in establishing the day-to-day distribution of this book out of my law and mediation office while it was self-published.

For this edition of the book I am very appreciative of my editor, Rod Chapman, for his patient and friendly guidance (and painstaking attention to detail) in editing this book. Thanks also to Nelson Vigneault for creating an exciting cover design that far exceeds my expectations.

Now that Janis Publications has turned this book into a professional product, I especially want to acknowledge Janis Magnuson for gently moving me forward, and for adding the structure and confidence I lacked to take the next, bigger step. I thank Ray Sobol for helping me focus my energies more productively and helping me believe this can happen on a large scale.

I really appreciate Jennifer Kresge for linking me up with Janis Publications in the first place, as she was one of the first to attend my seminar in 2002 and to see that understanding high-conflict personalities will be important to the future of resolving difficult disputes in a wide range of settings.

Last, my training in problem solving has been most influenced by my parents. My deceased mother, Margaret, was the first social worker I ever knew and the greatest role model of my life. My father Roland, a research scientist, taught me to analyze problems before trying to solve them, and to always consider alternate explanations. My stepmother, Helen, is an inspiration of spiritual and social values and service to others.

PART 1
UNDERSTANDING HIGH-CONFLICT PERSONALITIES

The Problem: Personalities Drive Conflict

"I'd rather be a huge part of the problem than a tiny part of the solution."

Everybody knows someone with a HCP.

- "How can he be so unreasonable? So totally rigid and self-centered?"

- "Why does she keep fighting so much? Can't she see how destructive she is?"

- "Can you believe they're going to court over _____?" (You fill in the issue).

H ow often have you asked yourself these questions about clients, or even about co-workers, friends, neighbors, family members or someone who is taking you to court?

For the past thirty years I have asked myself these questions while handling disputes in communities, schools, businesses, families and the courts. Over the past decade I have observed a dramatic increase in high-conflict legal disputes—an increase driven more by personalities than by legal or financial issues. Perhaps half of all legal cases that go to trial today involve one or more parties with a HCP. In these cases, the conflict is driven more by internal distress than by external events.

After handling more than a thousand legal cases from three professional points of view—as an attorney, mediator and clinical social worker—I have recognized some surprising patterns to the high-conflict cases that are threatening to overwhelm our courts:

- The level and cost of conflict is not based on the issues or on the amount of money involved: personalities drive conflict.

- High-conflict personalities have a life-long, enduring pattern of behavior and blame, typically denying responsibility for their problems and chronically blaming others.

- Many HCPs fit the criteria of Cluster B personality disorders described in the *Diagnostic and Statistical Manual* of the American Psychiatric Association.[2]

- People with HCPs are more likely to escalate their disputes into court, either as plaintiffs bringing suit over misplaced blame for events in their lives, or as defendants due to interpersonal misconduct that harms others and needs to be controlled.

- The disputes of HCPs are generally misunderstood and mishandled, and continue to escalate at a huge cost to our judicial system and our society in terms of time, money and emotional distress for all involved.

PERSONALITY DRIVES CONFLICT

I used to think that disputes were about issues—that bigger issues drove bigger, more difficult conflicts. Wouldn't a million-dollar dispute be harder to resolve than a conflict over $5,000? Wouldn't an argument over a small family inheritance be simpler to settle than the terms of an international business contract?

Not necessarily. Let me give you an example of two hypothetical families going through a very similar dispute—divorce. Let's call them the Smiths and the Greens. They are based on the types of cases commonly seen by family law attorneys and mediators. Suppose both families involve a businessman husband who makes $150,000 a year, a teacher wife who makes $50,000, two children, a family residence, a rental condo and retirement investments worth half a million dollars. The parties themselves can choose whether to go to court or to settle their divorce completely out of court.

The Smiths

Mr. Smith calls a divorce mediator and says that he and his wife want to try to handle the divorce out of court. After meeting together for five or six sessions in the mediator's office, they reach complete agreement on all issues. He moves into the rental condo with plans to buy a house in a year or so, while she stays in the family residence and the children reside primarily with her with flexible visitation rights for Mr. Smith. He agrees to give her child and spousal support in the monthly amount of about $3,000, based on

---

[2] Material presented in this book is based on the DSM-IV-TR version of the Association's manual.

guidelines the court might consider given the differences in their incomes. He gets more of the retirement investments, since she gets to keep the house. They each have an attorney review the Marital Settlement Agreement that the mediator prepared, resulting in some minor edits. Their divorce takes six months and costs them about $4,000. When they come in to sign the final divorce papers, Ms. Smith brings the children to the mediator's office for a visitation exchange when they are done. They get out crayons and draw pictures while their parents sign the papers for their divorce in the other room. When the parents are done signing, there are a few tears and a brief discussion of some visitation arrangements for an upcoming holiday. When they exit the office, the kids show both parents what they drew. They give Mom a kiss goodbye and leave with Dad.

It's not always like that, but it's not uncommon.

The Greens

Mr. Green calls a family law attorney for a consultation. He wants to mediate his divorce and use the attorney for outside consultation. But his wife won't agree. Gloria Green is really angry and wants immediate payment of spousal support far above the guidelines. Within a week she files for divorce and, without his presence or knowledge, obtains a court restraining order against him because of an incident two months prior when he apparently broke the lock to a shed behind the family residence to get some belongings when she wasn't home. She demands that the court require him to have supervised visitation with the children for just two hours a week because he is a "violent" person, since he broke the lock to the shed. She gets a temporary order for supervised visitation.

He says he was surprised to find that she had changed the locks. He says he was never physically abusive with her, and she never claims he was. He says that she was never afraid of him, but that she was frequently angry at him and the children—often over minor events or misunderstandings. He retains the attorney to represent him in court.

Over the next two years there are eight temporary hearings regarding various issues, including the restraining order, the parenting plan and support. Finally, there is a full-day trial. Ms. Green's second attorney (she fired the first one because he wasn't aggressive enough) presents evidence on multiple issues acquired through numerous subpoenas, depositions, professional evaluations of their parenting plan and appraisals. At trial, his attorney argues that several of the issues they have contested for two years have been long-settled under the law and not worth disputing. Ms. Green makes several contradictory statements during cross-examination, and is easily angered over minor issues.

Finally, the court orders the restraining order terminated. Mr. Green gets regular visitation, although his ex-wife still yells at him when he picks up the kids. The retirement investments are split equally. Mr. Green is ordered to pay his ex-wife spousal support in the amount of $3,000 per month (about the same as Ms. Smith received by agreement). However, they have to sell the family residence. The legal fees for both sides of this two-year battle end up at about $80,000—ironically, the entire amount the Greens receive as proceeds from the sale of their house.

What is the biggest difference between these two types of cases? They are both divorces, emotionally stressful experiences with often-difficult communication. The incomes, assets and parenting issues are the same. Yet the Greens' case appears complex, seeming to require the use of many legal procedures—deposition, subpoenas, hearings and a trial. The Smiths' case appears relatively simple and costs significantly less—five per cent of what the Greens spent.

You can't blame the difference on attorneys, as both couples sought the assistance of attorneys at some point. In fact, Ms. Green's first attorney probably would have settled the case early on, with an agreement similar to the eventual outcome and a significant savings in attorney's fees. It was Ms. Green's decision to pursue a highly adversarial approach over two years. Her high-conflict personality determined the direction of the entire case.

HIGH-CONFLICT PERSONALITIES

High-conflict personalities stand out. Their emotions are often exaggerated. Their behavior is repeatedly inappropriate. Minor problems become major disputes. They persist long after others let go. There is an urgency and drama to their daily lives. And they always have someone to blame.

Some HCPs are more difficult than others, but they tend to share a similar preoccupation with blame—a pattern of blame—that is embedded in their personalities. This preoccupation drives them constantly into one dispute after another—and enables them to avoid ever looking at themselves or changing their own behavior. The best way to explain this pattern is with an extreme example.

The Brodericks

This high-conflict case escalated over a period of several years in the 1980s.

Dan Broderick had obtained a medical degree along with a law degree and built a practice as a highly paid medical malpractice attorney. He and Elisabeth (Betty) Broderick had four children and a wealthy lifestyle in the La Jolla community of San Diego.

When Betty found out that Dan was having an affair with his legal assistant, Linda, she became angry, a common response. However, she handled that anger in a manner that drew national attention. The following story was compiled from news reports in the *New York Times*, *People Magazine* and the *San Diego Union-Tribune*.

After finding out about his affair, Betty burned Dan's custom-made clothing in the backyard. She broke windows, spray-painted inside the house and wrecked his bedroom. She spread cream pie all over his fancy sweaters. When he moved into his own home after the divorce, she drove her car into his front door. When the divorce became final in August 1986, he received custody of their four children. Betty claimed that the system was stacked against her because Dan was so well connected as an attorney. She complained that he harassed her with legal paperwork. She complained that the financial settlement was inappropriately low. Her anger remained strong even years after the divorce, despite being encouraged by those around her to get on with her life. One of her young sons told her that two years was long enough for her to be mad at their father.

You would think she was doing well after the divorce. She had a car, a home in La Jolla with an ocean view, and she was getting $16,000 per month in spousal support. But apparently she bought a pistol in 1989 and even cleaned it in front of her sons, who were ten and thirteen at the time. She reportedly told them that she was going to use it to kill their father. It was around this time that Dan and Linda were preparing to get married.

After his wedding, Dan finally decided to let Betty have custody of their two sons in the hope that it would bring some peace. However, during her first weekend with the boys, she re-examined the legal papers and came to believe that there were loopholes that would allow Dan to prevent her from having custody.

On November 5, 1989, Betty woke up early, claiming she felt she could not go on. She went to Dan and Linda's house, opened the door with a key she got from one of her children, and confronted them in their bedroom. She says she intended to shoot herself in front of them, but apparently swung the gun around, shooting wildly. She was so agitated, she claimed, that she left the house without even realizing that she had killed them.

Two years later, at the trial, she considered herself the victim. Linda should not have allowed herself to get involved with a married man, she complained. And Dan shouldn't have bullied her with a flood of legal papers. She had no remorse and said she wasn't to blame for their deaths.

At first, many people felt sympathetic toward Betty. Her first trial ended with a hung jury because two jurors preferred a verdict of manslaughter, believing she did not intend to kill Dan and his new wife. One of those jurors was especially sympathetic to Betty's dramatic and tearful testimony—he said he was surprised that she didn't kill him sooner, after how he treated her.

Apparently the second jury saw the case as much more about Betty and her own behavior. They didn't accept her efforts to shift responsibility onto Dan. They believed that her problems were brought on by herself and that she distorted reality. She blamed her aggressive and destructive behavior on Dan. The second jury didn't buy it. They saw her behavior as aberrant and wondered about her sanity, but they determined that she knew what she was doing and made her own conscious decisions.

I believe that the driving force in Betty's actions was a severe personality disorder that distorted her thinking and led to her extreme behavior. This interpretation is supported by psychiatrists and psychologists on both sides. To paraphrase the news reports, the prosecution and witnesses explained the problem as a person with Borderline Personality Disorder who stalked her victim and premeditated his murder. Psychiatrists and psychologists testified for both sides. A defense psychologist said she got her only identity from her husband. One of the prosecution psychiatrists said that her hostility toward Dan would not have changed at all, even if she got everything she wanted in the divorce, including an increase to $25,000 per month in spousal support, because it was really about her pathological drive to stay connected, not about the money.

It seemed as though Betty got her identity and attention from her husband—at first by being married to him and then by fighting with him. After the fight appeared to be over, she couldn't stand it.

Later, I attended a program on stalking presented by the Deputy District Attorney, Kerry Wells, who successfully prosecuted her. She said Betty still doesn't believe she did anything wrong even years later—a conclusion that fits with the pattern of people with personality disorders.

LOOKING FOR THE PATTERN

These case examples (the Greens and the Brodericks) show that one high-conflict personality can completely drive the direction of a case. You may have noticed that I did not indicate whether the husbands had HCPs. From my experience, sometimes both parties in a dispute have HCPs, but in many cases there is only one HCP—the other party is fairly reasonable, simply trying to avoid the conflict or trying to get it under control. This is similar to the sober spouse who tries to cover up, apologize for, and manage the alcoholic.

Another characteristic of these case examples is how self-sabotaging these personalities can be. Ms. Green lost the family residence to attorney's fees because of her own decision to use a highly adversarial approach. Betty Broderick lost her freedom (she got a thirty-five-year sentence) and lost her $16,000-a-month spousal support. This is one of the most striking characteristics of HCPs—their actions are so self-sabotaging and out of proportion with external events that they seem beyond comprehension.

But there is a logic if the personality patterns can be identified. Personality is a familiar collection of thoughts, feelings and behaviors considered unique to each person, just like our appearance. However, our individual personalities have patterns, and there are many standard types of personalities across cultures and throughout the world. Traditionally, we pay little attention to identifying the personalities we deal with in daily life and we rarely change our methods of interacting to fit them. Instead, we just consider one person nice and another a jerk, and we go about our business.

Researchers and clinicians have studied personalities for over a hundred years, from Freud to Beck to Millon. They have determined that one's personality is mostly formed by age five or six. It is very difficult to change one's personality, although with psychotherapy, medication or other approaches you can change specific behaviors, thoughts and feelings.

The patterns of one's personality are often more easily identified by those around us. Our own patterns may be psychologically blocked from our awareness. However, most of us occasionally reflect on our own behavior and make efforts to change it in order to improve ourselves and our life situations.

The importance of looking for the pattern in understanding personalities— to analyze past behavior and to predict future problems—is demonstrated in the following case example decided by the Supreme Court of California.

Mr. Gossage

Eben Gossage graduated from law school in 1991 and passed the Bar exam on his first try. However, when he applied to the State Bar Court (California) to become a practicing attorney, a difficulty arose with the final requirement of the process: the moral character determination. Apparently he had had legal problems in the past, which he generally attributed to an addiction to drugs and alcohol.

Specifically, in 1975 when he was twenty, he killed his nineteen-year-old sister during an argument. He was convicted of voluntary manslaughter and served two and one-half years in state prison. After he got out, he stopped using drugs and alcohol and apparently turned his life around.

During law school many years later, he performed community service, volunteered with a battered women's support group and joined Amnesty International. After passing the Bar, he assisted nonprofit groups, lobbied about the harmful effects of pollution on city residents, volunteered in local political campaigns, volunteered as a university math tutor, and helped drug-addicted youth prepare for their high school equivalency exams.

In 1996 the Bar Court held a hearing on his moral character, and numerous people testified on Mr. Gossage's behalf. The Bar Court became convinced that he had sufficiently rehabilitated himself, and decided that he was qualified to practice law. However, the Supreme Court of California reviewed the case. They had concerns. The following quotes are from the court's decision in 2000:

> "Gossage presented testimony (to the Bar Court) by twenty lay witnesses, most of whom he met after he was last released from prison and many of whom said they knew him well. They included his girlfriend and other friends, college and law school professors and prominent public officials. The foregoing witnesses described Gossage as an honest person who had expressed remorse for killing his sister and for committing drug-related crimes. No one had seen Gossage under the influence of drugs or alcohol since he was last released from prison in 1983.

> "Five mental health professionals interviewed Gossage shortly before the State Bar Court hearing. These individuals opined that Gossage had successfully overcome any substance abuse problem or **personality disorder** afflicting him in the pre-1983 period, when he killed his sister and committed other serious crimes. None saw any sign that Gossage presently suffered from a diagnosable mental disorder or psychopathological condition. However, the committee's witness, Dr. Feinberg, could not eliminate the possibility that Gossage's failure to promptly resolve the traffic citations during law school was the product of a **residual inability or unwillingness to abide by societal rules**. One of Gossage's witnesses, Dr. Carfagni, similarly suggested that receiving four to six traffic tickets over a three- to five-year period might reveal the presence of an **antisocial attitude or personality**." (Emphasis added.)[3]

---

[3] In Re Eben Gossage, On Admission (2000) 23 Cal. 4th 1080, 1092-3; 99 Cal. Rptr. 2d 130

The Supreme Court of California ultimately denied Gossage's application. The Supreme Court was concerned that on his application for admission to the Bar he mentioned only four of his seventeen criminal convictions, which included forgeries, driving with a suspended license, failure to register his vehicle, several failures to appear in court for automobile violations, and failure to finish paying fines. The Supreme Court noted that many of these offenses occurred during the six-year period that included his law school education, from age thirty-three to thirty-nine, and that he "repeatedly violated state traffic laws and sustained several misdemeanor convictions for mishandling these matters in court." [4]

Perhaps most importantly, the Supreme Court disagreed with the Bar Court's approach:

> "The majority examined each incident during this period, but did so in isolation, finding excuses or mitigation in each case. However, the majority again omitted and misstated relevant facts, and it never confronted the ominous implications of the *pattern* of misconduct committed while Gossage was preparing to be a lawyer..." (Italics are the Supreme Court's.) [5]

Instead, the Supreme Court agreed with the dissenting opinion of the Bar Court panel:

> "The dissent observed that when his more recent misconduct is viewed in light of his prior crimes, there is **no meaningful period in Gossage's adult life when he has not incurred convictions and otherwise shirked legal responsibilities.** The dissent perceived a dangerous tendency in Gossage to excuse his misdeeds, including those committed after he entered law school, when he should have been more sensitive to the rule of law." (Emphasis added.) [6]

---

[4] Gossage at 1088
[5] Gossage at 1094
[6] Gossage at 1094-95

PERSONALITY DISORDERS

Knowledge about personality disorders is central to understanding the preceding cases, and to analyzing the past and future behavior of those individuals. The term personality disorder is a mental health diagnosis contained in the *Diagnostic and Statistical Manual (DSM)* of the American Psychiatric Association. This standard manual is used by mental health professionals, health care plans and insurance companies throughout the world. It continues to be updated, but the basic approach to diagnosing personality disorders has been in place since 1980. The fourth version of the manual (DSM-IV) was published in 1994 and a DSM-IV-TR (Text Revision) was published in 2000. This version added further explanations without changing the diagnostic criteria for personality disorders.

In the DSM-IV-TR, presenting problems are identified under Axis I—a clinical problem or surface issue that needs mental health treatment. Axis II is used for identifying underlying personality disorders or maladaptive personality traits—long-term patterns that impact or explain the causes of the Axis I problem. Without recognizing the underlying Axis II problem, a mental health professional may end up treating numerous Axis I problems without lasting success—sometimes even making matters worse. Alcoholism, drug addiction, depression and anxiety, for example, are Axis I disorders. They are generally obvious, effective treatments exist for them, and successfully addressing the Axis I problem causes a dramatic improvement in the person's life. On the other hand, personality disorders (Axis II) are generally not obvious, treatment is difficult, and successfully addressing the Axis I problems may not make a significant difference in the person's life.

Personality disorders have the following basic characteristics:

- An enduring pattern of behavior
- This pattern exists from early adulthood
- This pattern is rigid and unchanging
- It leads to significant distress or impairment
- It exists well outside the person's cultural norms

This concern about an enduring pattern was at the center of the Supreme Court's opinion in the Gossage case. He had a consistent pattern of legal problems that had existed since his early adulthood. Even though he never killed again and engaged in numerous community efforts, he had an enduring pattern of legal misconduct in many situations—forgery, missed hearings and acquiring traffic tickets. While he may have "successfully overcome any substance abuse problem," the Supreme Court concluded that he had not overcome "any...personality disorder."

Both Betty Broderick and Eben Gossage were identified as possibly having personality disorders. In 2002, a large study by the National Institutes of Health, National Institute on Alcohol Abuse and Alcoholism (NIAAA) determined that approximately 30.8 million Americans (14.8 per cent) have a personality disorder. Mental health professionals commonly believe that another ten per cent may have maladaptive personality traits that do not fully meet the criteria for a personality disorder but cause repeated problems. These disorders and traits are not necessarily obvious on the surface, and a person with such problems can still be successful in some aspects of his or her life, such as employment.

GETTING IT BACKWARD

Those with personality disorders have it backward. When problems arise in their lives, they cannot see their own part in the problem and therefore cannot solve the problem.

Mental health clinicians and researchers have long recognized this situation in the thinking of those with personality disorders. In the *Cognitive Therapy of Personality Disorders* (1990), authors Aaron T. Beck and Arthur Freeman state: "Personality-disordered patients will often see the difficulties they encounter in dealing with other people or tasks as **external to them**, and generally independent of their behavior or input. They often describe being victimized by others or, more globally, by 'the system.' Such patients often have little idea about how they got to be the way they are, **how they contribute to their own problems**, or how to change." (Emphasis added.)

According to Donald G. Dutton, author of *The Abusive Personality: Violence and Control in Intimate Relationships*, not only do they fail to see their contribution to their own problems, in many cases the problem is entirely of their own making—because they are constantly responding to internal emotional crises.

Because they think their internal problems are external problems, the difficulties of those with personality disorders continue and often become quite distressing. So they look for something or someone else to blame. If they can get that system or person to change–or stop doing something–they believe that they will feel better. But this doesn't work either, leaving them feeling even more distressed and helpless. So they escalate this unsuccessful method of problem-solving as far as they can, until someone or something stops them. In our society, it is often the court system.

For example, in a case of domestic violence, a batterer may think that hitting his wife will make her understand the problem, and she will be able to fix it. Except she never can, because it is his problem, not hers. Thus it becomes a repetitive problem, and eventually he is taken to court for a restraining order and domestic violence treatment–and perhaps a divorce.

Another example would be the parent who repeatedly complains to the school system that her child is not getting enough special treatment, in a class where the other parents are quite satisfied. It may not be the school's problem, but her internal perception of a problem. After taking her concerns to the teacher, to the principal and to the district administration, she finally takes the school district to court. She loses, but it cost the district funds that could have been better spent on education.

Betty Broderick blamed her husband when it was her own behavior that was extremely inappropriate and the true cause of her incarceration. Eben Gossage blamed his former self for a drug and alcohol problem. He could not see that his own continuing antisocial behavior is what prevented him from being allowed to practice law.

CONCLUSION

Many people with HCPs appear to have the characteristics of a personality disorder–or of the less-severe maladaptive personality traits. You do not need to diagnose a personality disorder or traits to see a pattern of dysfunctional behavior and to use the approaches in this book. Instead, just recognize that the problem is a personality pattern that is enduring (not situational) and that is unconscious (not open to ordinary feedback). Thus, the behavior of the person in question does not change, and the conflicts escalate.

By recognizing the personality patterns of the four HCPs described in the following chapters, you will be able to develop a working theory for managing and resolving their specific disputes. Otherwise, without understanding the dynamics of high-conflict personalities, you may inadvertently get these cases backward, unnecessarily escalating minor disputes and risking getting sued yourself.

Chapter One Summary
The Problem:
Personalities Drive Conflict

High-Conflict Personalities
Enduring Pattern of Behavior

1. Chronic feelings of internal distress
2. Thinks the cause is external
3. Behaves inappropriately to relieve distress
4. Distress continues unrelieved
5. Receives negative feedback about behavior, which escalates internal distress, but thinks the cause is external so behaves inappropriately, and on and on

This pattern of behavior results in the following:

1. Repeatedly gets into interpersonal conflicts
2. Constantly identifies self as a helpless victim
3. Is unable to reflect on own behavior
4. Does not absorb behavior-change feedback
5. Vehemently denies any inappropriate behavior
6. Denies responsibility for any part in causing conflicts
7. Denies responsibility for resolving conflicts
8. Avoids mental health treatment
9. Seeks others to confirm that behavior was appropriate
10. Focuses intense energy on analyzing and blaming others

As a consequence, the behavior continues unchanged and the conflicts escalate.

The Pattern: An Enduring Pattern of Blame

"So I blame you for everything—whose fault is that?"

Not everyone with a personality disorder becomes a high-conflict personality (HCP). Only those who are also persuasive blamers seem to become HCPs. Persuasive blamers persuade others that their internal problems are external, caused by something else or someone else. Once others are persuaded to get the problem backward, the dispute escalates into a long-term, high-conflict situation, one that few people other than persuasive blamers can tolerate.

From my experience, observations and legal research, the persuasive blamers most often involved in high-conflict disputes come from Cluster B personality disorders. The DSM-IV-TR identifies ten specific personality disorders organized by related characteristics into Clusters A, B and C. Cluster B includes the following four personality disorders:

1. Borderline—marked by extreme mood swings, fears of abandonment, frequent anger and manipulative behavior

2. Narcissistic—involves an extreme preoccupation with the self, a disdain for others, and a preoccupation with being treated as superior

3. Antisocial—has extreme disregard for the rules of society, little empathy, and a willingness to hurt other people for personal gain

4. Histrionic—is emotionally intense, similar to a Borderline, but often with less anger and more drama; sometimes fabricates events

Persons with Cluster B personality disorders appear to have characteristics that draw them into intense, ongoing conflicts on a regular basis—much more than the other clusters. Personality researcher Theodore Millon identifies most of this group as *interpersonally imbalanced* personalities. (He puts Borderlines in another category and includes Dependents in his interpersonally imbalanced group, but I find that Cluster B accurately identifies the four HCPs I most often see in legal disputes.)

The interpersonally imbalanced personalities of the people in this group may explain why they are so frequently involved in prolonged and escalating legal (and other) disputes. The DSM-IV-TR refers to those in this cluster as dramatic, emotional or erratic, which fits their high-intensity interpersonal mannerisms.

In contrast, Cluster A includes Paranoid (suspicious), Schizoid (asocial), and Schizotypal (eccentric) personality disorders. People with these personality types are much less likely to tolerate intense, ongoing conflicts.

Cluster C includes Avoidant (withdrawing), Dependent (submissive) and Obsessive-Compulsive (conforming) personality disorders. Those in Cluster C have generally adopted methods of avoiding conflicts, and do not seek to prolong disputes. However, I have seen Cluster C personalities reluctantly involved in disputes aggressively promoted by Cluster B personalities. They often seem to get into relationships with Cluster Bs as the more passive partner—one who tolerates ongoing abuse because he or she has a withdrawing, submissive or conforming Cluster C personality style.

Non-persuasive blamers from Cluster B do not last long in their disputes. No one believes them, or people just avoid them, or they get constructively re-directed and solve their problems. It's only the persuasive blamers of Cluster B who keep high-conflict disputes going. They are persuasive and, to keep the focus off their own behavior (the major source of the problem), they get others to join in the blaming. Thus, those with persuasive blamer personalities tend to be high-conflict personalities. This is their life-long pattern—blaming others for their own problems. It is part of who they are and they are good at it—good enough to keep the conflict going and going.

Eben Gossage, identified as possibly having Antisocial Personality Disorder, was able to collect at least twenty committed witnesses who testified on his behalf. Did they all know about his ongoing antisocial behavior—his continued violations of the law? Or were they swept up in the emotions of this man who had worked so hard to overcome his past? Whatever the reason, his drive to become an attorney (at the same time as he was continually breaking minor laws) kept a dispute going in the courts for almost a decade and ended up before the Supreme Court of California.

Betty Broderick was identified as possibly having Borderline Personality Disorder. She was able to gather a lot of initial sympathy after she killed Dan Broderick, thanks to her emotional drive. She was a persuasive blamer for a long time. It took two juries to convict her of murder, several years after it occurred. While she is no longer that persuasive, she still believes that Dan and Linda were to blame for their own murders.

Gloria Green spent two years getting the family court judge to seriously consider—and mostly agree with—her numerous allegations against her husband. It was not until the final trial that most of her blaming claims were fully analyzed and determined to be unfounded.

In reality, persuasive blamers' own actions lead to most of their own problems. This denial or "displacement" of responsibility keeps their lives in chaos, as well as the lives of those around them. They can't fix their problems because they can't see where the problems lie. Persuasive blamers have it backward, and they convince others to get it backward as well. The only way to avoid this enduring pattern of blame is to understand how it works.

COGNITIVE DISTORTIONS

Chronic internal distress drives those with personality disorders. But what causes this distress? There are many possibilities:

- Traumatic early life experiences—child abuse, addictions in family, loss of parent

- Biological predisposition—internal distress, depression, anxiety, aggression, etc.

- Learning self-defeating lessons—okay to hit family members; okay to yell at strangers

Regardless of the original source, the past does not control the present or the future. Most people with traumatic life experiences do not become HCPs. The source of their chronic internal distress is based on how they interpret their life experiences. It is current thinking that determines current feelings.

Unconscious and constantly negative interpretations of the past, of themselves or of the future, are what maintain or trigger the chronic internal distress of HCPs. Mental health professionals use the term cognitive distortions to describe these defects in thinking. Cognitive distortions interfere with establishing satisfying adult relationships and succeeding in today's world. Cognitive distortions are also common in depression and anxiety.

While all human beings have cognitive distortions some of the time in some circumstances, the thinking of those with personality disorders is dominated by cognitive distortions. According to David Burns in *Feeling Good: The New Mood Therapy*, some examples of these distortions can be put into simple terms as follows:

- All-or-nothing thinking—seeing things in absolutes, when in reality little is absolute

- Emotional reasoning—assuming facts from feelings
  (I feel stupid, therefore I am)

- Minimizing the positive, maximizing the negative—distorting reality to keep on being stuck

- Overgeneralization—drawing huge conclusions from minor or rare events

- Personalization—taking personally unrelated events or events that are beyond control

Projection is another important distortion for HCPs. Just as a movie projector in a hidden booth throws a large image onto a screen, those with personality disorders project their internal problems onto their environment. Then they claim another person has the problem that they in fact have. Spousal abusers claim the other spouse is being abusive. Liars claim the other is lying. One man who was diagnosed with Narcissistic Personality Disorder claimed it was really his wife who had this disorder—because she liked to shop! He was projecting.

In short, cognitive distortions involve a negative, self-sabotaging view of the world, a view that is not accurate. These distortions may be acquired as a person grows up, based on life experience and on the interpretation of life experience. For the average adult these negative thoughts can pop up automatically, but quickly be dispelled with more realistic information. For persons with personality disorders, the negative comments and experiences of their lives can be so strongly imbedded in their thinking that little new information can get in. Rather than challenging their distortions, they seek confirmation of their distortions. While this might be momentarily reassuring, it keeps the person off track and over the long run triggers more distress.

Cognitive therapy is now one of the most common and successful methods for treating a wide range of problems, from depression to anxiety. Subsequently, these same distortions have been identified in the thinking of those with personality disorders. Many of the treatment approaches for personality disorders emphasize self-help methods for challenging and correcting these distortions. However, because of their cognitive distortions, most people with personality disorders do not seek treatment unless it is for a crippling Axis I disorder.

Betty Broderick in the first chapter appears to have suffered from several distortions. The first is emotional reasoning—she felt abused by Dan's legal challenges, so she believed that she was abused. However, many people feel abused in the court process and don't kill their opponents. In the second distortion, minimizing and maximizing, she maximized the behavior of Dan's new wife, Linda, who dated Dan when he was still a married man. To Betty, this behavior deserved a death sentence, even though affairs occur in many divorces (and marriages) today. On the other hand, she minimized her own behavior. She has no regrets or remorse for killing her husband, the father of her children, as though her actions were completely appropriate. Betty's other distortion was projection. While Betty was feeling abused by Dan's legal paperwork, she was in fact burning his clothes, driving her car into his front door, telling everyone who would listen how terrible he was and screaming obscenities at him in front of the children, all of which could be seen as abusive. Nothing is reported that indicates that his legal paperwork was more than in other contentious divorces. It appears that she was projecting her own behavior onto him.

BLAMING A TARGET

Since those with personality disorders have it backward, they find something or someone else to blame. The selection of a target is driven by the cognitive distortions of the person, and not by ordinary logic. It is a psychological process of diverting attention from one's own unacceptable behavior onto the behavior of another.

The target might be the system, as the Unabomber, Ted Kozinski, believed. He blamed much on technology and targeted institutions, including universities. He mailed bombs that exploded in the hands of the researchers or staff who opened them. He lived in a small cabin in Montana. Some news reports suggested that he had Schizoid Personality Disorder, which involves being very detached from social relationships and showing few emotions. He was caught because his brother recognized Ted's style of distorted thinking in a manifesto published in the newspapers. It appears that Ted totally believed that his attacks on these targets were appropriate and necessary.

The target might be a stranger. In 1994, during her pending divorce, Susan Smith killed her two children in South Carolina. She went on television with a tearfully convincing appeal that a black man had taken her car and her two children. For several days there was a massive manhunt for this stranger, until she broke down after a lie detector test and told the truth: that she herself had drowned them with her car. Some reports suggest that she had Borderline Personality Disorder. While she knowingly made up this story, her reasoning was based on her cognitive distortions: apparently she felt so bad when a lover rejected her because she had children that her emotional reasoning told her to get rid of the children. Her cognitive distortions caused her to blame another person, rather than to admit or deny what she had done. This targeting of another for one's own behavior is extremely common for HCPs.

In most high-conflict cases the target is someone with whom the HCP has, or had, a close relationship—often this is a spouse, former spouse, neighbor, co-worker, business partner or professional, especially one with whom the HCP had an emotionally close relationship, such as a doctor, lawyer, minister or priest. Any of these persons can become targets over some misunderstanding—an unreturned phone call, for example, can trigger rejection feelings, causing the HCP to believe the non-caller "deserves" an attack.

The selected target could also be anyone, because "I've been taken advantage of all my life and somebody has to pay for it."

In divorce cases, the other spouse is an easy target to blame for all of the problems in the marriage—and for the divorce. High-conflict personalities have difficulty tolerating the idea that these problems could be partially their fault. Society assumes that marriages and divorces are partially the responsibility of both parties, except in cases of extremely bad behavior by one spouse. Therefore, HCPs typically blame their former spouses for extremely bad behavior. A wife becomes a totally unfit mother, a slut, a slouch, a controlling witch and so forth. A husband becomes a spousal abuser, a child abuser, a deadbeat Dad or a child molester.

These extremes of behavior fit the extremes of emotions that HCPs feel. Because HCPs feel badly about being rejected, or because they've had some other cognitive distortion, they believe their former spouse is capable of the behavior of a monster. In some cases the HCP knows that the allegations are not true, but feels driven by cognitive distortions to make them anyway. "She was always an unfit mother and the children don't feel safe with her," he says after she spent five years without incident as the primary parent. To feel in control over the divorce, he feels he has to dominate her and the children.

OBTAINING ADVOCATES

With their extreme internal distress caused by cognitive distortions, HCPs are often in a state of emotional crisis. While the average person spends some emotional energy on reflection and self-change, HCPs put all of their emotions into attacking the target—trying to get them to change, to stop doing something, to compensate them for their troubles, or simply to divert attention from their own bad behavior. Not surprisingly, targets don't respond positively to these emotional demands. Therefore, the HCP starts pursuing others to help blame the target. Essentially, they are seeking family, friends, and/or professionals who will help advocate for their cognitive distortions.

High-conflict personalities are not seeking help for problem-solving ideas and general support. When HCPs are in a conflict, there's nothing to discuss or negotiate. Problem-solving ideas are irrelevant. High-conflict personalities seek advocates of blame. Most people try to give them problem-solving ideas, but problem-solving ideas are not what they want. The problem-solving strategy simply makes them feel disbelieved, or partly responsible. Since HCPs cannot tolerate the idea that they might be part of the problem, they will keep searching until they find advocates who agree that they are totally blameless. To be totally blameless, they must get advocates to agree that the target is totally blameworthy. Such advocates can be family members, friends or professionals. Attorneys and mental health professionals are particularly attractive as advocates, because attorneys "have to represent you" and therapists "have to like you." At least, that's how HCPs seem to think—and this appears to be the general public perception.

EMOTIONAL PERSUASION

When potential advocates don't believe the HCP (which is initially very common), the HCP escalates the emotions even higher. This escalation can take the form of a louder voice, a higher pitch, getting more in the listener's face, blaming the listener for not caring, or coming up with ever-more dramatic allegations against the target. The HCP might become more manipulative: seductive, tearful, helpless, offering rewards. Or the HCP might give up and look elsewhere for another advocate. The goal of releasing internal distress gives the HCP enormous energy with which to engage in an ever-escalating, high-conflict dispute.

Customer service representatives have stories about HCPs who call with complaints about the oddest things, then let their emotions escalate. It would be laughable, except that the way the representative handles the call can make the difference between whether or not the company gets sued. Even though the lawsuit may seem frivolous to the company, it may feel deadly serious for the HCP. Even if the HCP loses, the time and money spent on the case can be enormous.

While most potential advocates may feel empathy for the HCP, they are not persuaded by the real facts of the dispute. It will take more persuasive facts to win them over.

For HCPs, the actual facts of the dispute or other person's behavior do not fit their emotions. Since they have it backward, rather than re-examine the facts to see if their emotions are appropriate, they seem to generate emotional facts that fit how they feel. This may be a conscious or unconscious process.

In fact, none of the above is true. But to others, the emotional intensity with which so many "facts" are presented makes these statements appear to be true. It's hard to say whether John knows these statements are false, or whether he really believes them. Nevertheless, when you meet Mary you will already have a negative image of her. How could she be so uncaring?

She's not. In reality, she is the target of his cognitive distortions. A target of blame.

Stephen Ceci and Maggie Bruck, two researchers into false allegations of sexual abuse, have studied "stereotype induction," the process by which young children are given a false impression of a specific man. In their 1999 book, *Jeopardy in the Courtroom*, Ceci and Bruck observed how the children spontaneously generate negative "facts" about that man, facts that grow and grow, but were never true.

If persuaded of the emotional facts against a target, advocates in turn feel a sense of urgency. They feel compelled to do things on behalf of the HCP. The advocate will persuade new advocates, and those advocates will persuade each other. Advocates will start generating new emotional facts themselves, and the case will escalate. Rumors are part of human nature, especially in a conflict.

Of course, the target generally has two choices: give in to the mounting attack—which many victims of domestic violence and small business owners do—or fight back and also obtain advocates. Interestingly, many targets are not HCPs themselves and do not have practical experience in the adversarial approach to problem solving. They are not by nature highly persuasive. They generally are trusting (sometimes overly trusting) of others, believing that others will see the truth without the need for persuasion. The target may decide to involve a dispute resolver—mediator, ombudsman, arbitrator or court—or simply wait and see if the HCP calms down or goes away.

PERSUADING DISPUTE RESOLVERS

Inevitably, many HCP disputes escalate to involve a dispute resolver, often the court. As the cases in the following chapters demonstrate, this can be either because the HCP brings the case to court as a plaintiff, or because the target takes the HCP to court as a defendant.

Some high-conflict disputes are resolved in mediation, if the mediator is able to handle the mediation in a way that satisfies the HCP. This may involve some emotional or financial concessions that are acceptable to the target. However, the HCP may be unwilling to negotiate meaningfully regardless of what the mediator does. If the target is an insurance company or other large organization, it may have a policy of not settling cases with little or no hard evidence. So the case goes to trial.

In court cases, those with personality disorders or traits start out convincingly about their cognitive distortions. They are usually much more aggressive than their targets. They know right away that this is an adversarial process. Some targets are shocked by the emotional intensity, and by the emotional facts generated by their former spouse, neighbor, co-worker or client. They didn't know this adversarial side of the HCP because they were previously in a collaborative relationship. Other targets, victims of previous blaming incidents, know exactly what to expect.

Targets are generally at a disadvantage in court. They trust the court as a fact-finding process and they know the facts are in their favor, so they are confident they will prevail. They start out trying not to escalate the dispute and generally take a problem-solving and settlement-oriented approach. They behave respectfully in court and defer to the all-knowing authorities.

Unfortunately, the authorities aren't all-knowing. They can only base their decisions on the information provided by the parties. The court system—an adversarial system—has many procedures that control how information is presented. In many cases this works well. However, in the case of HCPs, the process may be easily manipulated if the professionals and decision-makers are not aware of cognitive distortions and emotional persuasion.

COGNITIVE DISTORTIONS AND LITIGATION

After learning about HCPs and cognitive distortions, today's high-conflict court cases begin to make sense. High-conflict personalities are in court because they are difficult, not because they have legitimate disputes. I believe that over the past ten years our courts have become a prime playing field for undiagnosed and untreated personality disorders. This is because the adversarial court process has a similar structure to their disorders. The following comparison shows a perfect fit, one that may help explain why people with HCP disorders are showing up so much more often in court.

Characteristics of HCPs	Characteristics of court process
Life-time preoccupation: blaming others	Purpose is deciding who is to blame; who is "guilty"
Avoid taking responsibility	The court will hold someone else responsible
All-or-nothing thinking	Guilty or not guilty are usually the only choices
Always seeking attention and sympathy	One can be the center of attention and sympathy
Aggressively seeks allies in their cause	Can bring numerous advocates to court
Speaks in dramatic, emotional extremes	Can argue or testify in dramatic, emotional extremes
Focuses intensely on others' past behavior	Can hear or give testimony on past behavior of others
Punishes those guilty of "hurting" them	Court is the place to impose maximum punishment
Try to get others to solve their problems	Get the court to solve one's problems
It's okay to lie if they feel desperate	Lying (perjury) is rarely acknowledged or punished

Because the thought structure of HCPs and the adversarial court process are such a perfect fit, HCPs are often effective at making innocent people look guilty, while at the same time with their desperate charm and aggressive drive they often succeed at looking innocent themselves.

For example, how many people believed that O.J. was innocent after he stood up and persuasively stated that he, "could not, would not, and did not" kill Nicole Simpson? How many believed his claims that Nicole abused him?

How many people were initially fooled by the tearful pleas of Susan Smith on national television that her two young children were kidnapped, when she had actually drowned them herself? How many perpetrators of child abuse or domestic violence have convinced the courts that they were innocent and avoided consequences for their actions? And how many people have been wrongly convicted of child abuse or domestic violence by someone who was emotionally persuasive–but wrong?

THE PERSUASIVE PROCESS OF COURT

Diagnosis and treatment are the fundamentals of the health care and mental health professions. An accurate diagnosis of the problem is essential to provide the proper treatment. A good diagnostic process considers several theories of a case, with the burden of making an accurate assessment on the therapist or investigator, who in turn must know all relevant diagnostic criteria and who must test the evidence against each plausible theory. However, in court the process is based on persuasion, not diagnosis. In court, the process of persuasion is centered on proving or disproving just one theory of the case. The judge or jury is the decision-maker, not an investigator. The burden of knowing all the relevant theories and of gathering evidence and presenting it is on the parties and their attorneys. The judge or jury must decide who is most persuasive– usually with many restrictions on the information they are allowed to see and consider.

For decades, social scientists such as Lewicki, Chaiken, Petty and Cacioppo have studied two basic paths to persuasion, called the central route of persuasion and the peripheral route of persuasion. Each route affects our processing of information and judgment in a different manner.

The central route of persuasion is generally a conscious process involving facts, ideas and reasoning. The peripheral route of persuasion generally operates outside of conscious awareness, and depends on a variety of factors:

- Attractiveness of the messenger
- Aggressiveness of the messenger
- Confidence displayed
- Number of arguments made
- Language intensity
- Shorter sentences and simpler messages
- Use of distractions
- Relationship to the listener
- Social role and group identification
- Emotional appeal

When someone tries to persuade you, he or she may start out with facts, but if you don't agree the argument usually shifts to ever-escalating emotions. This is equally true in sales, politics, religion and court. As a law school instructor once said in jest, "If the facts are on your side, pound on the facts. If the facts aren't on your side, pound on the law. If the law's not on your side, pound on the table!"

Those with personality disorders often have a loose grip on the facts, so to persuade people they rely more easily on emotions. Unfortunately, many persuasive blamers have developed highly effective skills at short-term emotional persuasion, including charm, heightened emotions and the ability to persuade others that they are victims even when they are the perpetrators.

In court—especially with interpersonal disputes—factual information is often skimpy and directly in conflict. The primary source of evidence is what each party says about the other: "He said, she said." Important information may be excluded by legal objections, and the decision-makers usually do not see the parties interact—the most useful information about interpersonal disputes, aggressive behavior and personalities.

There are significant rewards for winning in court (getting money, staying out of jail). Consequences for lying are rare. Persuading the court to adopt one's own point of view, no matter how distorted it may be, becomes the primary goal.

In the absence of factual information, or when the facts are in conflict, the peripheral route can dominate decision making. Jury research by Reike, Stutman, Sigal, Braden-MaGuire, Hayden and Mosley shows that parties who appear more confident and attractive are more persuasive. Additional research on jury verdicts shows that attorneys who use an aggressive style are perceived as more effective, although the assertive style was equally successful in obtaining favorable verdicts.

A more emotionally aggressive party (or attorney) may be more successful in capturing the attention and sympathies of the judge and jury. The first side to cry victim may be able to trigger suspicion and anger toward the other side. A more emotionally reasonable or passive party (many a true victim) can appear less persuasive—even though more truthful and flexible in out-of-court problem solving. Ironically, studies by Reike and Stutman show that courts are more accurate when considering written information and documents only—screening out visual and verbal peripheral distractions.

We have all witnessed in the news and in courtroom dramas situations where a persuasive, aggressive person wins in court even though the facts clearly indicate they shouldn't win. Ironically, it appears that the Court of Appeals can often more accurately and objectively understand these cases, while trial courts seem to be more affected by peripheral persuasion. Perhaps this explains why the Bar Court in the Gossage case seemed so forgiving of so many misdeeds, while the Supreme Court seems to have taken a more objective approach and observed the enduring pattern.

PERIPHERAL PERSUASION AND HCPS

It appears that the enduring pattern of blame of HCPs may give them and their advocates a distinct advantage in the adversarial procedures of court—unless decision-makers are aware of the patterns of these personalities. There seems to be at least ten peripheral factors that help persuade people in legal disputes, even when the facts would indicate otherwise.

1. High Bonding—All human beings, including judges and juries, develop bonds with people, and these bonds can influence our view of the facts. High-conflict personalities are especially high bonders because they have to rely so heavily on others to handle their many interpersonal problems. They've spent a lifetime charming, manipulating and pleading to get other people on their side. Ordinary, reasonable people usually don't put much energy into bonding with or persuading the court, because they believe that the truth will simply come out and resolve the dispute. Unfortunately, in a system based on persuasion, this is often not the result. Just as HCPs may have it backward because of their cognitive distortions, they and their advocates often persuade others and the courts to also get it backward. Their internal distortions become external facts.

2. Heightened Emotions—One of the first things people notice about HCPs is their high-intensity emotions. They can be almost intolerable, and many people will agree with them simply to get them to calm down. If you disagree, they will more urgently escalate the situation. Finally, someone has to give in. High-conflict personalities usually outlast ordinary people because to them the problem feels so urgent and absolute. Yet these emotions are highly persuasive. We tend to think that when someone is really upset it is because something upsetting happened to them. "That's awful. Something should be done about that." But with personality disorders, especially the dramatic HCPs, it is more likely to be coming from their constant internal chaos of emotions and less likely to be caused by external events. On the other hand, the emotions of HCPs make them much more interesting than the average person.

3. Sense of Crisis—High-conflict personalities are always experiencing a crisis, often triggered by some internal event or by an exaggerated response to a relatively benign external event. Yet in a crisis we often feel that we cannot take the time to fully evaluate the facts; we must reach a decision with little information. We then make judgments based on presumptions, erring on the side of caution. This means that the HCP can get a lot done in his or her favor in a very short period of time—as long as the HCP can persuade others that there's no time to look beneath the surface. Many family court decisions are decided in this context of crisis and urgency. It used to be that you could get a change of child custody at an emergency ten-minute hearing by claiming a crisis, but now that is far more difficult.

4. Attractiveness—Research confirms that attractive people do better in court (and in politics). That is just a fact of life. This would be irrelevant in a research study, but it plays a huge role in a persuasive process. Dress nicely, smile at the judge, be respectful more than ever before in your life. Be appealing. This may be more important than the facts.

5. Size Matters–The number of boxes of documents, the number of witnesses and the number of arguments and allegations can make a big difference. These things intimidate and impress observers and decision-makers. If you have produced a lot of paper on the subject, judges and juries may automatically assume that you know what you are doing.

6. Aggressiveness–Research shows that the more aggressive attorney often wins. When people ask around for an attorney, they don't usually say "I want a really knowledgeable attorney." They say "I want a really aggressive attorney. I want to intimidate the other side." Most people know that court is really about drama and dominance. They want someone who will dominate the other side and impress the judge or jury with energy and power.

7. Simple Stories–High-conflict personalities tell simple stories of being victimized by others. The stories are easy to understand and have an all-or-nothing, victim-villain quality to them (one of the cognitive distortions above). They are easy to process, so that the decision-maker can focus more attention on what to do about the situation, rather than having to figure out what the situation is. "If it doesn't fit, you must acquit." Isn't that what Johnny Cochran said in the O.J. Simpson case? I still remember that phrase; it was so simple it stuck in my mind.

8. Fast Actors–High-conflict personalities are quick to act, quick to change their minds (or arguments), and fast talkers. They speak quickly–you are caught up in just keeping track of what they are saying, with no time to process what they are saying. It's a neat trick used frequently by advertisers and con artists. The point of view gets in under the radar. You sense something's not right in what they're saying, but you don't have time to stop and figure it out because they are already on to the next subject–still commanding your full attention. In one fascinating case, I discovered that the person was making a totally false statement, then quickly moving onto a reasonable conclusion and passionately arguing for the conclusion to keep attention away from the underlying false fact. "He was hitting the child and we need to stop this from happening in our community–there's just too much abuse to allow him to get away with this behavior. Don't you think you should do something about parents who abuse their children?" Now the focus is on what to do about abuse, rather than determining whether it happened in the first place.

9. Body Language–Tears, dramatic speech patterns, suggestive body movements and non-stop talking are all part of the dramas that often get played out in the confines of court. That's why court stories make such great television. The courtroom is a small stage where facial expressions and hand-wringing can mean the difference between life and death. We are drawn in by these simple physical gestures, because we can identify with them so easily and they are part of interpersonal engagement. We remember the dramatics much longer than the content of a dispute. We remember that he raised his voice and captured our attention, but we don't remember what it was about. A person pacing around the confines of a courtroom can be very contrived, but it can be a pleasant relief to a bored juror who needs stimulation in a long, fact-based trial.

10. Negative Stereotyping Labels–When making an argument, HCPs frequently use negative labeling and catch-phrases: deadbeat Dad, Disneyland Dad, abusive father, unfit mother, welfare Mom, absent parent. These may or may not have anything to do with the facts of a case. But if you hear the negative label often enough, it will seep in under your radar and become part of your view of the person. Politicians and advertisers know this. Researchers Ceci and Bruck have identified how children will adopt a highly negative view of a person and even generate non-existent facts if an adult in authority engages in negative "stereotype induction."

BARRIERS TO FACTUAL PERSUASION

The central route of persuasion would appear to be the proper focus for litigation. Interestingly, the adversarial court process makes many efforts to screen out peripheral persuasion. "Evidentiary objections" are built in to safeguard against the intrusion of inappropriate, often highly emotional information. Objections can be used as a shield against unreasonable, unfair or unreliable information. They can also be used to protect citizens against evidence obtained improperly by an over-reaching government (improper searches, seizures and intrusions into people's homes or cars) even if the evidence is true.

But objections can also interfere with the central route of persuasion. In a clever commentary on objections in the movie *A Civil Action*, actor Robert Duvall teaches law students how to use objections to repeatedly interrupt the decision-maker's train of thought when the facts are going against his client.

From my observations, most high-conflict cases are not resolved until the central route of factual information finally prevails over the peripheral route of emotions and dramatics. Due to often-complex court procedures, however, this usually takes quite a long time. It may not be until the second re-trial (Betty Broderick case), or the civil trial (O.J. Simpson case), or an appeal (Gossage case), that the facts prevail, the overall patterns become clear and justice is somewhat done. Of course, many high-conflict cases simply end when the target gives up and decides to do something else with his or her life. For HCPs, dramatic interpersonal conflict *is* their life, so giving up is much less likely.

High-conflict personalities in court cases present a triple threat: cognitive distortions plus an emphasis on peripheral persuasion plus court limitations on central route persuasion. In combination, these factors often equal high-conflict litigation. In these situations the escalation of emotions and legal activity can involve many others, and a great deal of time and money.

THE COST OF HIGH-CONFLICT DISPUTES

Can we afford the cost of these escalating and unnecessary conflicts at work, at home, with neighbors, in business and in our courts? Since I handle the same types of disputes in court as an attorney and out of court as a mediator, I get to see the comparative costs of resolving these conflicts—and not just in terms of money. The most striking aspect of HCPs is this:

High-conflict personalities involve a large number of people in resolving their disputes, which escalates the financial cost, increases the time involved, and drains the emotional energy of all of those in contact with the dispute.

Family and friends are often drawn into these disputes. Since they care about the person involved, they may spend countless hours listening to the details of the conflict and giving advice and feedback (sometimes the same advice and feedback, over and over again). If the conflict reaches the level of court, they often attend hearings in support of the person, and may provide financial assistance in hopes of ending the conflict. Instead, it often helps escalate it, as the HCP does not have a cost-benefit approach to the problem, but rather is driven by internal distress to confirm his or her cognitive distortions—at any cost.

Co-workers are frequently involved, as the dispute consumes the high-conflict person and spills over into every area of his or her life. Since a large part of our social contacts are at work these days, co-workers are a primary source of information and support. Some of the most common disputes are with those who work around us, simply because we have to contend with each other more than in other areas of our lives. Therefore, the cost of high-conflict disputes almost always impacts the workplace.

Professionals in dispute resolution (lawyers, mediators, accountants, mental health evaluators, judges) frequently become involved, because HCPs have such difficulty resolving their own disputes. The courts are also turning to experts to evaluate high-conflict cases, in the hope that an expert's recommendation will satisfy the parties or give a deeper explanation of the facts of the case. Unfortunately, if the expert's recommendations put any responsibility on the HCP, the recommendations may be rejected by the HCP and the case may escalate while the HCP searches for another, "better" expert.

Using the court system itself does not cost the parties very much—often just a one-time filing fee which may even be waived in low-income cases. But high-conflict cases cost the public a great deal, as more and more of these cases seek the courts to resolve their irresolvable disputes. As taxpayers we pay for judges, court reporters, clerks, bailiffs, buildings, paper storage, security equipment and so forth, at the rate of thousands of dollars per day per courtroom. And most of our court cases today are about interpersonal disputes.

Take, for example, criminal court cases. How many of these are about interpersonal relationships gone bad? Murder, attempted murder, extortion, stalking, property destruction, betrayals in criminal operations, family fights over land and inheritances, conflicts between jealous lovers and spouses, disputes between disgruntled business associates and so forth.

What about civil court cases? Business deals gone bad. Betrayed trust and promises. Competition that got too personal. Lawsuits brought by unhappy clients against professionals, businesses, private institutions and government agencies. Many of these cases may have some legitimate issues, but a significant number are driven by personalities intent on getting revenge, obtaining huge amounts of money or gaining excessive control, not solving a problem. "I'll see you in court!"

Family courts are specifically focused on interpersonal relationships gone bad. Divorce, custody battles, restraining orders, property division—all involve high-intensity issues determined by personalities. While the vast majority of people in these cases are able to move forward after a year or two, from my observations the ones that exist in a state of high conflict for more than two years are almost certain to involve one or more Cluster B personality disorders.

The cost to the future of our society may not be known for years, especially when children's upbringing is dominated by anger and legal conflict. The research shows clearly that children in contentious divorce cases are at higher risk for drug abuse, criminal involvement, teenage pregnancy and premature death.

But I have focused here on the judicial system. The vast majority of conflicts do not get filed with the courts. Businesses, professionals and public and private agencies routinely deal with HCPs who are intent on blaming someone or something. The way these disputes are handled generally determines whether they end up in court. Rumor control is essential, as the cognitive distortions of Cluster B persuasive blamers generally cause them to focus on emotional facts—minor issues, absurd claims and non-existent events that can be quickly addressed with immediate and realistic fact finding.

CONCLUSION

Without understanding HCPs and their enduring pattern of blame, we as a society face ever-increasing costs as these disputes escalate into high conflict. However, with some basic understanding, empathy and the application of certain skills, HCPs can be identified, their energies redirected and their disputes resolved. The next four chapters describe in detail how to identify the characteristics of the four most common HCPs (Cluster B persuasive blamers—Borderline, Narcissistic, Antisocial and Histrionic) with several case examples of each.

Chapter Two Summary
The Pattern:
An Enduring Pattern of Blame

High-conflict personalities have an enduring pattern of blame:

1. Cognitive distortions cause internal distress
2. External target is blamed for the distress
3. Emotional facts are created against target
4. Advocates are sought to help blame target
5. Emotional persuasion wins advocates
6. Advocates persuade new advocates
7. Using peripheral persuasion, advocates persuade dispute resolvers to blame target

In this manner HCPs avoid accountability and do not change their own behavior. Worse, real problems remain unaddressed, and conflicts escalate.

Borderline Personalities: Love You, Hate You

"What sort of flowers say, 'I promise to obey the restraining order'?"

Approximately two per cent of the adult population is reported to have Borderline Personality Disorder (BPD), but they appear much more frequently in mental health settings: about ten per cent of outpatients and twenty per cent of inpatients according to the DSM-IV-TR. In my experience Borderline personalities (BPs) cause most high-conflict cases, whether in litigation, mediation or family counseling. They are pre-occupied with issues of abandonment. They frequently perceive abandonment in ordinary daily life events. To prevent feeling abandoned, they react with efforts to control and manipulate, or they rage against those they believe have abandoned them.

Borderlines have frequent mood swings. They quickly switch back and forth from extremely positive feelings to anger and hate—mostly at the same people they loved or liked. When they have strong enough feelings of being abandoned, they often go to court, either to punish or to feel in control. On the other hand, because of their tendency to act impulsively, they may be brought to court as defendants after they lose control and hurt others—from minor offenses such as shoplifting to major offenses such as murder.

Linda's Mom

I met my first Borderline when I was in graduate school for my master's degree. I was working for an outpatient clinic of a children's hospital as a clinical social work intern learning child and family therapy. One of my many clients was a seven- or eight-year-old girl—I'll call her Linda—who came straight to the clinic after school once a week. She often waited more than an hour for our appointment time, quietly doing her homework and carefully combing her straight blonde hair.

My job was to help Linda manage her symptoms of anxiety, mostly through the use of play therapy. She loved to create scenes with the dolls and toys and drawing paper in my office, like a young movie director in charge of the set. She was very imaginative and particularly enjoyed structured storytelling, when we took turns changing the story with therapeutic lessons. Linda was a lot of fun and very responsible about cleaning up when we were done. I wondered why she was in counseling.

Then I met her mother. Her mother's therapist had warned me that she had BPD. I was meeting with Linda when the receptionist said her Mom had arrived. I went out to the waiting room, but before I got there a short, round woman came barreling down the hallway at me. "The parking here is terrible. Why can't you people have a parking lot of your own?" she said. "Are you Mr. Eddy?"

At least that's how I remember it. I invited Mom into my office. There couldn't have been a bigger contrast in appearance. Linda always wore a neat dress (often the same dress) and black shoes. Mom's white tee shirt was hanging out over her shorts and she was wearing flip-flop sandals. She sat down in the empty chair, swung her left leg over the arm, and commanded attention. She was furious.

"Linda makes me so mad. She was bad last night. She left the kitchen a mess and needs to be punished."

Linda sat straight in her chair and stared at her shoes, silent.

I asked Mom what kind of mess, and she described some spots on the counter when Linda scrubbed it after doing the dishes. Apparently this young girl also scrubbed the kitchen floor each night. It wasn't enough for Mom.

"What kind of punishment have you tried for this?" I asked.

"She doesn't get dinner the next night."

I restrained myself from yelling at Mom. If I had any hope of helping Linda, I needed to find a way to work with this woman.

"Let's ask Linda what kind of punishment would work best with her," I suggested. If I could work with Mom's stated goal, maybe I could find a way for Linda to implement that goal in a healthier way—a family counseling technique I was learning. Linda instantly caught on.

"I think if you make me sit in the corner facing the wall I'll do better next time," Linda said.

"How long would you have to sit there to learn your lesson?" I asked.

"Maybe fifteen minutes."

"It won't work," Mom replied.

"Why don't you try it this once?" I said. "Sometimes when kids get to pick their punishment they learn more from it. Maybe I'm wrong. But if Linda's learned anything from this therapy, I think she'll do her best. Of course, she won't be perfect–heck, no one's perfect. Not even you or I, and we're the adults. If this doesn't work, we'll try something else."

Somehow Mom was satisfied. After that she started using me as her parenting consultant over the phone. She never came in again. Even though her moods swung widely, she started buying into my non-threatening suggestions. When I didn't get upset, and just focused on what to do next, she almost always calmed down.

Linda didn't make her mother mad. She wasn't being bad. Mom was. But Mom blamed her many frustrations in life on Linda. She had a history of telling people that her daughter was terrible.

If I didn't know Linda's personality, I would have believed her mother. Her complaints were intensely emotional and very detailed. And Linda's silence in response could lead one to believe the complaints were true. Mom could have been a persuasive blamer and Linda her target. Fortunately I had excellent supervision at the clinic, and I learned how to work with her disorder.

One of the most important lessons I learned was that Borderlines tend to put people into two extreme categories: extremely wonderful and extremely terrible. As a helping professional I had to be careful not to let Borderlines idealize me and put me up on a pedestal, because I knew that I would surely disappoint them eventually, and be blasted with anger for being terrible.

Mediators, attorneys and even helpful family members and friends must be watchful for this dynamic. If you accept the praise at how wonderful you are for helping out, you will risk getting an equally damning blast of anger when, in their eyes, you fail. And you will fail in their eyes, because their expectations are unrealistic and real life always sets in. However, if you can keep a stable balance you can work with them, as described in the second part of this book.

Maryann's Cup

A good example of a Borderline explosion in a mediation occurred in a divorce I was handling. The details and names have been altered.

Maryann and Sam had a house, a two-year-old daughter and some basic furniture to divide in their divorce. I had already met with them in two previous sessions and there was progress, although it was slow. Both parents obviously loved their daughter. However, Maryann occasionally felt rage at Sam. In fact, she once broke a window in his car. Child Protective Services had also been called out once when a neighbor heard her screaming at her daughter and throwing things around the house. I should have realized how unstable the situation was from those incidents.

During the third session, we were discussing where the child would primarily reside, and who would get the house. It made sense that the child would stay with the house. Sam was generally quiet and unusually calm. He was equally involved in caring for their daughter, as he often worked at home and Maryann worked out of the home part-time. I was asking for their thoughts on what could be done.

"Give me some ideas, some alternatives we could consider," I said. "Any idea will do for now, as we're just brainstorming possibilities. An unrealistic idea could lead to a good idea we hadn't thought of before." I sat ready to make a list of ideas.

Sam had the first idea. "Okay. Well, I think it makes sense for me to keep the house and for our daughter to stay here primarily, so you can get established in your new job," he said quietly.

"How dare you take her from me!" Maryann suddenly screamed. "I hate you." She stood up and tossed her cup of coffee onto Sam—and onto my wall, my table and my papers. Fortunately, by then the coffee was cold.

"That's it!" I jumped up. "We need to separate for a few minutes. Come with me!" I escorted Maryann out of the office into the waiting room. I asked my assistant to get a towel and mop up Sam. He had remained almost frozen from the moment she stood up. I suspected he'd been through this before.

Maryann was still furious at Sam. "How could he even say that?"

I felt like explaining that in mediation any idea is okay, and we don't judge any proposal. But I realized we were no longer in mediation. I terminated mediation on the spot and sent them to separate attorneys.

In retrospect, I might have kept working with them by going back and forth in separate rooms. By now I knew that her personality disorder was too serious and too unpredictable for me. I did not want to place her in an overly stimulating environment. Some people just cannot hear an opinion that conflicts with theirs—it feels too abandoning and threatening. And the fact that she had broken Sam's car window in the past and that Child Protective Services had been involved made it clear to me that much more structure was needed than I could provide.

What would you have done?

Identifying Characteristics

The term Borderline personality evolved among mental health professionals over the past century as a catch-all phrase for patients who do not fit other categories of psychiatric disorders, but who have significant problems in daily life. They have characteristics bordering between neuroses (minor adjustment problems) and psychoses (out of touch with reality, such as delusions). They are commonly identified as difficult and hard to treat. The use of the term Borderline Personality Disorder was formalized in 1980 with the DSM-III.

A study by Marsha Lineham in 1993 indicated that approximately seventy-five per cent of those with BPD are women. However, as Donald Dutton showed in 1998, BPD is also commonly identified in men who commit domestic violence. While both male and female BPs predominantly identify themselves as victims, their own intense anger and impulsive acts frequently get them into civil and criminal cases as defendants for offenses ranging from shoplifting to murder.

Conflicts (from mild to severe) between those with BPD and their advocates are to be expected. However, until you get to know the BP or observe one in a crisis situation, on the surface they often appear normal, even appealing. According to Dutton, their problems most frequently occur in intimate relationships and there may be a split between their frequently angry private behavior and their friendly public image.

Borderline Personality Disorder is characterized by extremes in emotions, in thinking and in interpersonal behavior. Borderline personalities are preoccupied with attachments to others and have a great deal of difficulty with being in close relationships and with ending relationships. One of the first books for the layperson about Borderlines, published in 1989 by Jerold Kreisman and Hal Straus, is appropriately titled *I Hate You–Don't Leave Me.*

Formal Diagnostic Criteria

The DSM-IV-TR identifies nine specific criteria that characterize BDP. An individual must sufficiently meet at least five of these criteria to be diagnosed with BPD. According to the DSM-IV-TR definition, **Borderline Personality Disorder** [7] is: *A pervasive pattern of instability of interpersonal relationships, self-image, and affects, and marked impulsivity beginning by early adulthood and present in a variety of contexts, as indicated by five (or more) of the following:*

1. *frantic efforts to avoid real or imagined abandonment*

2. *a pattern of unstable and intense interpersonal relationships characterized by alternating between extremes of idealization and devaluation*

3. *identity disturbance: markedly and persistently unstable self-image or sense of self*

4. *impulsivity in at least two areas that are potentially self-damaging (e.g., spending, sex, substance abuse, reckless driving, binge eating)*

5. *recurrent suicide behavior, gestures or threats, or self-mutilating behavior*

---

[7] Reprinted with permission from the Diagnostic and Statistical Manual of Mental Disorders, Fourth Edition, Text Revised. Copyright 2000 American Psychiatric Association.

6. *affective instability due to a marked reactivity of mood (e.g., intense episodic dysphoria, irritability or anxiety usually lasting a few hours and only rarely more than a few days)*

7. *chronic feelings of emptiness*

8. *inappropriate, intense anger or difficulty controlling anger (e.g., frequent displays of temper, constant anger, recurrent physical fights)*

9. *transient, stress-related paranoid ideation or severe dissociative symptoms*

Fear of abandonment is often evident from the nature of the dispute. Most of their legal disputes are about relationships gone bad. It is not uncommon for a BP to sue a person with whom she wants to reconcile. While the loss of a relationship with a spouse, friend, co-worker, doctor or other professional may be distressing to most people, BPs may remain absorbed for years in trying to get the person back (even when to everyone else this appears impossible) or to get revenge for abandonment. Even years later, being reminded of prior abandonment can trigger intense emotions almost as if it was yesterday. This fear of abandonment is potentially a major issue for attorneys, therapists, other advocates and possibly mediators with BP clients. Frantic efforts to quell the BP's fear of abandonment can include numerous phone calls, lengthy faxes and sudden appearances at the office. Clear reassurances and limits from the beginning of the relationship can significantly ease this problem.

While the BP may frequently express intense feelings of helplessness and anger at those close to them, it usually does not mean they want to terminate the relationship. Therefore, do not assume your relationship is over just because a BP is angry at you. It is important that you resist the urge to get angry back, otherwise the client may feel abandoned and sabotage the case, refuse to pay for services, threaten to sue or even stalk you. If you can remain unhooked by the client's intensity, listening non-defensively, giving some soothing feedback and focusing on what to do next, the BP's anger will usually subside.

Borderline personalities are known to be among the most difficult patients for mental health professionals, but many of them work hard in therapy and make significant progress over time. They can be engaging and enjoyable to work with when they feel secure in a healthy relationship.

When BPs get into a new relationship they often fantasize about how wonderful it will be. This can include intimate love relationships or professional relationships with doctors, lawyers and others who are perceived as powerful helpers. The BP may comment on how special and competent you are. However when reality sets in—as it always does—the BP can become demanding and enraged, in an effort to make the relationship fit the fantasy again. The praise unpredictably turns to blame and criticism, although this can usually be repaired by sufficient listening and reassurances.

Typically with BPs, just when you thought it was safe to settle back into the relationship, you will receive a new blast of anger at some perceived failure or abandonment. Then, just when you're ready to leave the relationship, the BP can be the most affectionate and nurturing person you've ever known. There are ways for coping with BPs, but there is a wide range of severity of the disorder and relationships with some BPs cannot be sustained. An excellent book for those in a relationship with someone who has the unpredictable mood swings of BPD is *Stop Walking on Eggshells* (Mason & Kreger, 1998).

Professionals and friends should not be deceived by a BP's unusually high regard for you at the start. As one therapist explains about BPD behavior: "What goes up, must come down." The higher you are at the beginning, the lower you will be when the devaluation occurs. Avoid reinforcing the high idealization as much as possible. Most professionals and friends love to hear how they're the greatest, but with Borderlines this is a sign of danger, not reassurance. You are being set up for devaluation. That's what happened to Sam, who was an unusually patient man. This characteristic particularly attracted Maryann, but when he wanted a divorce, she felt abandoned and he became the endless target of her rage. Let the BP client know there will be ups and downs in the case, and openly predict that you will each feel occasionally frustrated and angry—sometimes at each other. But explain that you can talk it through and work it out. With this prediction, the client may be less surprised by her own anger at you later on. You can't prevent this anger, so the most effective approach is to listen to the client and focus the conversation on what the next step should be.

Identity disturbance may become apparent when the client presents an unrealistic impression of herself. She may overly identify herself as a victim to gain sympathy and avoid criticism. This does not mean that she is not a victim, as approximately three-quarters of BPs were victims of physical or sexual abuse during childhood, according to Linehan. In adulthood, BPs often experience themselves as constant victims. Yet many of the adult crises they experience are ordinary events, or over-reactions to the benign actions of others. A fixed identity as a helpless victim can prevent BPs from taking responsibility in their legal disputes, and from improving their lives.

In a legal dispute, the BP may get a sense of identity from being a legal victim, whether or not it is true. In a court there are tasks to do, friendly court personnel to talk to, and clearly defined advocates and adversaries. The legal victim's role is elevated, with a lot of attention and sympathy. At times the legal system even appears to validate the BP's victim identity, after a lifetime of invalidation. A BP has many cognitive distortions and may use fantasy to soothe herself, but having just one other person accept these as true makes them become real to a BP, as Dr. Charles Ford found (1996). For a person with an unstable sense of identity, being cast in the starring role of litigant can be tempting. Betty Broderick in Chapter One appears to have been a prime example of this dynamic.

A parent may identify her child as an inseparable part of herself, referring to "us" when she really means "me." For example, when Mom was too enmeshed with her daughter, Linda, she claimed that she knew exactly what her daughter was thinking and feeling and she believed that these feelings should be identical to her own. Linda sensed her mother's moods and tried to feed back to her mother what she wanted to hear, a common mechanism for coping with a BP family member. Many people try to escape the unregulated emotional intensity of a BP, but children do not have this option. Therefore, they often adopt the opposite approach of compliance with the BP's emotional demands, attempting to soothe and reduce the BP's internal distress.

This dynamic causes a great deal of misunderstanding in family court cases involving allegations of abuse against a parent—abuse that may not have occurred as well as the cover-up of abuse that has occurred. The child's identity becomes lost as she tries to please the emotional demands of the BP, whose chronic internal distress is repeatedly triggered by the litigation process. In a dispute between parents, the child frequently tries to please the most disturbed parent to calm her (or him) down. Since she feels more secure with the less-disturbed parent, the child worries less about saying things that please him or her. Examples of this dynamic are presented later in this chapter.

When I was a therapist, self-harm and suicidal behaviors were a common threat and a common concern with many of my BP clients. However, in my experience as an attorney and mediator, these self-harming behaviors are less frequently present in the BPs who go to court, since the BP litigant is generally focused on blaming another person for the problem, rather than herself or himself.

However, impulsivity in other forms is common for BPs in legal disputes, and it often gets BPs into trouble before they realize what has happened. They may engage in impulsive sexual involvements, domestic violence, child abuse or substance abuse. The most common form of domestic violence (a cyclical, repeated pattern of abuse) is associated with men identified as having BPD. They impulsively strike out at their partner/spouse, then feel remorse, and then build up anger again. Despite their promises—to themselves as well as to their victims—they strike out again because they cannot control their angry emotions and impulses.

Often with a BP it is the extreme emotions that first get your attention. The emotions may be positive (sudden feelings of love) or negative (sudden feelings of hate), but they occur out of proportion with related events. Linehan (1993) says this "emotional dysregulation" has usually existed from childhood. Borderline personalities experience intense sadness, sudden infatuation and overwhelming anger, often in cyclical patterns that sometimes include violence against themselves or against their loved ones. A simple conversation can trigger a flood of emotions, possibly confusing and distressing the listener.

Even though someone with BPD may seem friendly and positive at the start, sooner or later there will be displays of intense emotions, especially anger and helplessness. These emotional displays may catch you by surprise. It is not uncommon for the advocate to also feel intense anger and helplessness—and to be tempted to direct these feelings back at the BP. But by understanding and expecting the outbursts you can help the BP soothe his or her emotions while focusing on the next task.

The most difficult—and most important—thing to remember is that this emotional intensity does not mean you did anything intensely wrong. Avoid getting defensive. It simply confirms that your client is a Borderline. This is not to say that you could do nothing differently in the future. Borderline personalities often help us see where our procedures need to be tightened up. Their insights may be good, it's just that their intensity is out of proportion—and that will probably change soon, when their moods swing again.

Paranoid "ideation" (thoughts) may occasionally occur for BPs. Sometimes a BP is under so much stress that he or she is convinced that another person did something—except that it could not have occurred, or it can never be known. One day Maryann was convinced that there was a prostitute in front of the house when she dropped off her daughter to her husband. She spoke to the neighbor about it, who said no one else was even around when she dropped off the daughter, and no one fitting that description had ever been seen in the area.

It apparently was an example of a Borderline delusion, which can occasionally occur. Maryann later displayed an obsessive concern about her husband's sexuality which cast doubt on her complaints. While no one can be absolutely sure there was no prostitute, Maryann's certainty (despite the denial of a neighbor who had no interest in the case) seems more like a BP's paranoia than the report of a surprised and concerned person who wants to investigate further.

Borderlines often do not understand why their actions get negative responses, although this may be blatantly obvious to everyone else. While they may be intelligent, there are gaps in their perceptions and a lack of common sense. At times they appear to have a childlike naiveté which alternates with an intense defensiveness.

Bordelines often have all-or-nothing thinking, which becomes irritating to those around them as they try to convince others that their thinking is accurate. They think in extremes—the negatives are too negative and the positives are too positive. Since facts contradict their all-or-nothing conclusions, BPs end up surprised and on the defensive. An important part of cognitive therapy with BPs, according to researcher Aaron Beck, is having them double-check their automatic thoughts for extremes so they can respond to these thoughts with more accurate information.

When interacting with BPs, it is important to work with them on these cognitive extremes, rather than to criticize them. One of the most effective treatment approaches is Dialectical Behavioral Therapy developed by Marsha

Linehan (1993). She encourages BPs to recognize their ability to change and to accept themselves as they are. Rather than blaming the BP for faulty thinking, she teaches them to accept that they (and the world) are not perfect, at the same time that they learn new skills. This acceptance of the dialectics (opposites) as co-existing in the real world has had research-confirmed success. The advocate (attorney, mediator, therapist, family member) working with a BP in a legal dispute can validate the person rather than criticizing the behavior, and then focus the person on alternative behaviors or on the next task in the case.

For example: "I can understand that you were just trying to protect your son from perceived dangers during the visitation exchange last weekend (when the BP started screaming at the other parent). I can see that you really care about your children. I can also see that there are some other more effective things you can do in the future. Let's talk about them when we meet tomorrow."

People v. Borrelli

In 2000, a Court of Appeal decision in a stalking case described behavior that might meet some of the criteria for BPD—especially impulsivity and anger. However, this case never discussed the issue of a personality disorder, so one should make no assumptions, but may approach it with the idea of developing a working theory of personality patterns to try to understand Mr. Borrelli's actions. There is no one right answer in developing a working theory of a high-conflict personality pattern, but developing a possible explanation for the person's behavior will help you decide what methods to use in handling that personality.

Annette Borrelli separated from David Borrelli in 1995 after first obtaining a restraining order against him. One day a few months later she was at her parent's house and he showed up unexpectedly early to pick up the children.

> "While Ms. Borrelli was putting the children in the appellant's [Mr. B's] car, he was threatening her and telling her that he was going to kill both her and her parents. Before she could finish strapping the children in, he began backing up his truck as though he was going to run over her feet. He then left with the children.
>
> . . . .
>
> A few hours later, [Mr. Borrelli] arrived unannounced at Ms. Borrelli's Turlock home. [He] was angry because the children had fallen asleep

and he had nowhere to take them. He stomped on her foot, kicked her and screamed obscenities at her. He then took off with the children still in the car.

. . . .

[A few months later he contacted her] and complained that the clothes she had packed for the children were inappropriate. He wanted new clothes. So Ms. Borrelli hurried home and packed some clothes. She had just sat down in her car to retrieve something when she felt it move and realized that appellant had rear-ended her. He hit her car hard enough to cause Ms. Borrelli's neck to go back and 'cause a good feeling in it.'

. . . .

One of the times he threatened to kill her, he said he would blow her head off with a gun. She was very frightened and became a nervous wreck each time she was threatened. She knew [he] owned a couple of firearms and she had seen ammunition around the house during the time they were together. He told her that he kept one of his guns in his car.

To her knowledge, the only other person [he] had ever threatened to kill was himself. Ms. Borrelli had contacted the police more than once when this occurred since [Mr. Borrelli] seemed likely to carry out the threat.

On May 1, 1996, she moved to another location and did not give [him] her new address. From that point on, she and [Mr. Borrelli] exchanged the children at the Turlock Police Department.

On May 7, 1996, [he] showed up at Ms. Borrelli's place of employment. He barged into her office, called her several names and blamed her for his inability to have surgery on his arm. She did not know why he was blaming her. As far as she knew, [he] was working with some type of program that was going to pay the costs of the surgery.

. . . .

[On December 22, 1996, sometime after 10 pm, two men noticed a fire across the street.] They ran over to investigate and found a burning car smashed into the building. They contacted [Mr. Borrelli], who was the only person nearby, and asked if he knew what happened. [He] said he did as it was his car. They asked [Mr. Borrelli] if he had lost control of the car. [He] said no, **he was making a statement** to his girlfriend who worked in the building. He left before the firefighters arrived on the scene." (Emphasis added)[8]

---

[8] People v. Borrelli (2000) 77 Cal. App. 4th 703, 708-710; 91 Cal. Rptr. 2d 851, 854-855

Mr. Borrelli was tried and convicted for arson and stalking. At trial he tried to explain what he did on the night of December 22, 1996.

> "He said he had been drinking and went to Mervyn's to do some Christmas shopping. He got upset when he discovered he did not have enough money to pay for his children's presents. He decided that, since he could not get the money his wife owed him [in the coming divorce settlement], he might as well give her the car too; particularly since it was having a lot of mechanical problems.
>
> So he drove it through the front doors of his wife's workplace. He then got out of the car, which he left running, and sat on the curb twenty-five yards away to wait for the police." [9]

Photographs indicated that he then set the car on fire, although he denied it. Since he was not challenging his arson conviction on appeal, the appeals court did not deal further with that subject. So guess what the appeal was about, since he had been convicted with overwhelming evidence of arson and stalking?

> "Appellant contends section 646.9 [stalking statute] is unconstitutional because it infringes on the free speech rights guaranteed under the First Amendment to the United States Constitution and article I, section 2 of the California Constitution." [10]

Mr. Borrelli tied up the courts—and Ms. Borrelli's life—with the following claims:

> "That the statute kept people from expressing their feelings and ideas, under circumstances where no one will get hurt."
>
> "Appellant next argues that the statute violates his due process rights because it forbids the doing of an act in such vague and overbroad terms that persons of ordinary intellect must speculate as to the meaning of 'safety.' " [11]

The Court of Appeal flatly rejected all of these claims with a brief analysis of constitutional law. From Annette Borrelli's first restraining order to the final judgment in the Court of Appeal, this case was in the courts for five years. By the way, in case you're wondering, the sentence Mr. Borrelli was appealing for his crimes was three years of probation. Apparently, he could not let go until the Court of Appeal ended his case.

---

[9] Borelli at 712; 856
[10] Borelli at 712-713; 857
[11] Borelli at 713, 857; 717, 860

Self-Sabotage in Dispute Resolution

It is surprising how often a BP will engage in behavior that has a sabotaging effect on his or her life—and on a legal case—but not recognize its effect. In a divorce, the BP may "accidentally" sleep with the party she or he is divorcing, or violate the restraining order you worked hard to obtain on her or his behalf. In a criminal case the BP may make a veiled threat of violence, but deny it meant anything. In a civil case, the BP may "forget" to accomplish an important task or appointment. Mr. Borrelli felt that his constitutional rights of expression were violated, yet it was his own violent actions for which he was convicted.

It is hard to predict self-sabotaging behaviors, as the BP usually is not consciously aware of them. Yet in working with BPs it is important to be aware of the potential for self-sabotage. Impulsivity combined with an extreme lack of insight into personal behavior are key reasons that their distress and social impairment are so enduring—thus the diagnosis of Borderline.

Kristin H.

A good example of self-sabotage is a case in which a mother with BPD lost her parental rights because of extreme neglect and endangerment of her young daughter, Kristin.

"Dr. Sazima told the social worker that the mother suffered from **Borderline Personality Disorder**, which was currently acute. She was not manic or psychotic but she did not show good judgment, particularly when she used drugs or alcohol.

The mother contends that these hearsay statements by her parents and her two doctors do not support a finding of mental illness. We disagree. It is well settled that hearsay evidence contained in the social worker's report is admissible. Moreover, there was additional evidence from Dr. Seeman, who evaluated the mother approximately six months after the incident of September 20, 1994. He found her to be a 'very troubled woman' and diagnosed her as having a generalized anxiety disorder and a 'high profile' of **personality disorder**.

Dr. Seeman concluded that without treatment the mother's care of her child 'might be problematic' and that her potential for impulsive and neglectful behavior 'might be a hazard.'

. . . .

Her parents told the social worker that 'the mother needs her medication and can't stay level without it.' Dr. Chamberlain stated that the Zoloft 'definitely helps.'

The risk of harm to Kristin is evident in that the mother had apparently stopped taking her medication shortly before the incident on September 20, 1994, when she succumbed to a severe anxiety attack, ingested illegal drugs and neglected to care for her daughter. **The mother did not feel she needed medication, preferring instead to rely on her "inner strength."** (Emphasis added) [12]

Apparently, all that the mother had to do was stay on her medication. Yet she refused to do this, even though she risked forever losing her rights to parent her child. She sabotaged herself in the simplest way, and then fought hard to avoid the consequences by opposing her own parents and her own doctors up to the California Court of Appeal. Could she avoid losing her child?

"...the mother has attempted suicide on at least three occasions, and the minor reports seeing the mother lying on the floor on several occasions.... As to lying on the floor, she explained that this is where she does her recommended back exercises.

The mother's most recent suicide attempt in June 1994 clearly posed a risk of harm to Kristin, who was in her mother's care when the mother took an overdose of her prescription drug Xanax and had to be rushed to the hospital. The mother downplays this incident, explaining that this was a stressful time, and that she was just trying to get some sleep.

She would not regularly take her medications which could have been helpful in stabilizing her mood swings and she **refused to acknowledge that her problems could be internal rather than external.**" (Emphasis added) [13]

Kristin's mother lost her parental rights. She fit many of the criteria for BPD, including her impulsive nature and mood swings. Unfortunately, she was unable to face these problems and deal with them through the use of medication, which in her case had been very helpful. Although most BPs do not have such severe problems and severe consequences, this inability to see the self-sabotaging nature of her own behavior is typical of those with BPD.

---

[12] In Re Kristin H (1996) 46 Cal. App. 4th 1635, 1651-53, 54 Cal. Rptr. 2d 722, 731
[13] In Re Kristin H at 1653-54

Sexual Abuse Allegations

Some BPs have a preoccupation with sexual issues. They can be at times highly seductive in establishing relationships and at times sexually desperate to hold onto relationships. Many were sexually abused as children. Yet when a relationship ends, the BP may focus her anger on the feeling that she was sexually abused or victimized, even if she wasn't. As Ford has shown, this sometimes leads to false allegations of rape or sexual harassment and the actual filing of charges against an innocent target.

These false cases by some BPs seem to be the result of growing public concern over real sexual abuse (which society denied for a long time), combined with their enduring and unconscious self-perception as victim. They may truly believe that abuse occurred, even if it did not. On the other hand, because of their manipulative nature, some BPs knowingly make false allegations in an effort to get revenge of the most extreme type. After all, their all-or-nothing thinking does not allow for mild allegations. Instead, their angry allegations tend to the extremes of sexual abuse and domestic violence.

One particularly troublesome area in family courts over the past decade has been allegations of child sexual abuse that arise during angry divorce or custody disputes. Just because a person has BPD does not mean that child sexual abuse did not occur. But in some cases there has been a direct connection between BPD and false allegations of child sexual abuse, such as the following two cases.

Patroske v. Patroske

In their divorce trial, Ms. Patroske alleged that Mr. Patroske sexually abused their two-year-old daughter. Regardless, after weighing all the evidence, Mr. Patroske was given custody of the child. She contested this decision on appeal. The appeals court upheld the decision for the following reasons:

> "On the third day of trial, Wife's attorney informed the court of an allegation that Husband had sexually abused the child the preceding weekend. According to the evidence, the first indication of potential abuse occurred when Husband returned the child to Wife's grandmother the night before trial commenced after having exercised visitation privileges.... [The grandmother] testified that the child was acting 'wild'

the next day (the first day of trial) and that she (the child) later pulled her panties down and began playing with her genitals while they were at the courthouse. That night, when the grandmother was getting the child ready for bed, the child allegedly said, 'Daddy saw my jaybird'; 'he kissed me down there'; and that she had slept with her Daddy.

...The case was recessed.... In the intervening time, the child was examined by a doctor with no findings indicative of sexual abuse. An interview of the child was also conducted by a deputy juvenile officer, during which she made statements and gestures that could be interpreted as indicative of sexual abuse....

The Division of Family Services also conducted studies of the home environments of both Husband and Wife.... The recommendation was that Husband be given 'positive consideration as custodian for his daughter'.... The guardian ad litem appointed to represent the interests of the child actively participated in the trial and recommended that custody be awarded to Husband.

The trial court acknowledged the allegations of sexual abuse, stating that, 'from the evidence presented, the Court cannot determine nor find that the allegations are true,' and awarded custody of the child to Husband with generous specific visitation privileges to Wife. It did so after having had the opportunity of seeing the witnesses and hearing all the evidence.

. . . .

There was evidence from which the trial court could have found that Wife had been diagnosed as having major depression and **Borderline Personality Disorder**; that as a result of her abuse of medications she had, in the past, slept when she should have been caring for the child, her ability to concentrate and carry on conversations was impaired, and she would become easily agitated; and that she had used not only marijuana but also cocaine and 'speed' on occasions.

Wife, however, argues that the allegations of sexual abuse were sufficient evidence to exclude Husband as a potential custodian of the child. She cites [another appeals court case] for the proposition that where there was physical manifestation of signs consistent with sexual abuse, custody should not be awarded to a 'suspected' sexual abuser but should be awarded to the non-offending party even though the party's conduct and lifestyle may not be stellar.... [The other case], however, was not a mandate requiring the award of custody to the other parent any time there is an allegation or suspicion of sexual abuse. In that case, the appellate court merely held that it was unable to find an abuse of discretion in the award of the custody to the mother under the circumstances existing there." (Emphasis added) [14]

Mr. Kipp

In another case in another state around the same time, four mental health professionals testified for the father on the issue of alleged child sexual abuse by the father. The appeals court reversed a conviction of child molestation primarily on procedural grounds, but the testimony is particularly interesting and may have played a part in the reversal.

"A psychiatrist testified that she had evaluated the family and concluded there was no indication that abuse had occurred. She further testified that the child's mother suffered from **Borderline Personality Disorder**, had a distorted view of reality and projected those views and her feelings onto the [child] who was suggestible. A clinical psychologist testified that the [child's] mother had **Borderline Personality Disorder**, that she had trouble with reality and that she might project her feelings onto her child. She further testified that preoperational children will believe something is reality if repeated enough times, that in her opinion there was no evidence of abuse in this case and that the [child's] allegations were the product of the [child's] mother's distortion of the facts in order to retain custody of the [child]. An associate professor of psychiatry testified that in his opinion the [child's] mother was **projecting her own sexual problems** with [Mr. Kipp] onto the [child's] relationship with [Mr. Kipp], and that the [child] did not exhibit any of the characteristics of an abused child. He also testified on redirect that it was possible for a mother to lead a child to believe the father had abused the child, even though not true. Finally, a psychiatrist testified that the [child] was suggestible and that the [child], torn between her mother and father, chose to please her mother." (Emphasis added) [15]

[14] Patroske v. Patroske (1994) 888 S.W. 2d 374, 382-83
[15] Kipp v. State of Texas (1994) 876 S.W. 2d 330, 224-35

In the Kipp case a fifth mental health professional testified for the prosecution, stating that he believed there had been sexual abuse. This demonstrates the difficulty of discerning the truth in these cases. As a result, there can be no presumption that such allegations are necessarily false—even if the accusing party has BPD. I have represented mothers and fathers in cases of child sexual abuse allegations and they are extremely difficult to resolve. One has to approach them with an open mind, recognizing that true allegations and false allegations are possible and that we may never know with certainty. Some cases involve actual child sexual abuse, while other cases involve allegations that spring from the internal distortions and fantasies of a BP, rather than from external events.

Conflicts With Professionals

Given that BPs have such difficulty with relationships, it is not surprising that they also have a love-hate relationship with their attorneys, mediators and therapists. They are particularly vocal about how they have been harmed by previous professionals, against whom they may have a lawsuit for malpractice by the time they come to you. Again, this does not mean they have not been wronged, but it should serve as a warning sign to the next practitioner to dot all the I's and cross all the T's.

Kristin H.'s mother is a good example of a Borderline in conflict with her own parents and doctors. It sounds like they all tried to help her, but she was unwilling to acknowledge any problems, and therefore blamed them rather than using them for support.

There will sometimes be pressure on the professional to bend the usual boundaries with BP clients in an effort to soothe and reduce their emotional intensity. Be careful. Remember, they are frequently in some kind of crisis—often triggered by their own actions, but not consciously. Some professionals let themselves be seduced in one way or another by BPs. For example, one attorney spent numerous unpaid hours helping a highly emotional new client find a new apartment after being evicted for various reasons—possibly related to the client's own behavior. This can appear on the surface like a generous act for a needy client, or this can be just the beginning of a high-demand, low-pay relationship for years to come.

Since BPs raise expectations extremely high, when the devaluation comes the professional will be hated even more so—and possibly sued for malpractice. It is best to have firm boundaries in advance, so that emotional pressure will not bend them. When in doubt, consult with another professional to evaluate your own judgment before making unusual commitments.

Causes and Treatment

The causes of BPD are not clear. However, current theories emphasize two components: biology and early childhood environment. Studies have found a greater incidence of Histrionic, Antisocial and Borderline Personality Disorders among the first-degree relatives of BPs. Whether these are caused by genetic links or social factors is unknown at this time. However, some research by Marsha Linehan indicates that those with BPD may have some biological differences from other people, especially in the brain's regulation of emotions.

A chaotic early family life is often cited as a factor in the development of BPD. One major personality researcher, Theodore Millon, suggests that the increase in BPs in society is a result of the increase in chaotic families in recent years. Another author, Charles Ford, points out that a family may have been highly dysfunctional and disruptive to the child's development yet looked normal from the outside. Linehan describes the dynamics of "invalidating environments" as a likely cause, especially common in families with substance abuse and child abuse. The child does not learn to tolerate distress and form realistic expectations. Further, these families tend to reinforce extremes of emotion and behavior, while ignoring the moderate emotions and behaviors necessary for a successful adult life.

Linehan's studies show that about three-quarters of BPD women were sexually abused as children or suffered childhood physical abuse. Yet the majority of adults who were sexually and/or physically abused as children do not become BPs. While the development of the disorder is well under way in early childhood, the diagnostic criteria of the DSM-IV-TR generally discourage the diagnosis of personality disorders until age 18. Some highly regarded professionals view BPD as primarily a symptom of Post-Traumatic Stress Disorder.

It is possible that with corrective emotional and behavioral experiences, a person could overcome the disorder and have only occasional BPD traits in adulthood. The most frequently used treatment to date appears to be long-term individual psychotherapy. However, the most frequently researched therapies have used cognitive and behavioral approaches that are now being used in short-term individual therapy. Cognitive therapy of personality disorders uses successful techniques initially used for depression and anxiety over the past twenty years by a significant number of therapists (Beck, 1990). The Dialectical Behavioral Treatment approach developed by Marsha Linehan has been well-researched as effective. It includes skills training for self-regulation of emotions and behavior, self-acceptance and tolerance for the co-existence of opposites (such as being angry at someone and still loving the person, or making mistakes and still being a good person).

Medications have been largely ineffective at treating personality disorders, although many BPs have had other problems alleviated with medications, such as depression and anxiety. Surprisingly, many therapists have observed that one of the most helpful treatments for some of their BPs has been Alcoholics Anonymous and other similar groups. Apparently, the structure and ready availability of these group meetings can help the BP handle fears of abandonment as well as help them regulate their emotions on a daily basis.

CONCLUSION

Borderline personalities engage in extreme behaviors related to their preoccupation with an enduring and unconscious fear of abandonment. Their behavior patterns make sense when you realize that most events are interpreted through the eyes of this fear. This explains the excessively seductive or clinging behaviors that are unconsciously designed to reassure the BP that the other person is not abandoning him or her. This fear of abandonment explains the anger at those the BP loves, as well as the frequent manipulations of the BP such as pretending to be pregnant, misrepresenting the behavior of others or forgetting to mention undesirable information, all designed to keep the person close and avoid being abandoned. And this fear explains the rage that the Borderline feels when someone close does abandon him or her.

Not surprisingly, Borderlines sabotage themselves by pushing away those who are close to them with these extremes of behavior. Therefore, they are in constant conflicts. Since they are insecure with closeness (because of fear of abandonment) and devastated when they are rejected (actual abandonment), their relationships are generally conflictual. When their relationships terminate, they become high-conflict disputes. With this love-hate dynamic, their targets often feel like they are on a yo-yo. These targets are often lovers, spouses, close family members and professionals who are trying to help them. It is not uncommon for one professional (attorney, therapist or mediator) to help the BP deal with a dispute against another former professional, then to become a new target when the Borderline is disappointed in the outcome.

With these patterns in mind, advocates and dispute resolvers need to be especially careful about keeping a balanced relationship that does not reinforce extreme expectations or extreme blame against other targets. Being modest and matter-of-fact are helpful approaches to preventing the idealization which always leads to devaluation—and possibly to avoid becoming the next target.

Likewise, it is helpful to avoid responding to BPs with direct criticism, strong anger, ignoring them or abruptly terminating relationships with them. All of these methods trigger the fear of abandonment and the high conflict that follows. Ironically, out of frustration, advocates and dispute resolvers frequently use these methods and escalate disputes with BPs that could have been avoided. Misunderstanding and mistreating BPs may be one of the most common reasons that attorneys and therapists are sued for malpractice. It is not uncommon for courts to lecture and criticize these clients for their self-sabotaging behavior, which may inadvertently escalate the conflict. This approach often increases the likelihood that BPs will be back in court again and again, because they are driven to prove themselves "valid" to avoid feeling abandoned by the court.

Instead, key methods for helping Borderline clients include: respectful listening, moderate reassurance, realistic expectations, remaining focused on necessary tasks and avoiding over-reacting to the BP's mood swings. These skills and others are discussed in depth in the second half of this book. By understanding these dynamics and learning techniques for handling these clients, you can avoid unnecessary escalation of the conflict, reduce the BP's feelings of distress and reduce your own stress as well.

Chapter Three Summary
Borderline Personalities:
Love You, Hate You

1. Fear of abandonment is a driving force
2. Frequent anger and mood swings
3. Controlling, clinging, seductive and manipulative behavior to avoid abandonment
4. Impulsive and self-sabotaging behavior due to inability to reflect and change
5. Idealization, then devaluation of family, professionals and advocates is common
6. May attack with words, violence or lawsuits
7. Seek dispute resolvers for validation, control of others (to prevent feeling abandoned), or for revenge

Tips and Techniques for Dealing with Borderline Personality Disorder

1. Be modest and matter-of-fact
2. Listen respectfully, even to anger and blame
3. Provide moderate reassurance
4. Provide realistic expectations and boundaries
5. Avoid over-reacting to intense emotions
6. Avoid using strong anger or intense criticism
7. May need consequences, but handle carefully
8. Don't ignore or abruptly terminate the relationship

Narcissistic Personalities: I'm Very Superior

"In addition to our speaker's many and considerable lifetime achievements, she is widely known as a piece of work!"

Mental health professionals and the American Psychiatric Association estimate that less than one per cent of the general population has Narcissistic Personality Disorder (NPD), although up to sixteen per cent may be present in mental health settings. In general, Narcissistic traits are harder to work with than Borderline traits, for reasons I will describe below. After handling over a thousand disputes, I believe that those with Narcissistic personalities (NPs) are present in a large number of high-conflict cases.

Identifying Characteristics

Those with NPs often become involved in legal disputes because they are high risk-takers, disdainful of others and generally oblivious to the consequences of their own actions. They often feel like victims, when in fact their own behavior usually causes the events that upset them. With these characteristics, conflicts with their attorneys, mediators and therapists are also to be expected. Compromise and settlement are not.

Narcissistic Personality Disorder is less frequently identified in mental health settings than, for example, Borderline Personality Disorder. It is identified primarily in men. They generally do not pursue mental health treatment, except for help with a separate problem, such as anxiety or depression. They cannot see themselves as contributing to their problems. If you confront them with their own behavior, they will become extremely defensive and often go on the offensive by verbally attacking you.

Formal Diagnostic Criteria

Narcissistic Personality Disorder is characterized by an extreme sense of self-centeredness and superiority. The DSM-IV-TR describes **Narcissistic Personality Disorder**[16] as: *A pervasive pattern of grandiosity (in fantasy or behavior), need for admiration, and lack of empathy, beginning by early adulthood and present in a variety of contexts, as indicated by five (or more) of the following:*

1. *has a grandiose sense of self-importance (e.g., exaggerates achievements and talents, expects to be recognized as superior without commensurate achievements)*

2. *is preoccupied with fantasies of unlimited success, power, brilliance, beauty or ideal love*

3. *believes that he or she is "special" and unique and can only be understood by, or should associate with, other special or high-status people (or institutions)*

4. *requires excessive admiration*

5. *has a sense of entitlement, i.e., unreasonable expectations of especially favorable treatment or automatic compliance with his or her expectations*

6. *is interpersonally exploitative, i.e., takes advantages of others to achieve his or her own ends*

7. *lacks empathy: is unwilling to recognize or identify with the feelings and needs of others*

8. *is often envious of others or believes that others are envious of him or her*

9. *shows arrogant, haughty behaviors or attitudes*

Narcissistic personalities should be distinguished from successful people who have achievements and talents generally recognized by others. It is the over-inflated sense of one's achievements and talents that mark the NP and often cause the NP to alienate those around him or her.

---

[16] Reprinted with permission from the Diagnostic and Statistical Manual of Mental Disorders, Fourth Edition, Text Revised. Copyright 2000 American Psychiatric Association

Many successful people including politicians, businesspersons, artists, doctors and lawyers have some traits of narcissism. However, a general criterion for all personality disorders is that the person has "Clinically significant distress or impairment in social, occupational or other important areas of functioning." Therefore, if a person has been successful in important areas of functioning, he or she may not qualify for the diagnosis of disorder, even though he or she may have some traits associated with it.

For one reason or another, NPs have developed a coping mechanism of believing that they will achieve incredible success and that they have incredible personal qualities. Such persons can be very charismatic, as they catch the dreams of those around them and believe in their fantasies in a compelling way.

Unfortunately, the fantasies of an NP are usually not real. When reality hits—as it always does—the NP is devastated and cannot understand what happened. Since NPs are blind to their own responsibility and the unrealistic quality of their expectations and fantasies, they often feel like victims and blame those around them for their own troubles.

We all have "narcissistic injuries" from time to time. This is the extreme sense of hurt any person has when things feel personal—that there is something wrong with them. For example, a person applies for a job for which he is well-qualified. However, a hundred other well-qualified people also apply, and he does not get the job. He feels devastated, even though other people would see that he was unlikely to get it because his chances were one in a hundred. However, the jobseeker may take it very personally, because he sees himself as a superior person—even superior to the odds. This is a narcissistic injury. We all experience them occasionally, but this does not mean we have NPD.

In contrast, NPs are constantly feeling narcissistic injuries from life events, even routine events. Usually there is no one to blame, but the NP finds someone to blame because it must be somebody's fault, it cannot be his. Thus, he finds a target of blame to attack. This approach can lead to legal disputes from breach of contract obligations to domestic violence and even murder.

Demands for special treatment and admiration often earn the resentment of others around the NP, who often characterize him or her as being obnoxious, self-centered and rude. While many people in daily life have these qualities occasionally, those who cannot succeed in important areas of their lives because of these qualities qualify for a diagnosis of NPD. In employment settings, disputes may arise because the Narcissistic person cannot accept feedback and being treated as an ordinary person. An NP may be sued for harassment in employment, because he is oblivious to the impact of his insensitive remarks and demands towards employees.

In business relationships NPs may be sued for breach of contract, because they do not interpret their actions as negative or harmful when everyone else does. In criminal relationships, an NP may injure others because he does not feel he is being treated like the special person he is. On the other hand, others may injure the NP because they can no longer stand the NP's attitude and behavior.

In families, NPs may commit domestic violence and/or child abuse because they do not feel properly respected and admired by the "inferior beings" around them, or because they see themselves as above the law or rules for ordinary people. These qualities often lead to difficulties in the attorney-client relationship, because the NP may demand admiration and special treatment from the attorney that he cannot (or should not) attempt to obtain.

Whereas the attorney may expect the NP to share the same expectations as other clients, the NP may become angry or simply fire the attorney and seek one who is "more competent" when the attorney does not give him the special treatment he expects. In working with these clients, it is common for the attorney to feel criticized and incompetent, regardless of the quality of his or her work.

Mediators working with NPs may also confront the difficulty of making them feel special while treating them neutrally. The NP will expect the outcome of the mediation to include more benefits to him than the other party, because he is "entitled" as a special person. Compromise or admissions of responsibility are very difficult to obtain with this personality type. Therapists working with NPs involved in legal disputes must be especially wary of their need to be seen as superior. The NP is usually preoccupied with winning and being respected without doing the necessary work. Narcissistic personalities consider themselves superior to therapists and expect therapists to be allies in proving their superiority to the world, instead of treating them as patients.

The tendency of NPs to take advantage of others may be the quality that most frequently gets them into legal disputes. Since the NP feels superior to everyone else, relationships are seen as an opportunity for recognition of that superiority. This includes a disdain for others. In order to feel superior, the NP must constantly put other people down. Consequently, NPs sometimes are involved in child abuse, and even child sexual abuse. Their narcissism justifies (to them) the manipulation and control of those who are much weaker.

Domestic violence is also common, although verbal abuse and manipulation may be the primary form this takes. Lying and exaggeration are common in relationships with NPs. They may also feel a pleasure in the process of manipulating and deceiving others. At times this has a sadistic quality. Yet many of these behaviors are not designed to harm others as much as they are designed to reinforce the NP's sense of being a superior person.

This quality, of course, does not bode well for professionals working with NPs. Rather than seeking assistance to change their own behavior, the NP may be seeking an attorney, mediator or therapist to help them prove they are superior. And court is where we prove things in our society.

These qualities may make the NP "forget" to mention important negative information in a case. The attorney, as well as the NP, may be caught by surprise by the information and evidence obtained against them. Because of the NP's grandiosity and charm, the unwary attorney may be swept up in the story presented by the NP. This story usually involves being a victim of others and having no personal responsibility. When the information about the NP's responsibility in the case is discovered, the attorney may feel lost, overwhelmed and enraged with his or her client. The client, on the other hand, will plead ignorance of what is now obvious to everyone else.

Once the NP realizes he or she can no longer manipulate the attorney, the NP may simply terminate the attorney-client relationship and look for a new attorney who will agree with him or her. In contrast to the stormy attorney-client relationship with Borderline Personality Disorders, NPs may not bother to get angry with the attorney, who may not be worth it in their eyes, so they simply move on. With this in mind, when it comes to getting paid it is important for the attorney not to bend the rules and treat the NP as special. Firm expectations should be maintained from the start.

In adult relationships, for the relationship to be successful each person needs to be able to empathize with the other's feelings. While NPs can be quite charismatic at the start of a relationship, they are quite poor at maintaining intimacy within ongoing relationships. Narcissists may have many acquaintances and appear to be popular. However, relationships for the NP are often seen as competitive opportunities to use others to boost themselves.

Yet because of their lack of empathy, NPs are often caught by surprise when the other person becomes resentful and angry, because NPs incorrectly assume that everyone else sees them as special and superior and will therefore tolerate their exploitative behavior in the relationship. They simply become angry back, or feel devastated and completely victimized—which justifies "acting out." Divorces are common, business relationships often go bad, or they lash out in anger by verbally or physically attacking those closest to them.

In extreme cases, this lack of empathy may allow them to sexually abuse children with a variety of justifications: that the child wanted it, that the child initiated it and is responsible, or that it is somehow good for the child. In such a case, the NP cannot identify the child as having any different feelings or thoughts from the NP himself. Self-gratification is predominant to the exclusion of any sense of responsibility or empathy for the feelings of others.

Some NPs are involved in domestic violence. In contrast to Borderline Personality Disorder, NPs are more likely to be violent inside and outside their intimate relationships. As Dutton has shown, this sense of superiority and lack of empathy allows the NP to harm others with little internal conflict. Once the NP feels unfairly treated, normal doubts and inhibitions may not arise and therefore the NP feels justified in harming others.

As the NP is preoccupied with feeling superior, he is frequently envious of the attention, possessions and images presented by others. He will try to be close to those who are considered superior, such as politicians, actors, wealthy business persons and anyone else perceived by his social group as having high status. The NP hopes that the high status will rub off on him, so he will frequently drop names and brag about his intimate relationships with those of high status—some of whom he has barely, or never, met.

The NP frequently exaggerates or lies to impress others. He automatically assumes that others are envious of him, or he attempts to elicit their envy. Narcissistic personalities can be irritating because they are constantly blowing their own horns. The smallest success will be advertised by the NP as an incredible accomplishment. At the same time, the incredible accomplishments of others will be characterized as insignificant events by the NP.

Narcissistic personalities may display behaviors such as impatience, lack of eye contact, lack of listening skills, and constant discussion of themselves. These arrogant behaviors and attitudes are easily identified by anyone who has spent much time around someone with NPD. Relationships with them are unsatisfying and uncomfortable. Over time the buildup of resentment by those around the NP may reach the level of a legal dispute. Yet when the NP is fired, divorced or excluded from a promising business deal, the NP is caught by surprise and feels completely victimized by the other's insensitive behavior. The NP's inability to compromise often leads to the initiation of a legal dispute or the escalation of an existing legal dispute.

The CEO

From time to time, I am selected to handle a business dispute as a superior court mediator. One such case involved two small high-tech companies in a bitter conflict over a key employee who left one company and went to the other. I have altered the names and facts to protect confidentiality.

Mr. Theodore, CEO of TedTronics, flew from Seattle to San Diego and arrived with his attorney well before the scheduled mediation was to begin. He had filed a lawsuit for $200,000 against MannTronics for fraud, patent violations, unfair competition and so forth, and the judge had referred the case to mediation before a trial date could be set.

The attorney for MannTronics, the defendant San Diego firm, arrived on time and assured us that Mr. Mann, the head of the firm, would arrive soon. But twenty minutes after the hour Mr. Mann had still not arrived and Mr. Theodore was extremely insulted. "I flew in for this mediation and my time is extremely valuable. How dare Mr. Mann make me wait like this!" he fumed.

I decided to start the mediation with those present. I focused on explaining the mediation process and offered to answer any questions about mediation while we were waiting.

Mr. Theodore wanted to know all about my background as a social worker. "What does a social worker know about business, anyway?" he challenged. I explained that I had successfully handled many business mediations because my background provided me with training and experience in helping people communicate and solve problems together. As the mediator, I relied on his knowledge of the issues at hand to construct a workable solution to the problems that had arisen. I also reminded him that I had been selected by the parties from a panel of mediators to handle their dispute.

"Yes, I agreed to use you, because I didn't know anyone from the list of choices and the other side thought it would help that you were a social worker. But what do you know about business matters? Inventory? Budgets? Personnel problems, like the one we're here about?"

His tone was condescending. The angrier he felt about Mr. Mann's lateness, the more demeaning he became toward me. I could feel myself beginning to resent his belittling manner. Then I reminded myself to develop a working theory of his personality. I realized that his arrogance and need for recognition were strong Narcissistic traits. I decided I could work with him if I gave him recognition for his "superior" achievements.

With the consent of the attorneys, I got Mr. Theodore talking about his background and the creation of his company, avoiding the legal issues at hand until Mr. Mann arrived. He calmed down immediately, appreciating my interest and awe at his accomplishments. He had created a multi-million-dollar business from nothing, based on his scientific skills and some bold business moves. He had been very successful, although his business eventually hit the skids.

Then the Chief Financial Officer of MannTronics arrived, a Mr. Short.

"Where's Mr. Mann?" Mr. Theodore demanded.

"He was unable to make it so he sent me, as the CFO," Mr. Short replied.

"What can you know about this problem?" Mr. Theodore challenged. "This is a personnel issue."

I inquired about Mr. Mann, as he was the named defendant in the lawsuit as CEO of MannTronics, and to have a productive mediation all parties should generally be present. It was obvious that Mr. Theodore had flown in to San Diego for this meeting, while Mr. Mann lived and worked nearby. "What do you all propose that we do about this situation?" I inquired, looking back and forth at Mr. Short, Mr. Theodore and each of their attorneys.

"Can we meet separately with you for a few minutes?" Mr. Short asked me.

"I am always willing in a civil court mediation to meet separately with the parties in confidential caucuses. However, if I do so, I will also meet with the other side."

They both agreed, and I met with Mr. Short and the MannTronics attorney.

"Mr. Mann cannot work with Mr. Theodore in any face-to-face setting," Mr. Short explained. "Mr. Theodore is so easily angered and belligerent that nothing would be accomplished. That's why Mr. Mann left TedTronics in the first place. Mr. Theodore cannot see how alienating and confrontational he always is. That's why his business is doing so poorly. Even so, Mr. Mann has authorized me to settle this case with favorable terms to Mr. Theodore, just to get him out of our lives."

This feedback reinforced my working theory that Mr. Theodore had a NP. He may have sabotaged his best efforts by being overly sensitive to those who did not see him as superior. If Mr. Mann left Mr. Theodore's "superior" company, that would have been a narcissistic injury to Mr. Theodore's self-image, which a NP cannot tolerate. But I decided to wait and see. I then met separately with Mr. Theodore as I had promised.

"I demand that he be here to face me," Mr. Theodore glowered.

"Mr. Short made it clear to us all that he cannot come today," I explained. "As a court-referred mediator, I have the authority to require that he be here, so we can reschedule the mediation for another date—or we can proceed and see if an agreement can be reached today. If not, then we can reschedule. I know how busy you are and it might be the most productive use of our time today to give it a try. I don't want to waste your time today without attempting a resolution to the problem you came so far to resolve. But it's up to you."

I knew that one of Mr. Theodore's strengths was that he was, in fact, very productive. I had learned that he was a tireless worker, which was part of why he demanded so much of those around him. He liked my thinking—and my deference to him. He agreed to proceed.

We spent the next hour and a half in intense discussions over the insult to Mr. Theodore of a former sales employee going to MannTronics to work for his betrayer, Mr. Mann. No damage had yet occurred—no evidence of misuse of secrets, no contact with former clients—but Mr. Theodore feared that this was inevitable.

By focusing the discussion on developing a very structured "non-compete" agreement regarding customers, non-disclosure of TedTronics secrets, procedures and patents, we were able to construct a complete settlement of the issues of the lawsuit. It would be dismissed and neither party would be held liable for any misdeeds. Mr. Theodore was satisfied by the controls put in place in the agreement we negotiated, and Mr. Short readily agreed to give Mr. Theodore a letter of apology for "miscommunication." I had suggested that some form of apology might help in a case like this where one party felt so personally offended, because an apology can also ease a narcissistic injury.

During the negotiations, it became obvious that a financial settlement was never really an issue. Mr. Theodore was insulted and frightened by his belief that Mr. Mann had stolen a key employee, and he wanted to confront the "bad guys" and get some control over the situation. He wanted to be recognized and respected.

However, there was one unresolved issue: $7,000 in attorney fees that Mr. Theodore had spent so far. This was a far smaller amount than the $200,000 lawsuit he had just negotiated away. But Mr. Theodore adamantly believed he should be paid something for his trouble, and he would settle for having his attorney fees paid by MannTronics. It appeared to me that this would satisfy what remained of his narcissistic injury. If he didn't get this (he was probably thinking), it would appear that no one had done anything wrong, and that he had been a fool. He still strongly believed that he had been betrayed by Mr. Mann.

On the other hand, Mr. Short said there would be no payment or admission of liability for any wrongdoing. MannTronics had paid its own attorney fees for this "unnecessary lawsuit," so Mr. Theodore should really pay his own legal fees, he suggested.

"All we need to do is reach an agreement that both sides can live with," I said. As they remained stuck on this point, I suggested one last caucus with each side.

I met with Mr. Short first. "Look, is there any reason you can think of to throw some small change at him? It doesn't have to be an admission of anything. It seems to me that he needs something, no matter how small, to help him let go. And besides, you've already saved yourselves the costs and delays of going to trial."

Mr. Short turned to his attorney. "What have we paid you so far?"

"I haven't done much yet, since I strongly believed this case needed to be settled. About $2,000."

"Mr. Theodore had to fly down here for this mediation," I pointed out. "Your company kept him waiting. And the mediation rules say that all parties must be present, although we agreed to try this without Mr. Mann. Even a token might settle the case."

"All right. Let's split the difference," Mr. Short said to his attorney. "Let's give him $2,500–half of the difference in attorney's fees that he's spent and we've spent. We'll call it costs of settlement and an adjustment for his travel costs."

I then met separately with Mr. Theodore and his attorney. "You know, court is always a roll of the dice. No matter how great your case, you could lose. And you can't prove any damages. It would cost you much more to take a high risk in court. Your legal fees are lower than those in a lot of cases I mediate. Your attorney has been wise to encourage a low-cost resolution to this problem. You have better things to do with your time than spend it in court."

Mr. Theodore was adamant. "I want something for what they did to me."

"Okay, let's meet one last time and see whether we can reach an agreement on this last issue."

I got everyone back together and asked for any new proposals to resolve this minor issue. As a good negotiator, Mr. Short started with a lower offer than he was aiming for. "We'll give you $1,500 for your attorney's fees and for your trouble in having to come down here and file this lawsuit."

Mr. Theodore's face tightened, and he blurted out. "I demand at least $2,000! Nothing less."

"Oh, all right," Mr. Short reluctantly replied. "$2,000–it's a deal."

Mr. Theodore was satisfied. To him it was an admission of guilt and compensation for his hurt. Mr. Short was satisfied. To MannTronics, it was an adjustment for his travel costs and a low-cost resolution of a potentially expensive legal dispute. Both sides agreed that the settlement would be confidential.

To me, it was a case of one NP and three other reasonable people. If Mr. Short and the two attorneys hadn't been so flexible and recognized the need to butter up Mr. Theodore a bit, it would have gone to court. Mr. Short was flexible and had been forewarned by Mr. Mann about Mr. T's difficult personality. If there had been two or more NPs present, this case would probably have gone to court, even though it was really about hurt feelings.

I don't believe that Mr. Theodore necessarily had a personality disorder, because he was generally successful in his life. But he appeared to have enough traits of a NP for my working theory to succeed: he responded favorably to recognition of his true accomplishments, and to a focus on his being highly productive, both of which were emphasized throughout the mediation. I purposely avoided direct confrontation of his self-sabotaging behavior, which would have backfired completely with someone displaying Narcissistic traits.

Self-Sabotage In Dispute Resolution

Because they perceive themselves as superior, NPs have a difficult time losing a dispute. When an NP is involved, the easy settlement of a minor dispute may become impossible. In defending against the claims of "less worthy people," the NP is driven to extremes. The Narcissistic person is oblivious to the effect of his drive to prevail, and may insist on testifying at trial even though his attorney advises him the result will be disastrous. In some cases, the NP simply fires the attorney and looks for one who will agree with him. In mediation the NP may have a hard time accepting any compromise or settlement. Even when a very generous offer is made, the NP may keep pushing for absolute victory. At times those involved in a dispute with the NP will simply give in, just to end the dispute. Attorneys with NP traits display the same rigidity in court, in judicial settlements or in mediation, as they persist in a manner that most others would consider unreasonable.

Yet by being so self-consumed, the NP simply replays his frustration with others over and over again. Since few disputes are resolved in a satisfying manner, the NP constantly feels victimized—which he uses to justify his arrogant behavior and responses. Internal conflicts and unresolved hopes keep the cycle continuing.

Conflicts With Professionals

NPs frequently seek out relationships with professionals because this helps them feel superior. Eventually, the professional-client relationship disappoints the fantasies of the NP. The NP feels victimized, and sometimes retaliates. This retaliation may include verbal attacks, suits for malpractice or even violence. If the professional abruptly or angrily terminates the relationship with the NP, there is a risk that the NP will sue or repeatedly attempt to contact the professional and convince the professional that he or she is wrong, to maintain the NP's self-image as superior or innocent.

Some successful techniques with NPs have revolved around giving the NP positive feedback and admiration. By stroking the ego or boosting the self-confidence of the NP, the relationship between the professional and client will generally remain stable. While a professional may dislike engaging in such behavior, the price of rejecting the NP may be much higher. In many cases the most effective technique is using a lot of respectful and interested listening skills. This will be discussed further in Part II of this book.

Causes and Treatments

Mental health theorists and researchers such as Beck and Ford generally consider that NPs develop in early childhood, possibly from child-rearing that lacks emotional nurturing while over-inflating the child's sense of being special for some unique talent or personal quality—a talent that may or may not be recognized by the larger society. One example would be the abusive parent who only praises his son for his fighting skills at school, when he shouldn't be getting into fights in the first place.

This life experience may drive the child to obtain nurturing by overly emphasizing imagined personal qualities. Ford and many other researchers believe that NPD is on the rise, primarily due to the social breakdown of consistent family environments and the decreased opportunities to receive nurturing for children in today's society. Narcissistic personalities are less likely than Borderline personalities to seek mental health treatment. When NPs do seek treatment, it is usually because of depression, substance abuse or anxiety disorders. They may become depressed because of the gap between their high expectations and real life. Those around them may demand that they get treatment. As Beck in particular has found, they may also become attracted to and destroyed by high-status drugs such as cocaine.

When NPs do receive treatment, according to Lester (1998) the most successful treatment appears to be long-term individual psychotherapy with an emphasis on confronting and interpreting inappropriate behavior, and discussing alternative behaviors for more effective relationships.

When a legal professional wants to recommend therapy for a client with NP, it may be most effective to suggest counseling "for dealing with the stress" of their legal dispute, rather than implying that there is something wrong with the person. Even short-term therapy may aid the NP in relieving stress and finding areas in which he can be more flexible. When a secure, positive relationship can be established with such a person, he can be a very stimulating and interesting client.

David

Aaron Beck, a cognitive therapist and researcher, provides a rare example of an attorney with NP who entered therapy. His description helps understand this diagnosis:

David was an attorney in his early 40s when he sought treatment for depressed mood. He cited business and marital problems as the source of his distress, and wondered if he was having a midlife crisis....

Feeling worse at work was associated with a heightened sense of discomfort in doing routine work, and the thought that such work was beneath him. He would think about how he really deserved better, and how he was not getting appropriate recognition for his talents and aptitudes. Consultations with colleagues often triggered thoughts of their failure to give him appropriate recognition, or their "nerve" in saying something even marginally critical about him. David believed that because he was "different" from other people, they had no right to criticize him. But he had every right to criticize others. He also believed that other people were weak and needed contact with someone like him in order to bring direction or pleasure into their lives. He saw no problem in taking advantage of other people if they were "stupid" enough to allow him to do so....

David felt better when someone flattered him; when he was in a group social situation where he could easily grab the center of attention; and when he could fantasize about obtaining a high-level position, being honored for his great talent or just being fabulously wealthy. The composite picture produced by the assessment of David's clinical history, his current symptoms, and his attitudes and automatic thoughts thus indicated a major depressive episode, of mild severity, with concomitant NPD.[17]

Those with NPD tend to get into trouble with the law because of their superior attitudes—that somehow the law does not apply to them. As Beck further says:

"Narcissists are apt to become most resentful and contemptuous of anyone who tries to hold them accountable for their exploitative, self-centered behavior.... When in a position of authority, the narcissist may misuse power to exploit those under his or her influence. One likely example of this is sexual harassment. Another example is a stockbroker who excessively buys and sells or

---

[17] Cognitive Therapy of Personality Disorders (1990) pp.245-47. Used with permission.

otherwise "churns" a client account to generate commissions, regardless of whether money is made or lost for the client. Other public examples might be found among political figures who behave as if their authority exempts them from generally accepted norms of conduct."[18]

With this type of behavior, it is easy to see how many Narcissistic people end up in court—often to their complete surprise. They are truly oblivious to the impact of their behavior and insensitivity to others.

It was after Beck wrote those words in 1990 that we had some of the biggest political scandals of the century. Newt Gingrich was driven from office as Speaker of the House of Representatives by legal action against him for his financial affairs. Bill Clinton was impeached as President of the United States with legal action against him for his sexual affairs. These were two of the most brilliant political minds in recent history. Yet it was not their politics (from opposite ends of the political spectrum) that left them in disgrace; it was their personalities. Their own apparently Narcissistic traits sabotaged them in high-conflict legal cases, and cost taxpayers tens of millions of dollars.

Gingrich and Clinton are two excellent examples of how Narcissistic traits probably helped them repeatedly succeed. They appeared to believe in themselves so highly that they were able to survive the endless criticisms and oppositions that politicians must endure. Both of them are known for their ability to bounce back and reinvent themselves. But this also tells us that they kept getting into trouble, which made these skills necessary. Did they have personality disorders? I doubt it. They were (and still are) highly successful and powerful people. If my working theory is right, and they were to understand and treat their traits, they could become even more successful (depending on your political persuasion, this could be a good or bad thing).

---

[18] Cognitive Therapy of Personality Disorders, at 244-45

The Father

An extreme case of someone diagnosed with NPD in a legal case is that of a father who lost his parental rights in part because of the disorder. Since cases involving young children in juvenile court keep last names confidential, I will refer to this man simply as the father.

Jasmon O. was born in 1986. Her mother gave the child up to Child Protective Services in 1987 because she was unable to care for her. The father was also unable to care for her at that time.

"It is uncontested that Jasmon's father was then also unable to care for the child, as he was living in an "independent living center" for mentally disturbed persons and was also suffering from drug dependency. Jasmon was declared a dependent child on July 1, 1987, and placed in foster care in the home of the A's on July 7, 1987. The home proved to be a good one, and the child has resided there throughout these proceedings.

During dependency proceedings, the mother failed to comply with the reunification plan. Her parental rights have been terminated and she has not appealed. The father, however, after a period between a year and eighteen months after Jasmon was placed with the A's (foster parents), **transformed himself**. He overcame his drug dependency, underwent psychological counseling, secured employment, established a home and maintained regular visitation with Jasmon.

A permanency planning hearing began on February 17, 1989, and continued on various dates until May 12, 1989. The juvenile court referee heard evidence that despite his general recovery, the father had failed to establish a close relationship with his daughter, and that Jasmon experienced separation anxiety as visitation with her father increased. The referee heard evidence that the father failed to or **was unable to empathize** with his daughter's distress.

The father presented evidence that Jasmon's mother's social worker, also an employee of the department, was instrumental in securing the placement of Jasmon with the social worker's sister, who was the foster mother. The department did not inform the father or the court of this fact. The referee was sharply critical of the department for permitting this potential conflict of interest, but found it had not ultimately affected the attempted reunification of Jasmon with her father." (Emphasis added)[19]

In this case, the father overcame his drug dependency and significantly improved his life situation (which sounds similar to the personal changes Mr. Gossage went through in Chapter One). Yet something kept the father from establishing a close relationship with his daughter. Perhaps it was the lost time while he transformed himself, or perhaps it was the social worker's placement of the child with her sister—or perhaps it was his own personality.

> "There was evidence that the father **failed to comply with the specifics of the transition plan**, in that he told Jasmon she was coming to live with him permanently before her therapist had prepared her for this information. He also **failed to cooperate with the child's therapist in participating in therapy** with him. There was also evidence that the father did not notice or denied the obvious symptoms of mental distress exhibited by the child during the transition period."[20]

The father blamed the problem of establishing the bond between father and child on the Department of Social Services for placing the child with the social worker's sister. Clearly, the department acted inappropriately and each referee criticized the department for letting that happen. In other words, his target of blame may not have been totally innocent, but in typical NP fashion he could not see any fault in his own behavior. He did not follow the requirements for his reunification. He told the child things he was not supposed to tell, and he did not participate in the therapy with the child. These are easy things to do, but it appears that the father could not stop trying to do things his own way even though he risked losing his daughter.

This is a possible example of the self-sabotage of a NP, who is preoccupied with his own needs and unable to attend to the needs of his child. He spent years trying to get custody, yet failed to do the simplest things that may have helped him.

Eventually, the case went to the Court of Appeals, which found in favor of the father and gave him another chance. The case was then appealed to the Supreme Court of California. In 1994, the Supreme Court reversed the court

---

[19] In Re Jasmon O. (1994) 8 Cal. 4th 398, 408-09
[20] In Re Jasmon O. at 410

of appeal and agreed with the superior court that the father's parental rights should be terminated and the litigation ended.

"Many judicial officers have reviewed the facts in this **exhaustively litigated** case—a case which the dissent would remand for further seemingly endless litigation. Only one referee, with reluctance, concluded that the father might possibly perform adequately as a parent. The others disagreed. The juvenile court at the final 1991 hearing made a finding that he could not perform adequately as a parent, declaring the evidence to be 'overwhelming.' The superior court that ordered termination of parental rights also expressly determined that the father **could not perform adequately as a parent**.... It also included evidence of an independent psychologist that the father had **Narcissistic Personality Disorder**."[21]

The Supreme Court finally looked at the issue of "who's to blame."

"**The father is far from being the innocent victim** portrayed by the dissent. At age twenty-four he chose to enter into a sexual relationship with Jasmon's mother, who was then an emotionally troubled minor of sixteen, living in a halfway house for the mentally disturbed. The father admitted these facts under a promise by the court that they would not be used against him in any other proceeding, eg a statutory rape charge. When the child was born, the father had a ten-year history of drug and alcohol abuse, and had been hospitalized for mental illness. He had been living in an 'independent living center' for the mentally ill for a year and a half when he entered the liaison with the child's mother. He lived with the child and mother outside of the halfway house until Jasmon was four or five months old, but then he left. His excuse for leaving his family was that the child's mother would not 'settle down.' When Jasmon's mother brought the child to the department, unable to care for her alone, the father was again in a halfway house for the mentally ill and had problems with drugs.

The department was also not to blame for the fact that the child had to stay in foster care for an extended period. As the superior court declared in its findings in support of the termination order, 'Mr. O[ ] did not jump into the reunification plan with both feet. There was a passage of almost eighteen months before he could—it could even be reasonably said that compliance was had.' The court noted that even the father's expert

---

[21] In Re Jasmon O. at 430

placed the 'responsibility on Mr. O[ ] for having used the drugs and the medications and the alcohol such as to create **apparent personality disorders** and a state in which he was unable to take care of the minor during the initial period.' Again, the court declared that because of the father's inability to care for the child, '[t]here was a period of almost eighteen months or more when it would have been completely unreasonable to have even considered any kind of reunification.' During this eighteen-month period, it was natural that the child would bond with the A's, but this bonding occurred **because of the father's inability to be a parent**–not because of any improper acts of the department or the A's." (Emphasis added)[22]

CONCLUSION

In summary, the above case emphasizes several of the common issues of NPs in court cases. The father could not accept responsibility for the problems his own behavior had caused. He blamed others for problems he continued to have. He had great difficulty empathizing with his daughter's needs and distress, while focusing on his own needs and the expectation that others would simply accept them as primary.

He apparently "transformed" himself and overcame his drug dependency and many other problems. But he was unable to change his personality, or probably never focused on it as an issue. Yet his personality was his biggest, long-term "enduring pattern." He was willing to promote his fight in court for over five years, yet he sabotaged himself by his unwillingness to do the simplest tasks required by him in the reunification plan (not discussing certain issues with the child and not participating in the child's therapy).

While most cases I have seen with NPs do not involve such a seriously impaired person, this case demonstrates the basic pattern of blind persistence, lack of empathy, self-centeredness and self-sabotage when NPs go to court or engage in other high-conflict disputes.

---

[22] In Re Jasmon O. at 428-29

Chapter Four Summary
Narcissistic Personalities:
I'm Very Superior

1. Fear of inferiority is a driving force
2. Constantly demands attention and exaggerated respect
3. Very self-centered and self-absorbed
4. Expects special, superior treatment
5. Extremely negative reaction to any criticism
6. Frequent disrespect and disdain of others
7. Oblivious to other's needs and feelings

Tips and Techniques for Dealing with Narcissistic Personality Disorder

1. Avoid direct criticism
2. Recognize real strengths and accomplishments
3. Listen with empathy
4. Share decision-making
5. Explain benefits of following your advice
6. Explain consequences of future misconduct
7. May need consequences, but handle carefully
8. Don't ignore or abruptly terminate relationship

Antisocial Personalities: Con Artists

"For God's sake, think! Why is he being so nice to you?"

People with Antisocial Personality Disorder (ASPD) are fast and fast-talking. They win you over with charm and incredibly good deeds—or so it appears on the surface. They work hard to keep their true intentions and bad acts out of sight.

Antisocial personalities (ASPs) chip away at your doubts and replace them with their own confident certainties. You may sense danger or deceit around them, but they convince you to doubt yourself and to develop more confidence in their point of view. Thus the phrase "confidence man," or "con artist."

Antisocial personalities fear being dominated and therefore they desire to dominate and control others—it gives them a reassuring sense of power in the world. They often have a drive to hurt others to get what they want, as compared to the other personality disorders which involve primarily self-sabotage and inadvertent harm to others. This drive to hurt usually encompasses taking advantage of other people, such as the con man who marries several women at the same time for their money, or the psychopathic killer who feels comfortable killing you because he wants your attractive coat.

People with ASPD are skilled at fooling neighbors, spouses, legal professionals and even mental health professionals. They are often involved in cases involving criminal charges and appear to make up a substantial portion of the prison population, frequently estimated at about fifty per cent. They represent approximately two to four percent of the general population, with men appearing far more frequently than women, at a ratio of about three to one according to Lester, or four to one according to Ford.

Identifying Characteristics

By adopting the term Antisocial Personality Disorder in 1980, the DSM combined the use of two prior terms, psychopath and sociopath, into one comprehensive category. These terms have often been used interchangeably to cover a range of behavior against the rules of society—thus they are called antisocial and sociopathic.

Chronic lying and manipulation are key characteristics of the ASP. Frequently, an ASP will attempt to persuade mental health professionals and legal professionals that another person is guilty of behavior that is actually his or her own.

The case of Mr. Gossage in Chapter One may be a good example of this personality type. He recruited twenty advocates who testified on his behalf at the Bar Court. They were confident that he had changed. He showed remorse over killing his sister many years earlier. He did good work in the community. He overcame his drug addiction. But did they know that he continued to get and ignore traffic violations even during law school? Did they know that he only mentioned four of his seventeen criminal convictions on his application to become an attorney? Probably not.

While individuals with this disorder frequently end up in the criminal justice system, those with only a few ASPD traits often show up in civil disputes. As I have often seen in cases with ASPs, the people they con become confident advocates who adamantly defend the ASP when challenged by others. To succeed, they must use and deceive other people to get what they want—friends, lovers, family, mental health professionals, attorneys and even their own children. The examples later in this chapter show how this works.

Formal Diagnostic Criteria

The DSM-IV-TR identifies those with **Antisocial Personality Disorder**[23] as: *There is a pervasive pattern of disregard for and violation of the rights of others occurring since age fifteen years, as indicated by three (or more) of the following:*

---

[23] Reprinted with permission from the Diagnostic and Statistical Manual of Mental Disorders, Fourth Edition, Text Revised. Copyright 2000 American Psychiatric Association.

1. *failure to conform to social norms with respect to lawful behaviors as indicated by repeatedly performing acts that are grounds for arrest*

2. *deceitfulness, as indicated by repeated lying, use of aliases or conning others for personal profit or pleasure*

3. *impulsivity or failure to plan ahead*

4. *irritability and aggressiveness, as indicated by repeated physical fights or assaults*

5. *reckless disregard for safety of self or others*

6. *consistent irresponsibility, as indicated by repeated failure to sustain consistent work behavior or honor financial obligations*

7. *lack of remorse, as indicated by being indifferent to or rationalizing having hurt, mistreated, or stolen from another*

Most commonly, the ASP arrives in the legal system accused of a crime. It usually does not take long to discover a long history of criminal or almost-criminal behavior. A thorough history-taking is in order, whether the attorney is defending the ASP or prosecuting the ASP. It is not uncommon for an ASP to omit certain key pieces of life history when discussing the case with an attorney.

There are also occasions in which the ASP is initiating a legal case. The ASP may pursue a claim against a former partner in crime, or against a business partner, or against a family member whom he wishes to harm using the legal system. One example would be an ASP who brings a fabricated charge of domestic violence against a spouse or partner when in fact the ASP was abusive and violent.

In handling ASPs in legal disputes, it is most important to be careful about the characteristic of deceitfulness. With their life-long skills at deception, ASPs know how to make their stories sound credible. The nicest and most sincere people, the ones who like to help others, are often the most easily conned. In the brief period they have to get to know these clients, attorneys, mediators and therapists may be easily fooled.

Getting accurate information from an ASP may be difficult. In realistically defending or settling a case with such a client, gathering accurate information is necessary to avoid unpleasant surprises down the road. It is also important to gather information from those who know the ASP well. This may include family and friends, although one should beware of those who share the same antisocial tendencies.

In many ways, as Ford has found, ASPs are like small children who want instant gratification and cannot tolerate frustration. ASPs may get into legal trouble due to an overwhelming impulse to have some object they want, which they can only obtain immediately through theft or violence.

However, the ASP may be able to plan ahead to accomplish a short-term criminal scheme. It is the long-term consequences that the ASP has difficulty imagining—even after being caught in the past. For example, a bank robber may be highly effective at pulling off the robbery, but unable to understand the risks of engaging in the same behavior at six different banks in the same city around the same time.

Since ASPs are in a constant state of child-like desire, there is frequent irritability at delayed gratification. This may lead to violence or aggressive interactions with those close to them. In addition, the biologically heightened aggressive energy characteristic of ASPs appears to keep them engaged in antisocial behavior.

As indicated, there is usually a long history of physical fighting for one reason or another. Yet, in contrast to the Borderline or Narcissist, the ASP's physical confrontations are usually not highly emotional—instead, they are simply the means to an immediate end. For example, when a Borderline engages in domestic violence it is likely to be impulsive, a short-term release of tension followed by a period of remorse.

For the ASP, there may be an internal calm as the person focuses on accomplishing a task through violence, with no remorse following it. Studies by Dutton have shown that the heart rate of Antisocial batterers actually declines during intense arguments. They can be effective at lying without being detected on police polygraph tests, perhaps because their heart rate does not increase when they lie.

Since ASPs are absorbed with themselves and with immediate gratification, they have little awareness of others and little concern for them. This allows for a reckless disregard for consequences to themselves, as well as to others. For example, speeding in cars, high-risk drug use and other dangerous activities can be attractive to ASPs.

In families, ASPs may have their children removed from their care because of neglect or abusive behavior. Further, they may have difficulty maintaining employment and frequently get into trouble for not paying debts and fulfilling normal financial obligations. Professionals should keep this in mind when it comes to being paid.

Some degree of gang behavior may be associated with ASPs and the expression "no honor among thieves" fits many ASPs. Even when they work together with others in a criminal scheme, their relationships frequently go bad and they become enemies of each other, rather than allies.

Lack of remorse can be the most frightening aspect of the ASP. This quality allows the ASP to be potentially the most aggressive and violent of the personality disorders. Many ASPs are predatory in their violence, which means it is planned, purposeful and lacks emotion. Studies by Dr. Reid Meloy have indicated that they commit more crimes that are violent, use weapons more often, and are more aggressive in prison than other criminals without the Antisocial diagnosis. This characteristic allows little room for negotiation or cooperation from the ASP.

There is a sadistic quality to the behavior of many ASPs, a further characteristic of their lack of remorse. Antisocial personalities actually devalue others by physically controlling and harming them. Malloy has found that this is in contrast with Narcissistic personalities, who tend to only fantasize such devaluation of others, while maintaining a capacity for attachment and idealization of relationships. For the ASP, actually dominating and humiliating another person may feel necessary for them to feel secure themselves. The sadistic behavior of ASPs may include sexual abuse of children, planned and violent sexual abuse of adults and preoccupation with dominance of others—including forms of torture.

The Neighbor

Ten years ago, Manny bought a house in a pleasant neighborhood at the end of a cul-de-sac in a small mid-west city. He began to tear it down to build his dream home. He showed the neighbors how beautiful the new home would look, based on a well-worn magazine photograph. He had a recent and sizable inheritance to work with and he assured everyone it would be done within six months.

Before he was finished tearing down the old house he moved in with his new girlfriend, and stopped working on building his new house. Months went by without him being seen. Yet the rubble, boards, nails and broken glass remained on the site of his old house. One day, two of the neighbor children playing in the abandoned debris cut themselves on broken window glass. The neighbors were outraged and began meeting to decide what to do.

The neighbors decided to take legal action. The site of the house was now an "attractive nuisance" to their children. The neighbors went to town council and were told to try mediation first. Six of the neighbors attended the mediation, as well as Manny. He was extremely apologetic. "I got side-tracked with my business, which had a downturn. After I get the money together, I'm going to start right up again finishing the house. I'm really sorry for the delays. They were just unavoidable. Trust me; I'll take care of it right away."

"But we thought you had enough money to do the project from the start," said Fred, one of the neighbors, with some degree of irritation. "Didn't you have an inheritance?"

"Well, yeah," Manny admitted. Then he was all smiles again. "I had to use it to get my business through the downturn. I just need another $10,000 to get it finished. I'll start again after I raise the money. I always keep my promises."

"But the job site is dangerous now, especially to the children," replied Fred. "You need to start working again right now."

"Give him a break, Fred," said Carrie, another friendly neighbor. "Can't you see that he's struggling to handle his business? Maybe we can help him put up a high fence to protect the children."

"Oh, a fence is a great idea. Don't worry, I can take care of that myself," Manny said. "I'll put one up this week. I'm a man of my word, I assure you."

Afterward, Fred said to Carrie: "I don't trust him for a minute. He told everyone he would do it in six months, and that was a year ago. Besides, I get a cold feeling when I'm around him."

"But you know how many delays there can be in construction," Carrie countered in defense of Manny. "I'm sure he'll get a fence up this week."

Two weeks later, Carrie finally tracked down Manny's phone number. He had given them a cell phone number at the meeting, but it was no longer in service. She was furious.

"Get that fence up and start working, Manny," she exclaimed. "I want that project done within six months!"

"Sure, sure," Manny replied. "Calm down. I just got some more money in, so I'll get started this weekend. Business problems just came up again that I had no control over. Even you said to give me a break. Thanks so much for your understanding. I'm a businessman and I know how important it is to keep good relations going. You've really been wonderful to support me on this. Not everyone has been so understanding. Thanks again."

Carrie said later that Manny had completely reassured her, and that she believed in him again. He made her feel so good—that she was being so helpful to someone having business problems.

Finally, the fence went up and the rest of the house was cleared away. Then there was no sign of Manny for another year—except for the ugly seven-foot construction fence around the empty lot. The neighbors decided it was time to take stronger action. They did some research and found out that Manny was reporting to the city that the empty lot was his principal place of residence. They found out that he was living with his girlfriend on the other side of town. They finally found out his new phone number, a number that kept changing for some reason. But they couldn't find any record of a business in his name.

They finally decided to sue him. Ten neighbors were now furious about his inaction and his constant lying about working on the house. They decided to sue him in small claims court, for a maximum of $5,000 each. A $50,000 judgment would move him to action, they figured, and besides, they wouldn't need a lawyer in small claims court, so it would not cost them too much.

At court they were all ready with their papers and photos and other exhibits. When the small claims commissioner started the hearing, Manny announced that he thought he had a solution that he wanted to discuss with the neighbors. The commissioner said: "That's wonderful. I always prefer a good settlement to a court-imposed decision."

Manny told them he would sell the lot, someone else could build, and the problem would be solved. Since the neighbors weren't sure if they would ever see their $50,000 even if they won, they believed that this solution would get rid of Manny, so they agreed. They drew up a contract in which Manny agreed he would immediately sell the house. If his name was still on title after ninety days, then he agreed that they could enter a judgment against him in the full amount of $50,000.

Over the next three months, no For Sale signs went up and no listings could be found in any real estate office. After ninety days they discovered that his name had been removed from the title and that a woman now owned the empty lot. It was his girlfriend. So he manipulated them again, and they could not collect the penalty.

It was two more years before he actually sold the house. A total of three and a half years passed from the time that Manny started tearing down the old house until the new owner completed the new house and tore down the ugly fence.

Manny is a good example of someone with ASPD traits. He was charming and effectively manipulated Carrie several times. Fred had him figured out, down to the "cold feeling" that people sometimes get around an ASP, because they have no real empathy and don't care if they hurt you or your children. But Fred backed off because Carrie felt sympathy for Manny and advocated for him.

Manny demonstrated the classic ASPD characteristics of lying and switching stories. There was no evidence that he ever received an inheritance. He controlled situations through fast-talking and diverting attention from his behavior with new promises and excuses. He had a history of bad deals falling all around him, including his (probably) non-existent business. To continue dominating the situation he played at the edge of the rules, such as transferring the title to his girlfriend. ASPs seem to enjoy dominating others. When they are confronted, they appear to relish spinning a new con to get out of the old one. With charm and a series of manipulations, they often succeed—for a while.

Perhaps neighbors in a small city with a small zoning department would seem more vulnerable to a con artist who doesn't care about injuring small children or offending their parents. But what about big city businesses and courts?

The Stockbroker

In the following story it is never stated that any of the players has a personality disorder. Therefore, this is another opportunity for you to develop a working theory. See if it fits and consider how you would handle such a case.

Jeffrey Streich was a stockbroker in New York City in the 1990s. In his own words: "Before I was a broker I was a normal human being making an honest living. The only illegal thing I did, I think, was when I was young I used to steal Pop Rocks."

After he was a broker, however, he went a good deal beyond Pop Rocks.

During his career, Streich was fired from AS Goldman for improper trading. He was fired from Gruntal for promising investors that potential losses would have no impact them. He was fired from Beacon for his handling of a retired man's account:

"When Streich took over the account Shy Glass, who was in his seventies, had a $440,000 portfolio dominated by Amgen, an early biotech company whose stock was solid and, as it happened, about to become even more valuable. Through unauthorized trading and forging a margin-account application, Streich transformed the portfolio into house stocks that had the advantage of paying him a cash kickback but the accompanying disadvantage of becoming worthless. When it was all over, Glass's portfolio amounted to just $30,360."

There were no consequences other than losing his job for each of these instances of manipulating clients—until he met Marisa Baridis. Marisa was in her twenties earning about $45,000 a year as a control-group analyst at Smith Barney—a job that involved maintaining barriers (called a Chinese wall) against the release of stock trading information from one division within Smith Barney to investment bankers in another division. She was proud of her job, although she felt a lot of stress. She had a lot of insider information, but never used it despite occasional pressure from friends.

When Marisa met Jeffrey, he was working for himself as a stockbroker and was moving from apartment to apartment, apparently just paying the first month's rent and then staying as long as he could. He also was drinking, using cocaine and gambling. However, he carried lots of cash and was quickly able to impress Marisa.

"He's the kind of guy who, you know, if you, like, asked for a pack of cigarettes he would, like, give you $50 and tell you to keep the change." She meant it as a compliment.

Eventually, they agreed that she would leak him information and he would do the investing while observing some safeguards to avoid drawing attention—tell no one, trade moderately and stay away from options trading. They would split the profits.

However, Jeff didn't split the profits. He lied to her about how much he invested, about how much he made, and about how many other people he told about this insider information. Streich and a man named Napolitano each made about a quarter of a million dollars on Marisa's tips, and other people they tipped made hundreds of thousands of dollars more. Even though she suspected he was lying to her, she kept giving him bigger and bigger tips, especially after she left Smith Barney to move to Morgan Stanley in the same role, and was herself making $70,000 a year.

When friends told her he was playing her for a fool and he was cheating her, he persuaded her with bigger and better deals. Even when he stuck her with a $2,000 hotel bill after a romantic night together, he was able to keep their friendship going. Even when he made derogatory comments to her, she remained loyal to him.

Finally, they had a big dinner out and she confronted him. They talked about her split of the profits and about her suspicions that he was holding out on her. When Streich wanted to underline his sincerity he would say, "I swear on my mother's ashes." When Marisa wanted to do the same she'd say, "I swear on Heather's life." Heather was her Yorkshire terrier. "Why wouldn't you trust me?" Streich said at one point. "I never gave you a reason not to." Finally, he handed her twenty-five $100 bills—a down payment on the $36,000 he assured her she would soon get.

In a van parked just outside CS Barrington's restaurant, Investigator Walter Alexander of the Manhattan District Attorney's office trained a video camera on their table through the floor-to-ceiling glass and recorded the entire conversation on a concealed microphone.

Apparently, Jeffrey had finally been caught for the Glass case. He eagerly offered to get information on the more important criminals, such as Marisa. However, neither Marisa nor Jeffrey went to trial. Instead, befitting his experience at betraying others, Jeff turned state's evidence against his biggest trading partner, Napolitano. Marisa also testified at Napolitano's trial in exchange for a reduced sentence. She, at least, appeared to take responsibility for what she had done, and even the prosecutors felt sympathy for what Jeff had done to her.

"My friends blame Jeffrey Streich for what has occurred," she said. "I see it differently. He was no friend but I only blame myself. I have tried to understand why I acted the way I did and to deal with the pieces of my life that are left."

Judge Keenan gave Marisa Baridis two years probation. Napolitano got two-to-six years. And how did Jeff do? Could he con the court? Incredibly, the Assistant District Attorney, Adam Reeves, argued for leniency even after it was discovered that Jeff had misled the court under his agreement to cooperate.

Acknowledging that the crime against Shy Glass had been monstrous, Reeves argued that such monstrousness had to be weighed against cooperation that had been instrumental in the successful conclusion of two major investigations. Giving Streich a sentence that was as severe as the one given Napolitano, Reeves said, could have a chilling effect on the inclination of criminals to come forward with information on crimes that would otherwise go unprosecuted.

Reeves even reported detecting some remorse in Streich, and did not draw attention to the fact that the principal criminal scheme Streich's cooperation had brought down would not have existed if Streich hadn't concocted it. "I have radically changed my life," Streich said. "I am no longer involved with drugs and gambling. I no longer take shortcuts that have plagued my life." To use financial terms, Judge McLaughlin said, the sentence was deeply discounted—one-and-a-third years to four years in state prison. [24]

Just as Manny conned his neighbors (especially Carrie), Streich succeeded in manipulating Marisa. She was impressed by his generosity—throwing money around—and by his claims that he would never take advantage of her. When she had doubts, he quickly rebuilt her confidence in him with sweet talk that she was special and arguments that he never gave her a reason not to trust him. Yet all the time he was keeping most of the money and bringing other people in on the deal. A classic con, he was fast-talking the positive to hide the negative. He also had no empathy for her and was immediately ready to sacrifice her to help him escape consequences.

And he even appeared to con the prosecutor! Reeves detected some remorse in Streich. This helped divert him from the fact that it was Streich's scheme from the start. The key lesson about con artists isn't their misdeeds, but their ability to effectively divert attention from them with fast talk, charm and lies. To ASPs, lying is routine and carries with it no shame or even any recognition that it is bad. The ASP assumes that everyone is lying and that it is an expected part of the game of life. When confronted, ASPs quickly blame someone else—their target of blame—for something even worse, to divert attention from their own misdeeds.

One might wonder about Jeffrey Streich, considering that the assistant district attorney reported detecting some remorse in him. I would be skeptical. ASPs know exactly what to say and do: if acting remorseful works, they will do it. The way to tell if there is true remorse is to examine whether they expressed any remorse to anyone before they were caught. Antisocial personalities are big on remorse after they get caught—especially right before sentencing. Don't be fooled.

---

[24] Annals of Finance: Marisa and Jeff. Copyright © 2000 by Calvin Trillin. Originally appeared in *The New Yorker*. Reprinted by permission of Lescher & Lescher, Ltd. All rights reserved.

Conduct Disorder Before Age Fifteen

In contrast to the other personality disorders, a formal diagnosis of ASPD requires a childhood history of similar behavior. Conduct disorder is a DSM-IV-TR diagnosis for children who have participated in aggression to people and animals; destruction of property; deceitfulness or theft; and/or serious violations of rules, which causes clinically significant impairment in social, academic or occupational functioning.

Since adaptation to social rules and the development of empathy and responsibility begin in early childhood, the complete lack of these qualities would also start in early childhood. Since these qualities are part of the basic programming of personality, it makes sense that a child who already displays aggressive behavior and lack of empathy and remorse will be more likely to grow up to become an ASP.

The apparent increase in dramatic crimes committed by children under age fifteen does not bode well for society, as it indicates an increase in the future percentage of ASPs. When teenagers and children as young as six years old murder their schoolmates, it becomes clear that the qualities of an ASP can be established at a very early age. For those legal professionals working with child and adolescent clients, it may be helpful to think in terms of the dynamics of an adult personality disorder in understanding and handling their behavior.

Self-Sabotage in Dispute Resolution

The irony for ASPs is that they have the strongest drives and fantasies for being in control of others and for getting whatever they want. Yet they are the ones who are most likely to wind up in highly controlled environments such as prison. While they need the assistance of others to defend them when they constantly get into trouble, they have great difficulty developing relationships except for those based on manipulation and deception. Their efforts at manipulation and short-term gratification often sabotage any possibility for long-term success at any endeavor—including remaining out of prison.

Conflicts With Professionals

One can easily predict difficulties in working with ASPs. The ASP will want to be in control and will attempt to do so by manipulating the information provided to his attorney and other professionals. This will make the work of the professional difficult and the response of the professional may be quite negative.

Many ASPs can be effective at charming the unwary attorney or psychological evaluator. It is not uncommon for these professionals to discover after the fact that they were deceived. In some court cases, there are psychological experts with very strong opinions about the person—but the opposite of each other. Successful manipulations by ASPs have inspired many books and films. Examples of this are the docu-drama about the real life of Ted Bundy and the edge-of-your-seat movies *Jagged Edge* and *Primal Fear*.

While many people have believed that ASPs are more intelligent than the average person, the research does not support this. In reality, as Malloy (1987) shows, there is no evidence of a correlation between intelligence and psychopathic individuals. Apparently, there is the normal range of high intelligence, average intelligence and below-average intelligence in this population.

In any case, as a professional you need to be cautious about believing the information you are provided, and about any extra favors the ASP may ask of you. Their creativity is unlimited, and they have had a lifetime of practice at deception.

Causes and Treatments

Antisocial Personality Disorder appears to develop out of a combination of biological and environmental factors. However, in contrast to Borderline Personality Disorder and Narcissistic Personality Disorder, ASPD appears to have a strong genetic link. Studies reported by Ford of adopted children show that if a biological parent is sociopathic there is a greater risk of the child developing a sociopathic personality, even if the adopted parents are not sociopathic. This finding is supported by anecdotal reports I have heard from criminal defense attorneys, even in cases when the children were raised from birth by non-sociopathic parents.

Some research indicates that the biological differences of ASPs may be based in the central nervous system. They appear to have less of an ability to respond to negative events, during which they are less likely to sweat, their heart rate remains the same or decreases, and they feel less fear and less guilt. Of course, it is hard to know if these are a cause of antisocial behavior or a result of physiological changes as the ASP grows comfortable with antisocial behavior.

Early life experiences and environment cannot be ignored, however, although these factors may be less important with this personality disorder. It appears that chaos in the household and inconsistent reinforcement of social values may train a child for antisocial behavior. Children of severe alcoholics and addicts may experience this inconsistency, as they absorb the antisocial behaviors of addicted parents into their own personalities. Ironically, parents who become recovering alcoholics or addicts may stop showing signs of antisocial behavior (such as lying, violence or lack of remorse) but the child may have already learned them as permanent behaviors.

While most alcoholics and addicts do not have ASPD, a large proportion of ASPs are alcoholics or addicts. Under the law, drug addicts are engaged in antisocial behavior. However, if the drug use stopped, most addicts would not engage in other antisocial behaviors. For the ASP, drug use is just one of many high-risk and illegal behaviors.

Some research has indicated that learning to lie extensively in childhood may be a strong predictor of antisocial behavior in an adult. As the DSM-IV-TR criteria explain, antisocial behavior in the form of a conduct disorder prior to age fifteen is a necessary requirement for the ASPD diagnosis, and lying is one of the core criteria of a conduct disorder.

Treatment of the ASP is difficult. For those who do not meet the full criteria for ASPD, Beck (1990) has shown that some cognitive therapy methods have been successful at addressing traits of ASPD. However, for those who are diagnosed with the full disorder treatment is difficult because they have many qualities that make them antagonistic to personal change and to bonding with therapists—or with anyone.

Meloy has found that extremely low or extremely high intelligence are factors that decrease the likelihood of successful treatment in an ASP. This would make sense, given the lack of insight for the low-intelligence ASP, and the high-intelligence ASP's strong ability to manipulate.

However, group therapies have had some success. Some examples are batterers groups for treating perpetrators of domestic violence; long-term therapeutic communities for hard-core drug addicts; and prison treatment groups for child molesters. These programs are all based on direct confrontation by peers who share many of the same characteristics and therefore can see through the cons and connect with the true vulnerability ASPs feel deep beneath the surface. While these groups appear to be the treatments of choice for ASPs, the success rate appears far more limited than for the other personality disorders. This would make sense, given the inability of ASPs to form interpersonal bonds—in contrast to Borderline personalities and Narcissistic personalities, who form bonds (albeit negative and conflictual) upon which positive treatment can be based.

General Considerations

Attorneys working with this population must be wary of reinforcing their manipulative behaviors and must be attentive to protecting themselves, physically and legally. Mediators are less frequently involved in dealing with this population, but the same cautions will apply. Therapists may be called to evaluate ASPs for a variety of purposes related to allegations of criminal behavior. The likelihood of manipulation is extremely high and most therapists are not trained in or skilled at detecting deception. In providing psychotherapy to ASPs, therapists must be realistic and feel comfortable using consultation and feedback from other sources regarding the client's true behavior.

Perhaps the more likely concern for most attorneys, mediators and therapists is having clients with traits of ASPD. These are the clients who look good and do not yet have a known history of criminal convictions, but may have been engaged in criminal behavior without getting caught and may be highly manipulative and charming. Because they are so adept at appearing normal and credible, their claims of innocence or allegations against others may be believed by legal professionals and even the courts. Greater skepticism and training are needed in this area.

Antisocial personalities have no fear. They're not afraid of lying and getting caught; they're not afraid of using other people or hurting them; and they certainly are not afraid of authority, including the courts. They will lie and manipulate without conscience or concern for others.

Courts have a particularly hard time spotting ASPs, because they are so good at manipulating sympathy. They are the most persuasive victims—not because they are true victims, but because they have learned that this works. They do whatever will work, without being inhibited by reflection, guilt or fear, which would stop most of us from even considering such behavior.

Mr. Oliver

Even some professionals can have ASP traits and be difficult for peers to handle.

Mr. Oliver was a mental health professional with a substance abuse problem. One day he was arrested with a substantial amount of methamphetamine. Even though he was charged with selling the drug (the police had plenty of evidence), he claimed that it was just for his own use. He stated that he needed help with his addiction, and that he would agree to attend a treatment program and do community service rather than go to prison for ten years, which the district attorney was seeking.

Addiction is a commonly recognized problem in modern court systems. It is widely understood that addicts in recovery can be very productive citizens. He might have been eligible for some diversion programs, possibly under the supervision of a "drug court." He sought recommendations for such an approach from other mental health professionals.

But in reality, there were several warning signs of ASPD. A substantial quantity of methamphetamine usually indicates that the possessor is selling the drug. A drug dealer selling a powerful stimulant is qualitatively different from a drug user who only hurts himself (and those who have to cope with him). Drug dealers frequently have a history of increasing willingness to violate social rules, a lack of remorse for the drug's effect on others, a thrill from conning others and getting away with it and a life-time history of manipulation and deceit.

In this case, Mr. Oliver was arrested with a substantial number of automatic weapons, tens of thousands of dollars in cash, a highly sophisticated surveillance system and evidence he was selling the drug to teenagers. Despite his use of all the right psychological words for treatment, he was unable to persuade his colleagues to recommend that he should stay out of prison.

Family Courts

Over the past decade I have noticed a significant increase in ASP traits in family court cases—and they fool almost everyone, at least for a while. In recommending how to work with Antisocial clients, Sanford Portnoy in *The Family Lawyer's Guide to Building Successful Client Relationships* specifically advises family law attorneys to be on guard for shifting stories and aggressive behavior that violates or disregards the rights of others.

Mr. Halo

From my experience in family courts, I have seen at least ten cases involving individuals with ASPD similar to the following:

In September 1994, Mr. Halo became involved with another woman and divorced his wife. They did a simple divorce agreement, and he filed it with the court about a year later. Based on their agreement, the mother had primary physical custody of their son, Peter, who was six years old at the time. Two years later, the mother remarried a Mr. Johnson, who had two children who lived with them half-time.

Over the next five years Mr. Halo, a self-employed plumber, somewhat sporadically paid $200 a month in child support. He occasionally saw his son, but refused to follow any schedule. There were times when he went a couple of months without seeing Peter.

By January 1999 Mr. Halo's business was doing better and the mother found out what the child support guidelines would be. Based on her estimate of what he made, she could receive as much as $800 to $1,000 per month instead of the $200 he was paying. She wrote a letter to Mr. Halo requesting this increase, but received no reply.

On March 1, 1999, the mother was served with papers filed at court by Mr. Halo. The papers stated that a Family Court Services (FCS) counseling appointment was scheduled for March 8, and that there would be a hearing two weeks later about a change of Peter's custody to the father. When she and Mr. Halo met jointly with the FCS counselor, Mr. Halo pulled out a letter written by a therapist about Peter, now eleven years old, and read it to the FCS counselor:

"I interviewed Mr. Halo and his son, Peter, eleven years of age, on Saturday, February 1, 1999. I spent most of the session with Peter alone, then the last fifteen minutes with Peter and his father together. Peter told me that his stepfather, Mr. Johnson, inflicted a lot of emotional distress on him. Peter began crying and shaking while he related his story to me. He told me that his stepfather locked him in his room for hours at a time, and that his mother kept him from seeing his father. He said that his stepfather screams and yells at him all the time.

I became very concerned for his welfare, which is why I am writing this declaration. I am recommending that Mr. Halo immediately seek an order from the court appointing a mental health professional to begin therapy with Peter.

As you know, it is not my style to treat a child without the knowledge and, if possible, involvement of both parents. In an initial telephone conversation with Mr. Halo I told him of my policy and he agreed to tell Peter's mother about the appointment after it took place, when he returned Peter to his mother. During the session last Saturday, Mr. Halo expressed a reluctance to do so, stating that he felt repercussions from this would impact Peter in a negative manner.... I was not given the telephone number, so I remain unable to speak with Peter's mother."

After he read this, Mr. Halo told the FCS counselor that the therapist said that life was a "living hell" for Peter in the mother's household. The FCS counselor was so concerned for Peter that she took the letter.

The mother was aghast to hear of this letter from an unknown therapist who had never been to her house nor even spoken with her. The FCS counselor made a copy for the mother. The mother called the therapist and expressed her anger about the secret session. She said that Peter must have been coached by his father, because he had been doing fine in her home. His grades were sufficient and he was involved in sports. They spoke very briefly. The next day, the mother was served with a declaration written by her son, also signed on February 1—a month before the mother even knew there was a court case about to happen. Peter and his father had kept all of this a secret from his mother for a month. Peter's letter said the following:

"To the Family Court Judge: My mother treats me like a little boy. Sometimes she pulls my hair. I want to live with my father. We always have fun together. I hope the custody battle doesn't interfere with my trip to Alaska with my father this summer."

The mother was shocked to read her son writing words like "custody battle." She'd never even heard her son use such words before. Then she went back to look at Mr. Halo's declaration, signed March 1 and served with the papers announcing the "change of custody" hearing:

"The situation in Mrs. Johnson's household has adversely affected Peter. Peter has shown signs of emotional problems and instability. He has low self-esteem and self-confidence. This could probably be documented by a child counselor."

She realized that on March 1 he was pretending that no child counselor had been seen. "This could probably be documented ..." Then the mother received the FCS counselor's report.

"I spoke with the child's therapist. She told me that the mother was hostile and making accusations that the father had coached the child. The therapist said that she saw no sign of coaching and that she believed every word that Peter said. She expressed great concern about his welfare in the mother's home. The mother's negative attitude seemed to confirm what the father had said, the therapist told me.

I also considered the mother's allegation that the father has a drinking problem and has given the son an occasional drink. The father reassured me that he stopped drinking a year ago and that he never gave the son a drink.

I met with the son alone, while both parents waited outside in the waiting room. He denied ever being given a drink by his father and said that he enjoys his time with his father more than his mother. But that he loves both of them. He said that his mother annoys him and treats him like a young child sometimes.

Therefore, I am recommending an immediate change of custody to the father. The child seems to have a stronger bond with the father and has conflicts with his mother and stepfather. He also seems very frightened of his stepfather. I recommend that he only spend time with the stepfather in the mother's presence."

At the subsequent court hearing, the mother's attorney argued that the father had manipulated the therapist, the FCS counselor and the court process. He requested a psychological evaluation to thoroughly examine the situation before any such change of custody occur. However, the judge was persuaded by the father's apparent sincerity and interest in his son.

"We have two mental health professionals reaching the exact same conclusion: The child's therapist and the FCS counselor. Therefore, I see no need for a psychologist. This appears to be a very concerned father who has a strong bond with his son. The change of custody will be effective today."

The father immediately stopped paying child support to the mother. He never made any effort to set up counseling for the child. The mother insisted that counseling be set up, but the father refused and said the problems were solved by the change of custody. Besides, it would cost too much.

Friends of the mother said they still saw him drinking. In January 2000 there was a change of judges and the mother went back to court to again request a psychological evaluation and to explain to the court that the father was still drinking. She persuaded the new judge to order the evaluation and the parents were ordered to split the cost.

Not surprisingly, the father delayed agreeing on who the psychologist would be and then he delayed paying his share of the deposit for the evaluation. Over the course of the next year, the psychologist held many meetings with each parent, with the son, and with each parent and the son together.

Since this was going to start costing him money, the father decided to seek child support from the mother. But since another family court hearing would not occur until the evaluation was complete, Mr. Halo decided to go to a different court. There was a separate court in this county for family support matters involving the district attorney's office. He sought the district attorney's assistance, and they scheduled a hearing on child support. When the hearing date came, Mr. Halo didn't show up because the district attorney's office was taking care of it for him. Mrs. Johnson didn't show up because she didn't know about it. He never had her served with the papers for the hearing.

The family support court ordered a continuance and the mother was served with the court papers. She had to hire an attorney to assist her in preparing a written response and going to the hearing. At the hearing the father again wasn't present. The mother's attorney explained that the case was active in another court, and that the psychological evaluation was now held up because the father wouldn't make his final payment to the psychologist. Once he paid, the family court would address custody, visitation and child support. The family support court dismissed the case.

The father finally paid the psychologist and the report came out. There was nothing to support the allegations against the mother and stepfather, so the restriction against the son being alone with the stepfather was removed. However, since the son was established in the father's home, the psychologist didn't want to return to the prior schedule. He also observed that when they came to his office the son appeared more relaxed and play-ful with the father than he did with the mother. So the psychologist rec-ommended–and the mother reluctantly agreed–that the mother have forty per cent of the parenting time and that the father have sixty per cent. This was an increase for the mother from the twenty per cent visitation time she had had during the year and a half from the first change of cus-tody hearing, and she was not going to push it any further. Peter seemed happy with both his Mom and his Dad, so she decided not to put him through any more stress.

But there was still the father's request for child support. By then, the moth-er's payroll income was higher than the income the father was reporting–except that his income was completely unreliable. So the mother's attorney used subpoenas and document demands to obtain copies of his tax returns and financial records for the past three years. By now, her attorney sus-pected that Mr. Halo had antisocial traits, so he particularly wanted to ana-lyze his tax returns. Not surprisingly, Mr. Halo listed his girlfriend and her children as dependents on his tax return. He also seemed to report only about half of his actual income. This disparity in analyses of his true income was presented to the court, and the judge ordered a Special Master to determine his true income. He said that the party who turned out to be the most accurate would have their attorney's fees paid by the party who was most incorrect. Both sides remained confident in their calculations.

After many delays, manipulations and complaints by Mr. Halo, the Special Master submitted a report and recommendations to the court. His conclusion was that Mr. Halo was not being forthright about his income and was not providing documents requested by the Special Master. The judge decided the father's income based on the mother's calculations and made him pay her attorney's fees. With enough investigation, his deceptions and manipulations were finally made clear to the court. The judge ordered child support in the amount of $100 a month from the father to the mother.

The net financial result of the above case for the father was a saving of $100 per month in child support payments, when he had been faced with an increase of $800 to $1,000. But another strong reason for his actions would be his drive to dominate, rather than feel dominated by, the other parent. Whenever I see this pattern in a custody dispute, it appears to be triggered by a change in financial expectations. Either the Antisocial has had a financial setback, or the other parent has made a financial request. The urge to dominate—and the fear of feeling dominated—seems to emotionally drive the ASP to seek custody. It's not just about money.

Oh, and by the way: the mother and her husband, Mr. Johnson, successfully raised his two children in their home at the same time as this two-year custody battle was proceeding. The children got top grades in school and won some awards. This is in the home called a "living hell" at the start of the case, when Mr. Halo launched his secret bid for custody.

The overall pattern that I have seen in several of these Antisocial trait cases (primarily with ASP-trait fathers but at least one ASP-trait mother) is as follows:

1. There is a history of several years of fairly non-controversial parenting by the mother, with no serious complaints by the father.

2. The father's involvement with the child or children has been minimal or negative.

3. The father is usually self-employed or works primarily alone, with the ability to control most aspects of his work and manipulate his finances. There may be a history of lying on tax returns, sometimes even blatantly (as in Mr. Halo's reporting his girlfriend and her children as dependents).

4. A financial pressure occurs for the father. This often comes in the form of a request for support—or an increase in support—made by the mother.

5. Father secretly takes the child or children into his confidence. He promises trips, sporting events, cool gear (cell phones, etc.) He also reinforces or encourages criticisms of the mother: "She can really be bossy, irritating, annoying, controlling can't she?" These criticisms often focus on bonding with the child in an adolescent manner around issues of independence against the authority of the mother.

6. Father and child/children form a fun, child-like conspiracy against the mother—in secret. (So Mom won't get angry and punish you. I'm on your side.) The child feels torn, but it's usually easier to side with a demanding parent against an all-accepting and unsuspecting parent. The child has more to risk in challenging father than mother. And the sense of grown-up freedom is enticing with the father.

7. The child writes a declaration to the court against the mother with vague or unfounded complaints, or the child tells a therapist or FCS court counselor that he or she has complaints against the mother, even using the father's words. ("She's annoying, or she's too controlling.") Father may pressure the court to have the judge speak with the child or to have the child testify against the mother. (This alone is one of the most insensitive acts a parent can do, and almost always indicates a personality disorder and the lack of empathy that comes with it.)

8. Father may take a therapist into his confidence. Father finds a therapist who will see the child without requiring the consent of the mother. He may report a crisis requiring secrecy from the other parent to "protect the child." Father asks the therapist to write a letter to the court, because of the "crisis." The therapist may recommend counseling, but the father does not follow through. It's not his goal.

9. Father may involve other children or adults in building a case against the mother. He tells them extreme events will occur unless they take action on his behalf. (In one case, an apparently Antisocial father got a whole soccer team of children to write letters to the judge on behalf of his request to overturn a prior court order.)

10. Father manipulates court procedures, such as not notifying the mother of court hearings, trying to get hearings on an emergency basis so that mother cannot be adequately prepared, changing experts or decision-makers when results are not looking favorable, or going to different courts at the same time on the same issues.

The bottom line is dominance and control to obtain a very short-term goal by any means necessary. There is little empathy, little attention to long-term consequences, and no guilt or remorse. In many cases I have seen, there is no attempt to cover one's tracks or to keep stories straight. I am fascinated when I take depositions of those with antisocial traits, because they freely impeach their own testimony without seeming to notice or care. They confidently figure that they can explain away anything after the fact—and they certainly try. Since there is rarely a specific penalty for perjury, lying doesn't worry them. They don't always get what they want in court (Mr. Halo's effort to get child support from the mother), but sometimes they do (his getting custody).

Antisocials can be identified most easily by their patterns of repeatedly violating minor laws, such as traffic violations or IRS filings. One example was the traffic tickets of Mr. Gossage in Chapter One. In another example, in a divorce I handled, the husband told his wife and the court counselor that he had never been arrested for drunk driving—when in reality he had been arrested twice for this and had a trial scheduled for the following week! I easily found this out by researching public court records. I guess they do not expect that I will research their statements, or they believe they can talk their way out of the results.

Mr. Nu

The Nu family provides another example from my files of an ASP in family court.

Mr. Nu and his wife came to the United States from an Asian country. A decade and two sons later, the couple separated. Mr. Nu was an apparently successful small businessman who ran a cash business. He had numerous judgments related to his business against him at the County Recorder's office.

During the divorce proceedings he submitted tax returns showing his business grossed $500,000 in a year, but that his profit was only $2,000. However, the IRS had no record of any tax returns filed by Mr. Nu. It turned out that his accountant had been convicted of felony mail fraud. In the divorce, the court was persuaded of Mr. Nu's fiscal dishonesty and ignored his threats to declare bankruptcy. The wife was awarded an equalizing payment of $80,000 and alimony of $1,000 a month.

However, Mr. Nu prevailed on the parenting issues. The wife had left the family home so that their two sons, ages eleven and thirteen, would not have to witness the father's physical abuse of her. She returned to her country of origin several times before the divorce trial.

After she left the home, the father had obtained temporary custody of the sons and she was given alternate weekend visitation and Wednesday evenings when she was in the United States. However, the father involved the boys in his business and they were often not at home when the mother came to pick them up for visitation. At trial, the mother refused to mention the domestic violence, but the father accused her of child abuse, submitting damaging declarations signed by his sons.

A psychologist read the declarations and met with the boys, then met with the mother alone. The psychologist recommended minimal contact for the mother—on Wednesday evenings only, to allow time to "gradually rebuild" her relationship with the boys. The judge accepted the psychologist's recommendations for less time, but added several hours on Sundays as well.

Apparently feeling confident he had won, the father made no effort to follow the court visitation orders and several months later disappeared with the boys. Prior to disappearing, after we put relentless pressure on him, he paid $40,000 on the equalizing payment but none of the spousal support. In frustration, the mother returned to their homeland, returning occasionally to search for her sons. Four years later the mother found the boys, although the youngest refused to visit with her. The eighteen-year-old was apologetic and said the father told them that she had taken all of his money.

Now that we knew where he was, we went to court with an outstanding warrant for his arrest for non-appearance at a previous hearing. The father appeared without his former attorney. When the new judge called our case the father awkwardly stated that he needed his eighteen-year-old son to interpret for him. I objected, stating that in six years he had never needed an interpreter before. The judge overruled my objection with a smile. "If he wants an interpreter, he gets one."

When we were seated before the court, the judge directed his opening comments to the son. The father immediately interjected that he was paid up, that he thought this was all over, and that he couldn't understand why he was in court again.

The judge immediately told him to be quiet, as he did not understand English. "Tell your interpreter," he said. Then the father and son huddled for a few minutes, with the father whispering to his son whatever he wanted to tell the court.

My client leaned over to me, trying to suppress her laughter. "They are whispering in English. My son doesn't know the language of my country at all. We raised him here in the United States." Eventually, the son explained the father's various excuses to the court.

Then the judge became quickly serious and told the father directly. "If you don't start making payments on the $76,000 you still owe her, I am going to have to put you in jail. Do you understand that?" The father instantly answered "Yes." The judge took no further action that day. The father evaded service for the next hearing on his contempt of court orders. The mother again returned to her native country and no further action is expected in the case. There are no assets in his name and the children are now grown. By now he owes her nearly $100,000, but it is unlikely that he will ever be forced to pay it.

CONCLUSION

One of the most striking aspects of ASPs that I have observed in legal disputes is how easily and aggressively they use other people to their advantage in their disputes. Mr. Halo and Mr. Nu involved their children throughout their divorces in a way that most people would find highly disturbing. Jeffrey Streich turned against and used his girlfriend and his business associate to protect himself. Mr. Gossage involved over twenty community leaders and friends in his plea to become an attorney despite his ongoing violations of the law.

Family courts, attorneys and even mental health professionals often think that a manipulative parent's behavior toward the children is based on difficulty getting over the divorce. From my perspective, with ASPs it is much more likely to be that they want control over someone. If they can't control the spouse (who they have often abused), they frequently turn to the children and seek a change of custody. With their charm, childish behavior, false promises and threatening statements, they often win them over in their disputes. For the unwary decision-maker, the child's expressed desires often turn the tide and many ASPs get custody this way.

Another common characteristic is how they go from court to court seeking the decisions they want. I have had several divorce cases in which a party with ASP traits has gone from one court to another seeking diversionary restraining orders or child support reductions, when the case has been pending in the family court where they expect an unfavorable decision. The courts are getting better at keeping track of concurrent case filings, but ASPs are so quick in their actions that they may receive favorable orders before they are found out–if they are found out.

Why do ASPs act the way they do, aggressively pursuing their immediate goals without concern for danger to themselves or others, and without any fear of getting caught? It's their personality. They biologically seem to have extra confidence–and a lifetime of learning to con others. They are not worried about their trail of lies and harmed people. They are fast and skilled at diverting attention.

Antisocials can be very effective in the legal process, where verbal persuasion and suppression of evidence are the rules of the game. They've played this game all their lives.

Chapter Five Summary
Antisocial Personalities:
Con Artists

1. Fear of being dominated is a driving force
2. Repeatedly breaks society's rules and laws
3. Aggressive charm and deceit
4. Drive to dominate others
5. Enjoys harming or taking from others
6. Contemptuous of authorities
7. Lack of remorse and empathy
8. Believable lies and diversions
9. Falsely persuasive about being a victim

Tips and Techniques for Dealing with Antisocial Personality Disorder:

1. Maintain healthy skepticism
2. Avoid being swayed by charm
3. Avoid doing favors
4. Do not expect to change or save him from himself
5. Obtain corroborating information
6. Explain consequences of future misconduct
7. Be prepared to impose and enforce consequences
8. Pay attention to your fears and protect yourself

Histrionic Personalities: Always Dramatic

"He just isn't happy unless he's in the eye of the hurricane."

I suspect I'm dealing with a Histrionic personality (HP) when I spend an hour with my client but only get five minutes of work done.

"He's the most awwwwww-ful person you'll ever meet. It's just not fair how everybody listens to him! You know what he did last week? You have to help me stop him! If you can't make him give me the money he owes me—my rightful share—I'm going to the newspapers and to the police!" And on and on. High-intensity emotion, but few facts and little focus.

More often I hear from attorneys for the other parties, many of whom seem to have this personality disorder, and who dramatically focus their energy on blaming others for every little thing: "Your client is horrible, Mr. Eddy. Do you know what he did yesterday? He... !!!"

Usually the accusation is totally exaggerated, or the event in question did not even occur. After two or three calls like this, I let the other attorney know I empathize, and I try to explain personality disorders.

Identifying Characteristics

A good description of Histrionic Personality Disorder (HPD) can be found in two Court of Appeals cases, one in South Carolina and the other in Wisconsin.

> "According to Dr. Boland, persons suffering from Histrionic Personality Disorder display exaggerated and short-lived emotions, are flirtatious and flighty, lack insight and integrate the experiences poorly. Their judgment tends to be undependable and highly erratic. They may appear charming to casual acquaintances but those with more enduring relationships are likely to see them as testy, irritable, antisocial and manipulative." [25]

---

[25] Housand v. Housand (1998) 333 S.C. 397, 404

It is interesting to note the impact this has on those around them, including their children. The psychologist above, Dr. Boland, explained more after observing each parent with the children:

> "Parents with this style of interaction tend not to provide the structured discipline that children require to develop into healthy well-adjusted adults. They may fluctuate from being passive and ignoring problems to being excessively angry when things have gone too far. In these circumstances, the children merely learn to act out and do as they please until the parents verbally become angry and lose their temper.
>
> By contrast, Dr. Boland found no evidence of any psychological problems in the father that would interfere with his ability to be a parent." [26]

In Wisconsin, an appeals court case involving DeLaMatter v. DeLaMatter emphasized that this disorder does not prevent one from working.

> "Histrionic Personality Disorder affects the manner in which the individual deals with people and is characterized by a tendency to draw attention to one's self, be flamboyant, have shallow relationships with others, but does not affect the individual's ability to maintain employment." [27]

In the DeLaMatter case, the court reversed the trial court's award of alimony to the wife which the trial judge had ordered believing that she could not work based on her panic attacks and HPD. Further, the trial court believed that Ms. DeLaMatter's alcoholism had been caused by her mental illness. The Court of Appeals disagreed and determined that her refusal to get alcoholism treatment was a poor excuse. The court also said that her personality disorder did not itself prevent her from working.

> "Dr. Bjerregaard never opined that Barbara's mental illness precluded her from maintaining employment. To the contrary, he testified that the panic and personality disorders, absent the alcoholism, would not bar Barbara from maintaining steady employment. Rather, it is Barbara's alcoholism that precludes her from being employed. We conclude that the trial court's finding that Barbara's mental illness precludes her employment is clearly erroneous." [28]

---

[26] Housand v. Housand at 405
[27] DeLaMatter v. DeLaMatter (1989) 151 Wis. 2d 576, 581, 587
[87] DeLaMatter v. DeLaMatter at 587

Formal Diagnostic Criteria

Histrionic Personality Disorder is considered to be present in about two to three per cent of the general population and about ten to fifteen per cent of mental health treatment populations, according to the American Psychiatric Association. The majority are women, although there may be a tendency for men with these characteristics to be diagnosed as having some other personality disorder. Histrionic personalities share some similarities to the other Cluster B personality disorders: Borderline (attention-seeking), Antisocial (excitement seeking and manipulative), and Narcissistic (self-centered). Histrionic personalities are known for emotional intensity and drama. The DSM-IV-TR states: "If they are not the center of attention, they may do something dramatic (make up stories, create a scene) to draw the focus of attention to themselves."

In many ways, HPD is an extreme exaggeration of the qualities identified with femininity. Television and movie characters may affect these emotional qualities for dramatic or humorous results. Gregory Lester (1998) has shown how Scarlett O'Hara in *Gone With the Wind* and hundreds of fictional characters since then have demonstrated these characteristics, and how actors, actresses and models may be more likely to have these qualities than the average population.

The DSM-IV-TR defines **Histrionic Personality Disorder**[29] as: *A pervasive pattern of excessive emotionality and attention-seeking, beginning by early adulthood and present in a variety of contexts, as indicated by five (or more) of the following:*

1. *is uncomfortable in situations in which he or she is not the center of attention*

2. *interaction with others is often characterized by inappropriate sexually seductive or provocative behavior*

3. *displays rapidly shifting and shallow expression of emotions*

4. *consistently uses physical appearance to draw attention to self*

---

[29] Reprinted with permission from the Diagnostic and Statistical Manual of Mental Disorders, Fourth Edition, Text Revised. Copyright 2000 American Psychiatric Association

5. *has a style of speech that is excessively impressionistic and lacking in detail*

6. *shows self-dramatization, theatricality, and exaggerated expression of emotion*

7. *is suggestible, i.e., easily influenced by others or circumstances*

8. *considers relationships to be more intimate than they actually are*

Legal disputes provide the HP with an extraordinary opportunity to be the center of dramatic attention. With high-profile cases in the news, an increasing number of legal dramas and more real-life court TV shows, the attraction of HPs to litigation is almost magnetic. Again, in court anyone can be a litigant–simply by claiming an injury or crime Histrionics can be assured that advocates, experts, clerks, support staff and powerful judges will pay attention to them.

At the beginning of the relationship with you as a professional, HPs often present themselves with enticing sexual overtones or false intimacy. This may include affectionate touches, longer-than-usual eye contact and being physically closer than one would expect at the beginning of a client-professional relationship.

The HP may attempt to shock or surprise family, friends or professionals with provocative behavior, or reports of her provocative behavior with others. Legal disputes are often marked by frequent crises, emergency phone calls, or appearances by the HP, and their dramatic reports of the other party's misbehavior are the focus of many phone calls between opposing attorneys. It is easy for the novice attorney to become hooked by an HP, and to become absorbed in attempting to convince the opposing counsel to better manage his or her client's misbehavior. However, often it is the HP's emotionality and provocation at the source of the problem–the other party's behavior often does not fit the dramatic complaints.

Histrionic personalities appear to drive their emotions, in contrast to other personality disorders in which the individuals are often driven by their emotions. Histrionic personalities can be extremely intense in the expression of their emotions, but there is little depth and consistency.

Emotions may be used to get your attention, to make numerous demands upon you, and to try to persuade you of something. However, these emotions may quickly shift and appear to be under more control than those of someone with Borderline Personality Disorder.

The HP may make strong statements with great drama, but be unable to back them up with any detail. For example, an HP may dramatically claim that the other party is committing perjury, but be unable to provide any specific examples in support of this claim.

At times family members, friends and professionals may feel that they are witnessing a performance, rather than an authentic interaction with an HP. Beck (1990) warns that if you feel a lack of empathy for the dramatic display of distress by the person, it may be an indicator of HPD. If the client seems proud of, or excited by, a description of traumatic experiences, this may be a further indicator of HPD.

In its commentary, the DSM-IV-TR states: "Their opinions and feelings are easily influenced by others and by current fads. They may be overly trusting, especially of strong authority figures whom they see as magically solving their problems. They have a tendency to play hunches and to adopt convictions quickly."

I have observed numerous examples of this in legal cases, when an HP is alleged to be exaggerating or lying. The HP immediately and dramatically counter-charges that it is the accuser who is exaggerating and lying. Whatever is alleged against the HP becomes the HP's newest allegation against the other party. While this would seem like a simple retaliatory technique, with HPs it may be due to their suggestibility, rather than an organized response. Dramatic news events or stories by others may quickly inspire similar dramatic tales from the HP. In legal disputes, they may allege they are victims of the latest abuse trend in the news.

As HPs operate so much on an emotional surface, relationships with them are difficult and superficial. Those close to an HP usually maintain an emotional distance while taking care of them and the problems they cause. Those who remain in the HP's life are often very co-dependent, resigned to letting someone else's crises be the focus of their lives. Histrionic personalities can be fascinating and exiting. Romantic relationships with HPs usually start intensely but end up as disasters. They may be stormy for years, then have dramatic endings. Temper tantrums, manipulations and angry outbursts may be common.

While not a specific DSM-IV-TR criteria, fabrication is common and has been noted by psychological authors, such as Ford. Fabrication appears in a range of behaviors, from simple exaggeration to the complete description of nonexistent events. Researchers describe such HPs as unconcerned about truthful details if distortion does a better job.

While noted for their skills at lying, HPs are generally not considered to have the same hostile motivations as those with Antisocial personalities. However, some authors including Ford have found a close similarity with antisocial behavior for some HPs. Apparently some female prisoners, when deprived of the ability to engage in antisocial behaviors, will shift to hysterical behaviors instead.

Generally, this deceitfulness is intended to get people to pay attention to them, or to like them. Unfortunately, since most of their emotions are simply on the surface, their deception and shallowness eventually angers or irritates most people, who then try to escape being around them. True intimacy, therefore, is unlikely for these clients. They deceive themselves as much as anyone.

The Salesman

In 1986, Olan Guilbeau, a mobile home salesman in Louisiana, took sick after a new carpet was installed in his office with an awful-smelling adhesive manufactured by Henry Co.

Two days after the installation he went to his doctor, Dr. Clause, whom he had been seeing for over twenty years, complaining of "headaches, light-headedness, tingling sensations of the skin, and numbness in his chin.... Dr. Clause testified that he observed no distress, confusion, speech or learning impairments, or differences in Guilbeau's behavior." [30]

The next day he went to the hospital.

---

[30] Guilbeau v. Guilbeau (1996) 85F 3d 1149, 1154

> "Guilbeau was examined by Dr. Sabatier, who found decreased oxygen in Guilbeau's blood, which he attributed to smoking; but chest X-rays showed no evidence of organic solvents and no traces of such materials were found in his blood or urine. Mrs. Guilbeau testified that the doctors ran tests and said Guilbeau was fine, but that he should stay away from the office for a couple of days." [31]

He went to work one more day after that, but his wife said that he went home early because of the smell. [S]he then took him to see Dr. Fournet, who again X-rayed his lungs and tested his blood and urine, but found no abnormalities. In October 1986, Guilbeau saw a doctor at Tulane University, who referred him to an internist who referred him to a psychologist, Dr. Friedberg.

> "Dr. Friedberg administered the Minnesota Multiphasic Personality Inventory (MMPI) to Guilbeau. The results and Friedberg's analysis indicated that Guilbeau was a somaticizer, meaning that he complained of physical ailments without physical cause. The MMPI scales for hypochondriasis, hysterical components, conversion reactions, depression and psychopathic deviant (which measures impulsivity and poor impulse control) were elevated.... Friedberg testified that he had treated other toxic exposure patients, **and saw no parallels between those patients and Guilbeau....**" (Emphasis added)[32]

By 1987 a psychiatrist, Dr. Rees, had examined him a total of five times. By then, Guilbeau's symptoms

> "included smelling ether in the bathroom, seeing things that were not there, extreme anxiety, anger and complaints about at least eight parts of his body. Dr. Rees was concerned that Guilbeau might go into an uncontrollable rage. He did not think that exposure to toxins could have caused all the symptoms that Guilbeau was reporting, and could not have caused Guilbeau's unusual anger at every physician he had seen. He testified that he was absolutely certain that Guilbeau's symptoms had nothing to do with his exposure to adhesive, and that he was sure, as the result of his examination, that Guilbeau did not have organic brain damage." [33]

---

[31] Guilbeau v. Henry Co. at 1155
[32] Guilbeau v. Henry Co. at 1156
[33] Guilbeau v. Henry Co. at 1156

Yet Guilbeau's symptoms continued to dramatically escalate. By 1988, his wife testified,

> "his symptoms included impotence; vision problems; pain in his ears, nose, throat, chest and back; sleep disturbances; pressure in his head; penile lesions; sores in his groin area and on his buttocks; fizzy urine with red, white and brown crystals and mushroom-type things that looked like cotton balls in it; white particles in his stool; sores at his hair line which has started to recede; seizures and confusion.
> . . . .
> His diary contains a drawing of his vein, and he reported that he could feel chemical deposits moving through his veins, creating "a cool, itching, raw, burning pain." [34]

By 1989 Guilbeau was seen at the Tulane Medical Center by Dr. Black, professor of neurology and psychiatry, who examined him on two occasions.

> "Dr. Black conducted extensive psychological testing and found no brain damage, but found **somaticizing and Histrionic Personality Disorder.** Dr. Black's 1989 report states that Guilbeau's complaints are more likely than not **due to a psychiatric disorder** rather than to residual effects of any alleged toxic exposure." [35]

By 1989 the Guilbeaus also had posted a sign on the door to their house, which stated:

DO NOT ENTER if you are wearing the following: perfume; hair spray; cologne; aftershave; deodorants; new clothing; powder; makeup. There is a Toxic person living in this house who is allergic to all these above products. With your understanding, we can help him from having severe seizures and severe multiple pain.

However, the Court of Appeals was not impressed with his sensitivities:

> "Amazingly, the smoke from the one-and-one-half to two packs of cigarettes he smokes each day has no adverse effect on Guilbeau; and he is not bothered if others smoke cigarettes in his presence. He uses a lighter with lighter fluid to light his cigarettes, but has not complained about the smell from the lighter fluid." [36]

---

[34] Guilbeau v. Henry Co. at 1155
[35] Guilbeau v. Henry Co. at 1155
[36] Guilbeau v. Henry Co. at 1155

One of the lessons I have learned from high-conflict personalities is that they can eventually find a doctor, lawyer or other professional who will agree with them, although the professional may not be very well-respected. In this case the Guilbeaus found Dr. Callender, who became their expert witness. In 1987 they found attorneys and filed suit against the Henry Company. The case finally **proceeded to trial in January 1994** on its 13th setting, with the Guilbeaus being represented by their **third set of lawyers** since the suit was filed." (Emphasis added)[37]

At a previous trial date in 1993, the Guilbeaus were not ready but Henry Co. was. The court ordered one of the Guilbeaus' attorneys to pay $11,186 to Henry as sanctions, to cover Henry's expenses in preparing for trial for the December setting. The Court of Appeals had many negative things to say about the Guilbeaus' attorneys, citing the possible coaching of a witness as "a typical example of the numerous problems arising out of the conduct of counsel throughout the trial." [38]

At this point in our story, it would appear that so many doctors and other professionals had reached such similar conclusions—somaticizing and HP— that there would be no chance of success in court. No one in twenty years had been adjudicated to be harmed by the Henry Co. solvent, which had been sold to thousands of people. The person who replaced Guilbeau felt fine in the office. The two workers who installed the carpet said it smelled, but they also felt fine afterwards. But think again. The Guilbeaus won at trial! They convinced the jury that they had both been injured—Mrs. Guilbeau by loss of consortium with her disabled husband. The jury awarded Mr. Guilbeau $2 million and Mrs. Guilbeau $900,000.

How could this happen? Remember what I've said about "peripheral persuasion" and the emotional appeal of HPD. At the trial level, the judge and the jury get to see all the trauma that the parties can muster.

However, from the Court of Appeals' opinion, it appears that emotions played too big a part with the jury, and that facts were glossed over or simply not addressed. The Court of Appeals reversed the decision and found in favor of the defendant, Henry Co. They were particularly critical of the attorneys for Guilbeau. Henry Co. claimed that Guilbeau's "trial counsel engaged in improper trial conduct and made improper closing arguments to confuse and inflame the jury." The Court of Appeals appears to have agreed:

---

[37] Guilbeau v. Henry Co. at 1159
[38] Guilbeau v. Henry Co. at 1163

> "...the conduct by the Guilbeaus' trial counsel and appellate counsel causes more than great concern. Counsel is cautioned that such conduct in the future will result in the imposition of severe sanctions. But, this great concern goes beyond sanctions; the greatest concern is that counsel seems intent on winning at any cost, notwithstanding concomitant violations of long-established rules of practice and evidence (all designed to attempt to ensure fundamental fairness), and in disregard, it seems, of the truth." (Emphasis added)[39]

It cannot be known from reading the opinion of the appeals court if the attorneys were simply communicating the views and personalities of the Guilbeaus in their actions, or if they were independently acting badly. From my experience, the attorneys for Cluster B personality disorders tend to either share their proclivities for extreme emotional manipulation or are simply doing whatever their clients want—to their own detriment. But this observation by the Court of Appeals seems well put and similar to many other cases.

Karen's Support

Karen was in her early 50s with a teenage son when she decided to divorce her husband, Alan. She made many allegations throughout her divorce hearings and trial. Some were ignored, others were played down, and a few were accepted as completely true. Overall, the courts believed her dramatic words over her less litigious, generally deferential husband, Alan.

At one point after the divorce trial was over, Alan had to be out of the country on business for four months. His former family law attorney, Mr. Brown, agreed to take over paying his child support out of his paychecks, which were deposited into Mr. Brown's client trust account. The checks came and were dutifully paid to Karen for her monthly support. There was a minor mix-up the first month over the support amount, and she was underpaid. Mr. Brown retroactively corrected this by sending her an additional check the next month, on February 15.

After the corrected support amount was paid, to give the appearance that he fixed it at her demand Karen wrote Mr. Brown a letter demanding that he correct it. Her letter was dated February 10 and said: "Since you are the one writing the support checks I wanted to first notify you that I will seek out the help of the district attorney if the arrears are not paid by

[39] Guilbeau v. Henry Co. at 1171

February 20." However her letter was postmarked February 20–after she had received the payment. She also sent Mr. Brown a separate letter dated February 20 stating that she had "received a check written out of your account today..." This letter was also postmarked February 20.

When she learned that Alan was going to return a month early and that there was a new judge in family court, she rushed to court alleging that Alan was $4,000 in arrears on support. (While Alan was gone, the prior judge had set aside $8,000 of Alan's separate property funds from the divorce into a trust account managed by Karen's former attorney, in case his paychecks stopped and she got no support. She had convinced the court that he was unreliable.)

No one opposed her at this ex parte (emergency) hearing on March 30, since she failed to give proper notice of the hearing. Using her dramatic style, she was so persuasive about her poor child and herself that the judge didn't just give her the $4,000 "arrears" she requested, but gave her the full $8,000, which she promised she would put in a trust. She rushed to her former attorney's office with her new court order and got the funds released before Mr. Brown found out.

A week later, Mr. Brown went to court for an ex parte hearing (for which he gave notice to Karen) and explained to the new judge the support payment system and that Alan was totally up-to-date. The judge vacated his prior order and told Karen to immediately return the $8,000 to Mr. Brown's office to be held in his trust account until further hearing. Despite her promise to put it in trust, all that was left of the $8,000 was $2,000. She had spent most of it within one week.

Karen played the victim and was a persuasive blamer. She was able to make up emotional facts that sounded reasonable, then she would quickly draw a conclusion which was also reasonable–except that the facts upon which it was based were fabricated. She was so quick that she shifted the focus to her reasonable conclusion with an emotional intensity that demanded attention. As she said in bold black letters in her declaration requesting the $8,000:

"In addition to not providing support for the children, respondent has cancelled their health insurance, and ignored requests for daycare reimbursements....

Due to this court case, I have lost three jobs due to excessive time off for court, I am without credit, without money, and am in debt. Please release the money so that we can get on with our lives."

Given that she was so emotionally persuasive, the only issue at court became how much money to give her. By May, they had a hearing on this issue. Mr. Brown explained to the court that none of the above statements was true. They were all fabrications. In fact, he pointed out, Karen had submitted to the court her letters to him of February 10 and February 20, and even they were fabrications. Karen hotly denied this, and angrily accused Mr. Brown of lying.

So Mr. Brown submitted the envelopes to the court, which showed both letters were postmarked the same day, February 20. The February 10 letter was sent after he had paid her the support correction. The judge asked Karen why the letter she had submitted dated February 10 was mailed on February 20. She burst into tears and said she didn't know how that could have happened, but that she was a poor single mother who got no support from an absentee father. She desperately needed the money, she said.

Mr. Brown explained that Alan was not in arrears, had not cancelled the health insurance, and that she had never submitted any requests for day-care reimbursements. He explained that Mr. Brown had in fact been paying the support all along. The judge decided to have a neutral Special Master determine if there were any arrears. Another hearing was scheduled for September.

At the September hearing, Karen argued strongly that Mr. Brown had committed perjury and should be punished. Surprisingly, in response to his argument that she rushed to court to get Alan's money after she heard he had returned a month early, she said that she did not know that he returned until ten days after she got the $8,000. She didn't even need to lie about this, but she did. She had already stated on her initial ex parte declaration in March when she requested the $8,000: "He has recently returned from overseas."

At the September hearing, the Special Master presented a report stating that Mr. Brown had actually overpaid Karen for child support by a few dollars. Karen saw that the arrears issue was going against her, so she tried to dodge the subject. The judge had the same problem Mr. Brown did with getting her to focus.

The Court: *And the appearance for the ex parte was specifically to deal with what you perceived to be arrearages, correct?*

Karen Smith: *Actually, it was about the insurance and the need for medical attention.*

The Court: *On your document it says he has not been paying his support.*

Karen Smith: *Well, that was another issue. Right. I didn't realize because Mr. Brown holds the trust fund. He had substituted out. His only job was to pay the support out of the trust fund while Mr. Smith was overseas. He wasn't the attorney of record. He had substituted out.*

The Court: *But yet you wrote him about arrearages.*

Karen Smith: *Only because he was in charge of writing the check. Mr. Smith does not write me a check; Mr. Brown does.*

The Court: *I know. See, I'm concerned about your representations made to me at the ex parte which started all of this, and I still have some concerns about that. Proceed.*

Karen Smith: *So anyway, I was not aware that Mr. Smith had returned....*

At the end of the September hearing, the judge was convinced that there were no arrears. He ordered sanctions against Karen in the amount of $500, to be paid by Karen for Alan's attorney fees for having to litigate this issue. However, the health insurance and daycare reimbursements needed to be resolved. So another hearing was scheduled, which finally occurred in December. At the hearing, the court resolved all of these issues:

> "As of March 30th, the Court finds there are no arrearages based on child support, spousal support, medical expenses or daycare costs.

> Based on the Court's previous orders, Petitioner is to reimburse Respondent the sum of $8,000."

Unfortunately, it had cost Alan about $3,000 in attorney's fees over ten months to get this issue resolved. Karen never paid the $500, but Alan was able to get the rest of his $8,000 back through a wage garnishment through her employer.

This case is unusual in that Mr. Brown was able to show that one party was in fact acting inappropriately—in this case it was the wife. It slowed Karen down so that she stopped pursuing hearings, which she had done every few months for two years with the previous judge, who had avoided concluding that either party was acting inappropriately or lying.

Some important conclusions about HPD cases, from my experience and case research:

1. Histrionic personalities are driven by their strong emotions, and the intensity of their emotions can make them look, act and sound persuasive as victims.

2. Courts are especially concerned about helping victims and punishing perpetrators, so they are especially vulnerable to Histrionics.

3. Histrionic personalities are constantly bending or fabricating emotional facts. They often don't know where the line is between true and false— it's all based on dramatic effect; whatever works to achieve an immediate goal. False allegations can be made quickly, but getting the full facts out can take months or years. Even with Karen Smith's single issue, it took ten months to get it fully resolved.

4. Court conflicts often look like two high-conflict personalities fighting. Whenever Alan would say that Karen was lying, she would simply use that allegation back on him. From the outside, it could look like two people who liked to bicker. As occurred in the Smith and in the Guilbeau cases, the court concluded that one person was acting inappropriately and that the other was not.

5. Once this conclusion is finally reached, the case stops escalating and the principals may actually stop coming to court.

Dependency on Others

While dependency on others is not a criteria for a formal DSM-IV determination of HPD, it appears to be a strong characteristic noted by many authors including Beck (1990). Those with HPD generally have developed the belief that they cannot handle matters on their own. Therefore they constantly seek attention and assistance from others. They use this dramatic approach to handle problems they cannot handle themselves.

Karen Smith really was having difficulty balancing finances, work and children, mostly because of her own emotion-driven life. From the start of her case it seemed that she expected the court to solve all her problems, no matter how small. Mr. Guilbeau's life seemed to be on hold, as he expected the court to do something about his problem—which most professionals and the appeals court said did not exist.

Self-Sabotage in Dispute Resolution

Because of their attention-seeking and provocative behavior, HPs frequently find themselves offending others or feeling offended in a highly dramatic way. Yet they take no responsibility for their reactions, such as admitting they are inappropriate or exaggerating. They frequently remain engaged in a campaign of gathering allies against their alleged persecutors.

To resolve a dispute by compromise—with the HP making some concessions—would shatter the HP's fantasy that the problems are all caused by others. Since maintaining a false image of being lovable and competent is a preoccupation for the HP, any concessions may feel life-threatening. Therefore, negotiation and mediation may be difficult.

In court, HPs may enjoy performing and playing out the fantasy of a victim—modeled after one of the celebrity victims they have seen so often on television. However, this wears thin with the court personnel who must deal with the HP. They eventually become angry and reject her, resulting in exactly the experience she had hoped to avoid.

The interpersonal goal of the HP is to be loved and cared for. However, in reality, the HP's behavior triggers anger and intense desire to escape from the relationship. As each person around her eventually abandons ship, she must constantly be on the lookout for new people to care for her—and her drama continues and escalates yet again.

Conflicts With Professionals

For HPs, relationships with professionals quickly turn sour. This is often based on their high drama and excessive demands for time and attention. While at first they are seen as charming and even seductive, this wears off quickly as they turn on the heat of their intense emotions. Professionals may be easily charmed or drawn into deep concern about the HP's problems. One must be careful to ask for supporting details to corroborate all of the dramatic allegations.

It is important for professionals to understand that HPs do not remember events with attention to detail. Instead, their memories are emotion-driven and highly dramatic. This is not necessarily an intentional deception, and often it is a true self-deception. However, it is best to find corroboration for their allegations.

With intense emotions and dramatic claims, it is easy for the novice professional to be seduced into assuming the role of super-hero. Demands may be so endless that the professional is tempted to give in to them rather than resist the HP. This is a serious mistake. In this manner, warns Beck, the professional simply re-enacts a typical relationship pattern of the HP. To avoid falling into this pattern, the professional must help the HP focus on details and straight-forward assertiveness. One must avoid getting absorbed in the drama, focusing instead on specifically what occurred or specifically what needs to be done next.

If the Histrionic does not get her needs handled as she wishes, she will frequently seek other professionals to get assistance, including having others put pressure on the attorney, mediator or therapist. Ultimately, HPs frequently change therapists, attorneys and other professionals in order to avoid intimacy and to avoid risking rejection. In contrast to Borderline Personality Disorder, those with HPD do not maintain angry attachments, but instead lose interest and move on—on a frequent basis.

Causes and Treatments

Beck quotes the widely respected personality researcher, Ted Millon, as seeing HPD as a result of biology and social learning. Some studies have indicated that HPD may have some hereditary factors and be biologically closely related to Antisocial Personality Disorder. Some genetic studies by Ford indicate that families with Antisocial sons more frequently produce Histrionic daughters.

Some psychoanalysts see the development of HPD as resulting from unresolved early childhood issues. For example, rather than developing an identification with her mother, a girl may have developed an excessive competition with her mother for her father's attention. Perhaps she was so successful that she has remained stuck in this role. Most prevalent is the belief that HPD is caused by a combination of biological and social experiences in early childhood.

One of the key components of treatment for HPD is teaching the client to become more logical and problem solving, in contrast to her highly emotional responses to events. Research by Beck indicates there has been success with cognitive-behavioral therapy on an individual and group level. Learning to focus on facts and details, and to replace dramatic words and emotions with more realistic ones, are helpful aspects of the treatment. Fortunately, this focus on specifics and tasks is also highly compatible with helping the HP resolve her legal disputes.

Chapter Six Summary
Histrionic Personalities:
Always Dramatic

1. Fear of being ignored is driving force
2. Dramatic and exaggerated speech and stories
3. Demands to be center of attention
4. Theatrical mannerisms and appearance
5. Superficial emotions and relationships
6. Presents self as helpless, in need of being rescued
7. Lacks detail and focus
8. Will fabricate stories and lie for attention
9. Falsely persuasive as a victim of horrible abuses

Tips and Techniques for Dealing with Histrionic Personality Disorder

1. Maintain healthy skepticism
2. Listen respectfully, then try to focus on tasks
3. Empathize with feelings, not with alleged abuses
4. Maintain balance of interest and limits on stories
5. Provide structure and focus
6. Avoid over-reacting to intense emotions
7. Avoid using strong anger or intense criticism
8. Teach self-help skills, encourage self-sufficiency

The Enablers: Family, Friends and Professionals

"Edwina, we can't go on forever propping each other up like this."

This may be the most important chapter in this book. While those with high-conflict personalities (HCPs) have enduring patterns of behavior that are hard to change, those around them are usually more capable of making behavioral changes. This is where the most potential exists for change in high-conflict disputes.

High-conflict personalities don't get very far unless they persuade others to adopt their cognitive distortions and assist in their interpersonal battles. In substance-abuse treatment, we call these persons "enablers." They enable the abuser to stay stuck in negative behavior, negative thinking and avoidance of responsibility. I use the term "negative advocate" for enablers in legal disputes, because the adversarial process relies so heavily on professional and non-professional advocates. Enablers—often inadvertently—advocate for the cognitive distortions and negative behavior of HCPs.

High-conflict disputes don't occur without one or more negative advocates—at least I've never seen it happen. On their own, most HCPs lack credibility. They seek negative advocates to justify their misbehavior and misperceptions, and to assist them in blaming others for their life problems—to advocate for them.

Getting it Backward

Negative advocates are those family members, friends, mental health professionals and legal professionals who try to help but get it backwards—they adopt or agree with the HCP's backward thinking. They become persuaded—especially by Cluster B persuasive blamers—to focus all their attention on other people's alleged misbehavior. They help the HCP to avoid responsibility and to hold others responsible for their own problems and behavior. They agree with, and advocate for, the cognitive distortions of HCPs: their all-or-nothing thinking, emotional reasoning, personalizing events, exaggerating minor (or nonexistent) events and minimizing their own major misbehaviors. Negative advocates help HCPs stay sick.

Negative advocates absorb the high-intensity emotions of the HCP and often enhance them to a higher level of urgency—they amplify their distorted thinking and join in generating emotional facts. They have adopted the HCP's process of emotional reasoning. If family members, friends and professionals would become more skeptical and avoid becoming negative advocates, high-conflict disputes would significantly reduce the pressure on our legal system.

Betty Broderick

Betty Broderick in Chapter One gives us a good example of blaming and finding enablers. Two years after the murders of Dan and Linda Broderick, the news media reported that she still would not accept any responsibility for her actions. She claimed that Dan and Linda brought on their own deaths: Dan by "legal bullying" and Linda by having an affair.

Apparently, even twelve years later she truly believed it was Dan Broderick's fault that she killed him. And for a while she convinced many others of this as well—prolonging her case for two years and two juries. One juror from her first trial even stated that he was surprised that Betty "waited so long" before killing Dan after how he used the legal system against her.

Not only did that juror evaluate her behavior as acceptable, he became a negative advocate for her in the deliberation process, amplifying her distorted way of thinking. This is what often happens when an HCP persuades someone. The HCP's emotional drive persuades them there is a crisis, so the negative advocate picks up that sense of crisis and also becomes emotional and aggressive in defending the HCP. However, the negative advocate usually has more credibility, and therefore is more able to persuade others. It's the domino theory of negative advocates. In some cases, negative advocates are able to persuade a lot of other people to become negative advocates.

Eben Gossage

As we saw in the Gossage case, twenty well-respected people advocated for Mr. Gossage and convinced the Bar Court that he had reformed.

> They included his girlfriend and other personal friends, his real estate partner and other business associates, college and law school professors, and prominent public officials. Also appearing for Gossage were two

attorneys who had represented him in criminal court, one attorney who attended law school with Gossage, one attorney with whom he worked as a student clerk, and one attorney who was his landlord. The foregoing witnesses described Gossage as an honest person who had expressed remorse for killing his sister and for committing drug-related crimes.[40]

It appears that his friends didn't know about his on-going traffic violations and that he only disclosed four out of seventeen criminal convictions on his application to become an attorney. Yet their testimony had a powerful impact on the approving Bar Court, which otherwise was unlikely to accept his application. It took the Supreme Court of California to see the pattern in his actions, and to look beyond the emotional persuasion.

The Stockbroker

Jeffrey (Chapter Five) was able to recruit Marisa in his scheme. She was essential to helping him, and she had credibility where he did not, along with access to essential information. She thought he was great and defended him to her friends, telling them admiringly that he was the type of guy who would give you $50 for a pack of cigarettes and tell you to keep the change. She then assisted him in bilking her employers, then she defended him after he was caught—and even after he turned her in.

"He knew exactly how to play her personality," one of her friends said. "He'd tell her she was in a different category from everyone else. I think a lot of people would be like 'Give me a break,' but she believed him."

"My friends blame Jeffrey Streich for what has occurred," she said. "I see it differently. He was no friend but I only blame myself. I have tried to understand why I acted the way I did and to deal with the pieces of my life that are left." [41]

Perhaps she learned the lesson that blaming others doesn't work in the long run, and took responsibility herself. A reformed negative advocate?

---

[40] In Re Eben Gossage at 1092-93
[41] Annals of Finance: Marissa and Jeff

Similarities With Substance Abuse

In the 1980s I worked for six years in a psychiatric hospital and an outpatient clinic as a mental health professional in substance abuse treatment. One of the programs I worked with was the Co-dependency Program for family members of alcoholics and drug addicts who were in our hospital for thirty days. Family members and friends would come for two or three nights a week, after visiting the patient over dinner. At first I wasn't sure why they needed a program, but it soon became clear.

Co-dependents enable others to stay sick. They do it in hundreds of different ways, without even realizing it. In fact, they usually think that they are helping, because co-dependents are helpers. They can be family members, friends and even professionals.

A co-dependent will call in sick for a drunk spouse. A co-dependent will clean up the mess. Co-dependents cover for addicts and alcoholics, telling the children, for example, to ignore the behavior of the father or mother, or apologizing for it. Co-dependents pretend nothing is wrong. Without co-dependents, addicts and alcoholics would have to manage problems directly and develop better coping skills.

In our Co-dependency Program, one of the family members worked nights. He told me that he bought his alcoholic wife a six-pack of beer each night before he went to work because that's what she wanted. He figured that it kept her at home, rather than risking her driving home drunk from a bar or a liquor store. This was a good example of co-dependency. He thought he was helping her, but he was helping her stay sick. What she needed was treatment, not booze.

Another example was the divorced wife who called the treatment center at least three times a day to check on her ex-husband's progress. She insisted on knowing certain things and on deciding certain things for him. He was in bad shape, so it was tempting to let her "help." He had a history of using cocaine intravenously. He accused the entire staff of doing cocaine during the lunch hour—a good example of projection. The ex-wife thought she was helping him, but he had to do it for himself. He blamed her for everything, and her presence helped him continue blaming her. He had to learn to focus on himself. She told me that this was her fourth addict husband, and that she had buried the previous three. She was ready to try something different, she just didn't know how. The Co-dependency Program helped her let go of responsibility for him. She had already divorced him; now she had to let go of him, too. She learned to stop helping him, which—ironically—helped him.

Co-dependents are necessary for dysfunctional people to get by, to look okay in our society. Without a co-dependent covering up and otherwise enabling an addict, the addict's behavior would be obvious and the consequences unavoidable. Negative advocates are really co-dependents.

Negative Advocate Patterns

When a negative advocate supports the cognitive distortions of a HCP, the HCP becomes more confident and aggressive, which increases the likelihood of becoming involved in the legal system. The HCP is encouraged to blame someone else for events that may not have occurred. "It's horrible that this happened to you! You should sue them!" That's what I imagine Mr. Guilbeau heard from those around him—certainly from his wife. He sued for harm from a solvent which thousands of others—in fact, everyone else—had used without harm.

Slights from a co-worker may be misperceived as harassment. Neighbors may misperceive a theft. Clients may misperceive a professional's routine actions as a case of malpractice. These events happen every day. But when a HCP seeks reality-testing from the people around him or her, those people risk becoming a negative advocate or a positive advocate.

A positive advocate will empathize with the person while at the same time asking: "Is that really true? What's your part in all of this? Let's look into the facts of the situation." A negative advocate will ask: "When are you going to sue? Why did you wait so long?" When people are extremely upset, to calm them down it is easier to agree with them than it is to challenge their thinking. The easiest course of action is to pacify them. And HCPs are extremely upset much of the time.

It is particularly hard for family and friends who are dealing with a HCP on a daily basis. In many cases they have become worn down over time and eventually simply accept the HCP's cognitive distortions. They become regular negative advocates for them—enablers for the HCP.

Family

Family members are the primary advocates for those with personality disorders. In many cases they are positive advocates who are truly helpful, steering the dysfunctional person into responsible behaviors and setting limits on their misbehavior. As with drug addicts and acting-out adolescents, a "tough love" approach seems to work best.

However, there are many examples of negative advocates who have either given up fighting or who actually agree with the cognitive distortions and misbehavior of the family member who has a personality disorder.

Almost every time Karen Smith (Chapter Six) had a hearing at court, her brother attended. Regardless of what she did, he seemed to be a quiet supporter. Even though she was in her fifties, it seemed as though she was performing for him in a high school play. Alan Smith remembers walking past her brother one time while waiting for court to begin. Her brother said to Alan: "How can you face yourself in the morning?" The brother appeared to have completely adopted his sister's false allegations and truly believed them, despite repeated evidence that they were false.

It appears that he must have become worn down and taken the path of least resistance. He eventually wrote one half-hearted declaration to the court on his sister's behalf.

Mrs. Guilbeau (Chapter Six) appears to have played a highly active role in supporting her husband's belief system. Even though several professionals had diagnosed him as somaticizing his symptoms and having personality problems, she was a strong proponent of his "illness." She appears to be the one who wrote the "DO NOT ENTER" house sign, requiring others to be chemical-free around her (smoking) husband: "There is a Toxic person living in this house who is allergic to all these above products. With your understanding, **we can help him** from having severe seizures and severe multiple pain."

One expert also testified that Guilbeau "reported that he could smell chemicals coming out of his body at times, and that **Mrs. Guilbeau agreed** that she could smell them, too."

Mrs. Guilbeau was a key witness at the trial and her claim for loss of consortium won $900,000 before the entire judgment was set aside by the appeals court. One has to wonder if Mr. Guilbeau's claim would have gone anywhere if not for his wife advocating, validating and encouraging his apparently Histrionic beliefs.

Family disputes are notorious for recruiting children as negative advocates. Mr. Halo (Chapter Five) began his custody battle by influencing his son to tell a therapist that he was scared at his mother's house. Mr. Halo structured the situation so that there would be no competing information for the therapist, and persuaded his son to keep this a secret from his mother. His son became a negative advocate for the father. Did he really choose this role?

In their insightful 1999 book, *Impasses of Divorce: The Dynamics and Resolution of Family Conflict*, Janet Johnston and Linda Campbell describe some divorcing parents as enlisting their children in custody battles, with little awareness of the affect it has on them. Two-fifths of the children in one study tended to merge with the angry parent, blocking out the other. Total compliance is what seems necessary to get an angry parent to calm down, and children are too dependent to oppose a high-conflict parent.

If adults have difficulty with HCPs, and the HCPs are constantly seeking allies, imagine how hard it must be on a small child. Since HCPs have weak interpersonal boundaries, it is natural for them to enlist children in all of their disputes (with neighbors, with other family members, in business). Most parents I have worked with—even those going through divorces—are careful to protect children from adult disputes, so adamantly involving children is a special indicator of a HCP.

A common term in high-conflict family court disputes is parental alienation. The theory of parental alienation evolved to describe cases in which the child totally rejects one parent and totally admires the other. This process begins primarily between ages nine and fifteen. The extreme absoluteness of the child's opinion appears to be much more an expression of the HCP's point of view than the child's fear or anger at the other parent. The child is forced to make a choice.

Yet there is conflict among professionals about the existence of parental alienation. I believe it exists, from my years of experience as a therapist working with children and families, as well as a family law attorney. However, I do not believe it is an intentional act by those with personality disorders. Since they can't reflect on their own behavior, they are unable to see how damaging this is to the children. The alienation appears to be completely or mostly unconscious.

Ironically, in my private divorce mediation cases I rarely see serious disputes over the children. In fact, many couples start out by telling me they respect each other as parents and do not want to fight over the children. They are coming to mediation to keep the children out of it. On the other hand, most of my high-conflict divorce court cases include heated disputes over the children. High-conflict personalities go to court. And they recruit children as negative advocates, whether they realize it or not.

Whenever a parent brings a child to court to testify against the other parent, I strongly suspect a personality disorder. The small percentage of parents who try to do this—less than five per cent in my experience—are insistent, self-absorbed and seem to lack any empathy for what this does to a child. Fortunately, most divorce courts forbid children from entering the courtroom. They are not allowed to testify against either parent or even to meet with the judge.

Instead, a counselor may meet with the child and report to the court on the interview in general terms, so that the child is not involved in speaking publicly against one parent, and does not feel pressured to decide where to live. An exception to this prohibition against children testifying in court is in criminal cases of child sexual abuse or extreme physical abuse, when a child is the only witness to criminal abuse and may need to testify.

The Good Daughter

I once represented a father in a custody dispute and the mother brought their eleven-year-old daughter to court to testify against him. I observed her sitting at a table in the lobby of the court with her daughter, going over my client's most recent court declaration. The mother was standing over her shoulder, shaking her head and occasionally blurting out "How dare he say that! That's a lie! You tell the judge!" The daughter repeated almost the identical expressions of anger and disdain as they continued to read. It was like a student being taught by a teacher—a course in negative advocacy.

Later that day, when the judge refused to let the daughter testify, the mother was angry and disappointed. "Well, I brought her all the way down here and she really wants to tell you how mad her father makes her!" The mother was firmly admonished that she was not to show the daughter any court papers or even to discuss the court case with her. The child was to be protected from anything having to do with the court. Unfortunately, the mother appeared to have a personality disorder with enduring patterns of behavior, so this admonishment had little affect. Ultimately, only a change of custody allowed the daughter to really get to know her father.

Researchers have found that children are clearly influenced by what adults tell them—and especially by the way they are told things. A child is more influenced to agree with an adult against a suspected perpetrator if the adult is in a position of authority; if he or she repeats questions (Are you sure he didn't touch you down there?); and if the child is given a negative stereotype of the suspect (He does bad things—did he do bad things to you?).

In addition to the two cases mentioned in Chapter Three about false allegations of child sexual abuse, for much of the 1990s there were high-profile cases of child sexual abuse in daycare centers around the country. Most of these cases turned out to be completely unfounded, and most of the alleged perpetrators were released from long jail sentences. The courts ultimately found that the cases were based on suggestive interviewing methods that tainted the children's thinking—they simply absorbed and enhanced what they heard. They unwittingly became negative advocates. If adults easily become negative advocates, it certainly makes sense that children can as well.

Enabling in the Judicial System

For many years, the judicial system allowed drunk drivers to avoid responsibility after being arrested. They could beat a ticket by obtaining a letter from a therapist, by promising to stop drinking, or by convincing the judge that it would hurt the alcoholic's career. Unfortunately, this process was easily manipulated. Hundreds of alcoholics drove drunk again, and killed many innocent people. This was a good example of enabling behavior by legal professionals.

What the judicial system eventually learned was that alcoholics don't change by making persuasive promises to act better. Their behavior is embedded in their disease. It takes a program of change to help them. Many alcoholics and addicts are great talkers who can convince others of almost anything. So the courts developed zero tolerance programs and automatically put drunk drivers into supervised, structured treatment programs, programs that have been very successful.

Slowly over the past fifteen years, society and professionals have stopped enabling drunk drivers to stay sick. We required them to get clean and sober. This is one area of great success for the combined efforts of mental health professionals and legal professionals. A similar approach may be necessary for people with personality disorders. We do not help them by being negative advocates.

Mental Health Professionals

Over the past decade, mental health professionals have come to play a significant role in legal cases. They have evaluated, treated and managed numerous parties in court cases, from criminal cases to divorces. Their assessments have been invaluable in helping courts determine mental competency for trial, competency for signing wills, ability or lack of ability to form criminal intent, ability or lack of ability to parent abused children, and the best interests of a child after divorce.

Yet mental health professionals are generally trained to assist individuals who voluntarily appear for treatment of mental health problems. Therefore, they are often vulnerable to the manipulations of HCPs who don't want treatment at all, but just want to win their cases—and are willing to lie and manipulate to do so. Without even realizing it, mental health professionals sometimes become negative advocates.

Mental health professionals who evaluated Mr. Gossage played an important part in persuading the Bar Court to approve his application to become an attorney.

> "Five mental health professionals interviewed Gossage shortly before the State Bar Court (California) hearing. These individuals opined that Gossage had **successfully overcome any substance abuse problem or**

personality disorder afflicting him in the pre-1983 period, when he killed his sister and committed other serious crimes. None saw any sign that Gossage presently suffered from a diagnosable mental disorder or psychopathological condition." (Emphasis added)[42]

Yet, did they know that he had omitted thirteen out of seventeen criminal convictions on his application? Did they want to believe him? As they looked at each incident, did they interpret it in the most favorable light? Did he persuade them to overlook the pattern of his unchanged behavior? The Supreme Court of California criticized the Bar Court for missing the unchanged pattern:

"The majority examined each incident during this period, but did so in isolation, finding excuses or mitigation in each case. However, the majority again omitted and misstated relevant facts, and it never confronted the ominous implications of the *pattern* of misconduct committed while Gossage was preparing to be a lawyer." (Italics are the Supreme Court's)[43]

From my experience, Antisocials in particular are drawn to mental health professionals, perhaps because therapists believe so strongly in the inherent goodness of everyone that they are less likely to realize they are being manipulated and purposely deceived. Unfortunately, as I learned in treating addicts—several of whom were also Antisocials—they will lie to and steal from their own mothers to get what they want. They are very effective at acquiring negative advocates, and very aggressive about recruiting professionals.

In Chapter Five, Mr. Halo started his case with a secret meeting with a therapist. The therapist never met with the mother, but still wrote a declaration to court for the father. The therapist's declaration had a persuasive impact on the family court counselor, who then adopted the therapist's one-hour viewpoint and recommended changing custody of eleven-year-old Peter, which the court approved.

Ironically, almost eighteen months later, a full psychological evaluation found nothing wrong with the parenting at Mr. and Ms. Johnson's house. The psychologist who thoroughly investigated the matter found no reason to restrict contact with the children by the mother or the stepfather. However, since Peter had spent almost eighteen months primarily in the care of Mr. Halo, the psychologist recommended a nearly equal parenting arrangement.

---

[42] In Re Eben Gossage at 1092-93
[43] In Re Eben Gossage at 1094

I have seen this pattern many times: a fast and persuasive HCP parent starts a custody battle by secretly and individually finding a mental health professional to get the ball rolling. Even the family court judges now complain about therapists doing this. Yet there are still a few unsuspecting therapists who get fooled every year. They become negative advocates without even knowing it.

Legal Professionals

Attorneys often adopt and escalate the allegations of their clients based on their ethical standards to be zealous advocates. However, they also have an ethical obligation to speak the truth and not knowingly lie. Some attorneys are completely uncritical about their client's allegations, never examining the facts or motivations of their clients. High-conflict personalities thrive on attorneys who agree to be their negative advocates—fortunately, in my experience this appears to be a minority of attorneys.

At the beginning of a divorce case Ms. Blameworthy requested a restraining order with very weak evidence and it was initially denied until a full hearing could occur. At the followup hearing, she filed a declaration in which she stated: "I am no longer requesting a restraining order. My husband has been staying away from the house for several weeks now."

When it was time for her attorney to argue the case, he said she had withdrawn her request for a restraining order. However, during his oral argument he commented, "And the husband keeps coming around the house, making her feel unsafe."

Didn't he know what was in her declaration? Had he come to believe her emotions and enhanced the allegations? Or was he knowingly lying to give strength to his argument on another issue?

I believe that he had absorbed her emotions and therefore assumed the husband was coming around the house—which would have explained why she was so upset. But her upset was caused by her own HCP, not because he was coming around the house. The evidence didn't support the attorney's claim, but he absorbed her intense emotions and enhanced the facts to fit the emotions.

Mr. Litigation

Attorneys handle HCPs in different ways, although they usually do not know they are dealing with a HCP. Attorneys have an ethical duty to zealously represent their clients. On the other hand, attorneys are not ethically required to take any client who comes into their office. What would you do with this client?

"I'm really angry. I'm not going to let him get away with having an affair and then paying almost no child and spousal support. I want an attorney who will make him sorry he ever left me. I need an aggressive attorney who will make him jump through so many hoops that he won't be able to afford to fight with me any longer. I want an attorney who will make him beg me to stop taking him to court. I don't want to even suggest negotiating with him. He's like the devil, and you don't negotiate with the devil. I want lots of hearings, I want a big trial, and I want to pile him up with depositions and have all of his records subpoenaed."

Many attorneys I know say they would not take this client. That's not how they work. Instead, they would politely encourage the client to find another attorney. But a few attorneys in every county will take this client—and the client's money—with no question about it. Mr. Litigation would be a good example of this approach. This is essentially what he says:

"Everyone deserves a day in court. That's what they really want. So I help them have it. I know they won't be satisfied and I tell them that. But it's their right under the constitution, so someone's got to be their attorney. I'm only doing what they want. I'm representing them as a zealous advocate, like I'm supposed to do. It's not my job to verify that everything they say is true. That's the job of the husband's attorney. Our system of government works best when everybody has someone who will aggressively advocate for their interests and rights in court. That's all I do."

A big problem that I see with this approach is that Mr. Litigation will often be zealously advocating for his client's cognitive distortions and emotional facts. That's why I prefer a "Counselor at Law" approach, which I see as counseling the client to see the situation more clearly and to not make any claims that I have no confidence in. That's why I get fired from time to time by a client who wants a Mr. Litigation.

One client fired me because his wife was getting too comfortable negotiating with me. "Bill, she thinks she can work with you and reach an agreement with compromises from both sides. That's not what I want. I want her to suffer. I want her to cry before this is all over." I prepared a Substitution of Attorney form and we gladly went our separate ways. There will always be a negative advocate out there for those who really want one.

The Court

Given the aggressive energy and cognitive distortions of HCPs and their negative advocates, sometimes the judge or jury will adopt their point of view and get the case backwards. When this happens, one of these results tends to follow:

1. The victory encourages the HCP to have confidence in his now-validated (but distorted) thinking. His aggressive energy increases, along with the intensity of his belief that he is not responsible for his own behavior and that the other party is to blame. Perhaps O.J. Simpson is a good example of this, as he travels around playing golf and insisting on his innocence, occasionally in public.

2. HCP's victory motivates the target of blame (or the target's attorney) to act much more aggressively in stopping the HCP at future hearings or trials. At first the target was confident that the courts would recognize the obvious distortions and manipulations, but suddenly the target realizes that the court has been fooled and gotten it backward. He or she is now highly motivated to correct things. This is what happened in the Broderick case (second trial was a conviction), the Simpson case (civil trial was a conviction) and the Gossage case (the Supreme Court of California finally denied his admission to the Bar).

3. Professionals tell the target to stop fighting. They view it as an equal battle between two equally unreasonable people. They criticize both parties. "Why can't you both just stop fighting?" It appears to outsiders that both sides are being overly aggressive and therefore both parties must be at fault. Sometimes this is true, but much of the time this is not true and does not address the underlying problem: one party's HCP and attacking behavior against an innocent target.

It would be tragic for a real victim of abuse to stop fighting after the case has been decided backward. I have been involved in many cases that went badly at the first hearing, but were eventually resolved in a positive manner after many months or years. Sometimes this has to be at the appellate court level, after the HCP's emotional persuasion has distracted the trial court, such as in the Gossage case. Sometimes this just requires several trips back to court, as occurred in the following case.

Mr. Persistent

When Mr. Persistent and his wife divorced, she received physical custody of their five-year-old daughter and he had about thirty-five per cent parenting time. Over the next four years he returned to court twice, each time requesting custody of his daughter for various reasons. The mother's parenting had been fine, so the judge denied each request. When that didn't work, in the fifth year after the divorce he went to court seeking an order that the daughter attend an Irish dance class in his neighborhood, which met twice a week and sometimes had events on the weekend. They had a particularly inspired dance teacher and the possibility of attending national competitions.

The daughter enjoyed dancing, but she also liked other activities. The father wanted her to compete, but the mother thought she was happy with her neighborhood activities, which occasionally included dancing. The mother felt that the social aspect of playing with her neighborhood classmates was important too. The dance class would have been inconvenient as the father lived across town, and the mother was concerned that it was just a tactic by the father to build up to another custody request.

Before the court hearing, the parents had to meet with a family court counselor for a recommendation. The father intensely blamed the mother for being overly sensitive, controlling, lying and alienating the child from him by denying this opportunity for a father-daughter activity. The mother told the counselor that the father had been physically abusive before the divorce and that he had been ordered into a batterer's treatment program. She said he wasn't really interested in the activity as much as he wanted to ultimately get custody, and that he bullied the child much like he had bullied her. The father admitted the order for abuse treatment—which he attended—but denied that he was abusive and said that it was the mother instead.

The family court counselor reviewed the case. She treated it as a case of mutual blaming, and told them both to stop it. Because of the history of domestic violence and manipulation, the mother's attorney filed a Memorandum of Points and Authorities with the court claiming that the father may have an Antisocial personality, so that he was likely to bully the child as he had the mother—and that he was unlikely to change without strong court intervention. Her attorney also asked for attorney's fees as a sanction.

At court, the judge was irritated to have this family back again. He lectured both parents:

> "All I see in front of me are two stubborn parents who don't care about their child. If you cared about your child, then you wouldn't be asking me to parent her in court. Sir, your activity request may be reasonable, but you act like a bully sometimes. Ma'am, you are too stubborn and just want to win. You should seriously consider his request. It sounds like it might be a good opportunity to me. But I'm not going to make any orders about this activity, as there's already an order that the child's activities are in the neighborhood where the child goes to school—the mother's neighborhood. And I'm not ordering any sanctions, either."

After that hearing, the father sent demand letters to the mother, blaming her for the problem: "Just as the judge said, you just want to win." The mother didn't know what to do and considered giving in. After all, throughout their marriage he had bullied her into doing many things. But she discussed it with her own therapist and with the child's therapist, both of whom said it was reasonable for the child to play with children from her school neighborhood.

Then, after the daughter's grades dropped slightly at school, the father filed for his third change of custody request. She had taken on a lot of activities and gotten overwhelmed, her mother said. But the father said there must be abuse in her house, because a drop in grades can indicate abuse.

The court appointed an attorney for the child to investigate the situation and the attorney determined that the mother was correct. It was a temporary overwhelm, and the grades were already getting better by the time of the hearing, three months after it was filed.

At the hearing, the mother's attorney requested sanctions of $2,000 for all of the work involved in responding to a hearing that should never have occurred in the first place. For the third time, the judge denied the father's change of custody request. But this time the judge decided not to give a joint lecture—the judge focused on the father's behavior. He ordered the father to pay all of the mother's attorney's fees—$2,000.

> "And if you come to court again with a custody request, and you don't have an extremely valid reason, I'm going to sanction you again and again. Do you understand?"

After that, the case remained out of court for more than two years. The real source of the problem had been addressed.

When Advocates Get it Backward

If you are reading this book and have come this far, you are likely an advocate or dispute resolver (mental health professional, mediator, attorney or judge) I hope this book will help you become more discriminating and constructive in your advocacy. It is easy to be misled by the emotions of a HCP who is gearing up for court.

Blaming the victim is a common defense mechanism for HCPs. Finding advocates to help in denying responsibility becomes a major preoccupation. Since their thinking process is rigid and repetitive—and backward—they are not going to think about the consequences of their actions or be open to feedback. Therefore their energy is freed up to find others who will share their reverse belief system.

People with personality disorders would not get away with as much if they didn't also have co-dependents. Just as those who abuse substances are impaired in their behavior, thinking and decision making, those with personality disorders are also impaired. They need people to solve their problems for them, since they alone cannot see the real problem (their own behavior). They work hard at getting those around them to adopt their cognitively distorted view of the problem, and to advocate for them in solving it their way. This often means helping them go to court against their "enemies"—their targets.

From my experience, many long, drawn-out court battles involving personality disorders are funded by relatives or friends who are just trying to help. In messy divorce cases, often it is the parents who "help" one or both parties against the hated ex-spouse. They chip in with declarations against the other party, and with overall encouragement in the battle. They usually have a lifetime of experience with this.

Those with personality disorders are difficult to be around, even early in life. Many have a shocking emotional intensity or manipulativeness that is hard to endure. Family members and friends usually adopt one of the following three coping responses:

1. Confront the person and refuse to buy into his or her distorted thoughts, intense emotions and extreme behaviors. The person may learn to become more reasonable, or one of the parties leaves the relationship and significantly reduces contact.

2. Give in. Tolerate, accept, agree, cope and hope that with enough support he or she will eventually change. Family members who repeatedly come to court mostly seem to have adopted this approach.

3. Agree with the person's anger, arrogance and dramatic emotions, and encourage the acting out, maybe even participating in their schemes. Identify with their view of the world. This is how many criminal endeavors seem to occur: someone with a personality disorder teams up with one or more negative advocates (sometimes other HCPs) and takes on the world. They justify each other's actions, and they can become quite dangerous.

In the second and third responses above, HCPs are rewarded for acting out, for expressing inappropriate emotions, and for retaining their cognitive distortions. By the time they reach adulthood (if not before), they may enter the judicial system either as misperceiving plaintiffs or misbehaving defendants. The negative advocates who agree with their skewed point of view are an important part of their belief system. They help the person stay sick, and allow or encourage them to harm others by engaging them in the adversarial process of court. With their distorted, but persuasive, logic and with the help of negative advocates, they often "win."

By reinforcing and advocating for the HCP's cognitive distortions, negative advocates make matters worse for the HCP as well as for everyone around him or her. This negative advocacy is usually inadvertent and well-intentioned, but uninformed. Unfortunately, just one person advocating for the HCP's negative thinking and negative behavior makes it seem legitimate to the HCP–and to others.

CONCLUSION

Since the HCP's impaired behavior and perceptions may be obvious to others, they seek negative advocates to replace the ordinary doubts of others with the negative advocate's higher credibility. Negative advocates excuse the HCP's negative behaviors and advocate for (enable) their minor, absurd or non-existent claims in court. As one negative advocate persuades another, the conflict escalates. This encourages the negative thinking and negative behavior of the HCP, and often inspires the target to become much more active in the case.

As an alternative, those around a HCP can truly help. There are many concepts and skills that can be employed in being a positive advocate. The second half of this book focuses on what to do–and what not to do–as a positive advocate or professional involved in resolving a dispute.

Chapter Seven Summary
The Enablers Or Negative Advocates

1. Wanting to help is driving force
2. Misled by charm, hurt, fear or anger of HCP
3. Professionally/personally enjoys solving problems
4. May like taking charge and telling others what to do
5. May feel intimidated or was actually threatened by HCP
6. Inadvertently escalates a high-conflict dispute
7. Protects HCP from natural consequences of misconduct
8. May have HCP

Tips and Techniques for Enablers and Negative Advocates

1. Avoid making assumptions; investigate first
2. Avoid taking responsibility for others' behavior
3. Avoid doing more of the work than the HCP
4. Do not expect to change or "save" HCP from self
5. Obtain corroborating information
6. Explain consequences of future misconduct
7. Allow HCP to experience pain and consequences
8. Refer HCP to professionals who are positive advocates

PART II
FOUR STEPS IN RESOLVING HIGH-CONFLICT DISPUTES

Many of the examples described in Part I were extreme cases, chosen to demonstrate the dynamics of high-conflict personalities (HCPs). Most cases are not as extreme, but many disputes today involve one or more parties with traits of these personality patterns of extreme thinking, feeling and behaving. The next four chapters provide four key steps or issues to consider in managing any HCP in any setting—including legal disputes.

These four key steps also apply to managing those with other mental health problems common in interpersonal disputes, such as Bipolar Disorder (formerly known as Manic-Depressive Disorder), Obsessive-Compulsive Disorder and substance abuse. Having an idea of which type of personality is involved will help you be more effective, but these steps and related skills are applicable even if you have not developed a working theory of a specific personality problem. Examples are provided for each of the four HCPs discussed in this book.

These four key steps apply whether you are an advocate (attorney, family member, volunteer); dispute resolver (mediator, judge, ombudsperson); or target of blame (could be anyone). After explaining these steps, five specific skills are provided for implementing each step. At the end of each chapter, separate suggestions are made for advocates, dispute resolvers and targets of blame.

The four key steps to consider in handling any HCP or upset person are:

1. Bonding
2. Structure
3. Reality-testing
4. Consequences

Bonding

"We're really bonding now, aren't we, Dad?"

People with high-conflict personalities (HCPs) are in a constant bonding crisis. Their emotions and confusing behavior usually have more to do with their lifetime bonding difficulties than with the facts of their current dispute. In many cases, the bonding crisis behavior is a major cause of the conflict. If you do not understand this and do not manage bonding issues sufficiently, you will be unable to help the person resolve his or her dispute and you may risk becoming the next target of blame, perhaps even risking verbal or legal attacks on you. However, it is not hard to handle these bonding issues if you pay attention to the concerns addressed in this chapter.

High-conflict personality bonding crises usually stem from early childhood, when bonding may have been difficult or seriously disrupted. Bonding is one of the factors that can lead to a personality disorder. Through an absence of sufficiently positive bonding experiences, or for other reasons, HCPs develop a generalized mistrust of relationships and have great difficulty coping with relationship losses. To compensate, they develop rigid and dysfunctional coping behaviors which actually perpetuate the very bonding problems they are trying to avoid.

Overcompensating Relationship Styles

As described below, the difficulties HCPs have with bonding vary somewhat by personality type:

Borderlines are preoccupied with fears of abandonment. To feel secure, they overcompensate by being overly friendly, charming and sometimes seductive to get you to like them. If they receive a generally positive response, they will feel more secure—but they may also develop extremely high expectations of the relationship. If their high expectations are not completely fulfilled, their fears of abandonment are triggered. Sometimes this unleashes an intense rage much like a three-year-old's temper tantrum. This anger can lead to dramatic action such as intense verbal attacks, violence, self-destructive behavior or legal action.

Narcissists are preoccupied with fears of inferiority. To feel secure, they overcompensate by constantly promoting themselves as superior beings, characterizing their ordinary achievements as extraordinary and minimizing the successes of others. They constantly devalue people, and criticize those they consider beneath them. These behaviors alienate those around them, who then challenge or criticize the Narcissist. This criticism is interpreted as a narcissistic injury, which triggers their fears of inferiority. They respond with anger, or an escalation of demeaning comments, or blaming behavior toward the one who "caused" their narcissistic injury, or toward whoever is nearby. The drive to prove their superiority may include verbal put-downs, physical abuse, public humiliation and legal action.

Antisocials are preoccupied by the fear of being dominated. To feel secure, they overcompensate by trying to dominate others. To feel in control of their relationships they use cunning, lying, stealing, violence and constant manipulation. While they may appear exciting, confident and charming, it is really a manipulation to gain control and to feel unthreatened. They are insincere and are eventually found out, but often after it is too late and their short-term goals (and related harm to others) have been accomplished. They are highly mistrusting. Even when they gain somewhat stable relationships—in which they have the dominant role—they are not satisfied, and often leave to seek new conquests.

Histrionics are preoccupied with the fear of being ignored. To feel secure, they overcompensate by constantly seeking attention with dramatic and emotional appeals. After they have your attention, it is difficult to disengage them. Their anxiety is so strong that it is easy for the listener to just give in and tolerate them, or eventually to become forceful in rejecting them. Their dramatic claims are usually unfocused, simply an excuse to hold your attention a bit longer. They push away all but the most tolerant people.

Individuals with these personalities appear driven to have conflictual relationships, rather than none at all, so be prepared for a roller-coaster ride of anger, manipulation and conflict. They have experienced rejection and criticism hundreds of times, and as a result they have refined the initial impression they make to be more normal and less threatening. Many professionals are easily fooled at the beginning of the relationship with a HCP.

Just to be safe, I recommend that you use the following methods to manage the inevitable bonding crises and manipulations without over-reacting yourself. You may already do much of the following. However, with HCPs you will need to pay much more attention to bonding, because they are so sensitive to the slightest indication of rejection, criticism or abandonment. Be prepared for sudden over-reactions to routine events. This is an indication that the situation will require your utmost efforts to repair the relationship and to calm the HCP.

Skill #1: Listening to fear and anger (without getting hooked)

If you practice highly attentive listening with HCPs, most of your contacts can be quite brief. Your full attention should include direct eye contact and no distractions. Avoid interrupting with unnecessary questions at the beginning of each contact, when they are pouring their hearts out to you. Just listen and empathize for a minute or two. It is possible to be very attentive, even over the phone.

Respond with empathy, including sympathetic body language (use head nods and avoid closed arms over chest, for example). Respond with recognition of how the person may be feeling, using phrases such as "That sounds really difficult" or "That sounds overwhelming" or "That sounds really sad." Avoid agreeing with the content. Simply take it in as information. "Okay, I hear what you're saying. I understand how strongly you feel about that."

Skill #2: Being consistent

Maintain a consistent level of contact and emotional support over an extended period of time and in the face of widely swinging emotions. Avoid intense emotional involvement one day and cold distance the next. The more consistent you are, the more secure the HCP will feel. The more abrupt or inconsistent you are, the more likely the person will feel insecure and escalate clinging behaviors in an attempt to feel secure (more phone calls, faxes, sudden appearances at the office). Or the person will terminate the relationship in anger and seek some kind of revenge for the perceived slights by you (suing for malpractice, or spreading the word about how terrible you are).

Some professionals have a warm, friendly style of relating to upset people. However, be careful not to get involved to the extent that you over-react and later have to cut the person way back. Instead, be warm but limited in the time and emotional energy you spend on their upsets. Not abrupt, but limited. The person will get used to this and accept it, if it feels consistent and secure.

Other professionals have a more removed style of bonding. This is fine, so long as the expectations of contact are clear. Let the person know how and when you will be available, and if he or she can talk to someone else when feeling in a crisis. Otherwise, the HCP will escalate the demands to speak with you.

Being consistent is better than being especially nice and later abandoning the person, which is one of the most common errors in dealing with HCPs.

Skill #3: Anticipating crises

Because HCPs are so sensitive to bonding insecurities, at the beginning of your relationship there will be several bonding crises. Anticipate when these may occur. Common times are right after they start working with you; right before and after any court appearance (remember, their expectations are usually unrealistic); and right after dealing with the other party (getting served with court papers, responses to settlement offers, or any face-to-face contact).

Take the first crisis call. This will often come within 24 hours of starting to work with an HCP. This call is a test of your commitment—your bond—to the HCP. It will determine how secure the person feels for a long time to come. Calmly taking this call—as soon as possible if you can—will save you many hours over the long run. If you brush off your HCP from the start, he or she will feel compelled to get your attention with phone messages, faxes, escalating demands for action on your part and possibly threats of action against you.

Surprisingly, from my experience it is not how well you perform for the HCP, nor the outcome of the case, that matters most. It is how you pay attention to him or her, especially when the HCP is upset. Remember, HCPs really, really, really do not like to feel abandoned (Borderline), belittled (Narcissistic), dominated (Antisocial) or ignored (Histrionic).

Skill #4: Adopting an arm's-length bond

Just because you develop an attentive relationship with the HCP does not mean that you should be close. The closer you are, the higher the risk that the HCP will develop extremely high, and possibly intimate, expectations. Therapists describe this as *transference*, which is the term for unconsciously transferring the positive and negative feelings about a prior intense relationship (such as with one's parents) onto the present relationship, even if it is not supposed to be an intense personal relationship. Transference can backfire if you let the relationship get too intense.

Avoid being too responsive to the emotions of the HCP. He or she will try to convince you about how upsetting the situation is, or about how you urgently need to take action in dealing with his or her perceived crisis. Remaining calm and consistent is the best response. Proceed to take action in a typically professional manner. "Yes, I have already planned to work on that tomorrow" or "We'll need more information before taking any action. You can help by gathering some relevant documents for me to review."

Skill #5: Validating the person, not the complaint

Avoid agreeing with the content of what your HCP is saying. Your job is to support the person, not the complaint. Most high-conflict disputes lack witnesses and have little evidence, so the HCP makes up in emotion what is lacking in facts. It is easy to feel that to maintain your bond you must agree with the HCP. This is not true. Your bond is based on your relationship with the person, not on the complaint. Many professionals make this mistake, which only escalates the dispute. Gather information and present it to a decision-maker, but do not get caught agreeing with your client's cognitive distortions.

"Yes, I see how upsetting this situation is for you. I will advocate for you, but I can only present information that will seem reliable to others. We need more evidence. I can't just say that you feel it is true. My credibility with the court is based on facts, not on emotions. Even if you are completely correct about what happened, it doesn't mean a judge or jury will see it that way. My job is to do my best at presenting the facts of your case. You do not have to persuade me. In fact, we have to consider what the other people will say about you. What do you think they will say? And what facts can we respond with?"

This arm's-length approach will reduce your client's focus on emotions, stabilize your relationship and help your client provide more information that is useful. It will also reduce your client's expectations of outside favors and constant attention.

Balanced, Neutral Bonding

It is especially important for professional mediators, evaluators and judges to maintain balanced, neutral bonding with both parties when dealing with both sides of a dispute. This also applies to family members who are close to both parties in a conflict. You can be firmly neutral. Practicing all of the methods described above will help in dealing with both parties.

Mediators, for example, can say, "My role is to facilitate a resolution, not to evaluate who is right. My focus is on the future, not the past and who is to blame. It's always possible that one of you is really at fault and the other isn't. But as a mediator I do not have the means to determine that. So let's focus on finding a solution you can live with in the future, regardless of the truth about the past."

Evaluators, arbitrators and judges can say, "I am making this decision knowing that I can never have all the facts. I have tried to be fair and firm in resolving this dispute. I am constrained by certain rules and standards, and this result seems to be the best fit. Good luck to both of you in your future endeavors."

When judges use expressions such as the above it has a reassuring effect on the parties—even when one or both do not agree with the decision. This fits with the research, which indicates that most parties are more concerned with the way they are treated by legal professionals than with the actual legal outcome. I believe this is especially true of HCPs, who are very sensitive to being criticized and immune to negative feedback.

Family members and friends can say, "You're both my friends (relatives) and I hope that you are able to resolve your dispute. I care about both of you, but it's better that I do not get involved in trying to decide who's right."

Avoid Anger

Avoid getting angry with HCPs, even though it is hard. Since they are un-aware of their highly irritating behavior, your anger is usually a complete surprise. To them it feels like a rejection or putdown, and for this slight they will feel compelled to punish you in some manner. However, you do not have to be perfect. If you are prepared to repair any perceived breaches of the relationship by effective listening to the HCP's anger and hurt, the HCP will usually respond favorably and recover quickly.

Focus on Strengths

High-conflict personalities are often successful people in some areas of their lives. They have developed coping skills and strengths. By acknowl-edging their strengths, you will have an easier time working with them. We all like a little recognition from time to time. This is especially true for HCPs, who often grew up getting little respect—or getting respect for the wrong things.

Frustrating Farrah

The following illustration gives a simplified example of how an advocate can better help a high-conflict client by anticipating bonding crises, and as much as possible by dealing with these crises directly. Using these simple and brief methods of responding will usually calm the client down. Plan to manage bonding crises, not to eliminate them. This is a core issue for HCPs. It does not just fade away.

Farrah is a thirty-four-year-old woman who hired Anne Amsterdam to be her divorce attorney. After she left Anne's office, Farrah remembered that she needed to tell Anne about a secret bank account she thought her hus-band had. She immediately called Anne, but Anne was busy working on the paperwork for a hearing in another case the next day.

"Farrah's a real talker," Anne thought, worried the call would take too long. She told her assistant to tell Farrah she was out of the office, figuring she would call her back in a day or two. Farrah wanted to leave a long message, but the assistant cut her off and said Anne would get back to her when she had time.

By now, Farrah was angry at being brushed off. She decided to send a fax to Anne with her information about the secret bank account. This made Anne angry and she dictated an angry fax back. "I have an important hearing tomorrow. Your information is not urgent. Please leave us alone until I contact you when I'm ready to work on your case."

The next day, Farrah showed up at the office urgently wanting to speak with Anne. Since Anne was at court, Farrah waited in the office waiting room, even though the assistant said Anne had a full schedule for the day when she returned from court. Finally Anne came back, and Farrah started to tell her that her husband spent the evening at a bar, which she knew because she followed him there.

Anne was furious. "I don't care where he spent the evening. We don't have an appointment and I'm very busy. I'll call you when I need your information."

By the time Anne and Farrah went to court for their first hearing, there had been several negative interactions. Farrah had sent numerous faxes and called almost every day—and Anne and her assistant brushed her off almost every day.

At court, Anne argued that Farrah's husband was a drunk and had failed to pay the mortgage on the residence where Farrah continued to reside. However, the husband's attorney pulled out documents showing that the husband had paid the mortgage until he started giving money to Farrah for spousal support. The judge concluded Farrah could certainly afford to pay the mortgage herself out of the $2,500 a month her husband gave her in support.

Anne was again furious with Farrah after the hearing. "Why did you tell me your husband abandoned the house and didn't pay the mortgage? You made a fool out of both of us at court this morning."

"I forgot when he started to give me money," Farrah said. "I thought it was the next month."

I think you simply lied to me, Anne thought to herself.

A couple of weeks later Farrah fired Anne Amsterdam. However, Anne had done a lot of work on her case by then, and had exceeded Farrah's initial retainer deposit. Anne sent her the bill, and Farrah was instantly angry. She decided to go to fee arbitration under a program run by the county bar association, and Anne's fees were reduced. In addition, Anne did not get paid for the time she spent preparing for and attending the fee arbitration.

Farrah then found attorney Betty Bailey to take over her case. Betty asked how Farrah felt about working with the prior attorney, to get an idea of any problems that might arise in their new relationship. She got an earful. "That's too bad," Betty said, without criticizing the other attorney. "Sometimes it just doesn't work out."

Betty paid particular attention to Farrah's statement that she felt abandoned by her husband, and then abandoned by her attorney. Given Farrah's intensity on first meeting her, Betty figured she might have some Borderline personality traits. Best to avoid triggering those abandonment fears from the start, she figured, even if I'm wrong about her.

Betty told Farrah to call anytime, and that she valued her information about the case. "After all, you know him better than I ever will." If she was busy, Betty told Farrah, it would be fine to leave a detailed message with her assistant or to leave her a detailed voicemail message. Even faxes were okay, she said, although it might be a while before she would have a chance to read them. Her assistant would let her know one had arrived, though. Betty's staff knew not to lie about her being out of the office if she was really there. "If I'm unavailable, just say I'm unavailable—which is true."

When Farrah left Betty's office she felt much better. She decided that Betty would be perfect. Then she remembered that she had not told Betty about the affair her husband had last year. She called Betty's office. Betty was busy working on a hearing she had for the next day, but she took Farrah's call. "I just have a couple minutes, since I'm working on a hearing for tomorrow—just like I will be when I'm working on yours. Tell me what's up." Betty mostly listened for a couple of minutes.

"Okay, well thanks for letting me know about that," Betty said. "It's not a large issue the court will want to focus on, but it helps me understand how your husband thinks and acts—which is extremely important in handling your case. It may help in negotiations, too. Well, I've got to get back to my paperwork, but feel free to call me or send me any notes you want in writing. Also, my assistant can take a detailed message. Whatever works best for you."

Farrah felt reassured at how interested Betty was in her case. It was a week before she called again. And by the time they went to court, Betty had a more thorough understanding of Farrah as well as of the husband. She predicted that the judge would probably give both sides something, so she advised Farrah not to be surprised or to have high expectations.

After the hearing, even though Farrah benefited from the outcome more than her husband, she was angry at Betty for not telling the judge about the affair. Farrah felt that Betty was not that good after all. Betty was tired and this irritated her after all her hard work. But she remembered to mostly listen. Then she said, "I can understand your frustration. There's a lot I wish I could have said, too. But the judge would have been angry with you and me if I had done that. The judge really doesn't like to hear about misbehavior that doesn't directly relate to the decision to be made."

"But the other attorney said bad things about me," Farrah replied. "You should have defended me and told the judge he's really the one who behaved badly."

"Yes, but don't forget that the judge paid no attention to it. It might feel good for a few seconds, but that's not the way I work. I think you'll agree that it's better that the two of us take the high road."

Farrah agreed. After that, she did not call for two weeks.

Specific Concerns For Specific Roles

Advocates

Attorneys need to be concerned about being too emotionally close or too emotionally distant with HCPs, who usually have high expectations of advocates, which generally leads to a falling out when those expectations are not fulfilled. High-conflict personalities frequently have conflicts with their attorneys, and may have several attorneys before a legal dispute is resolved. By maintaining a professional relationship, you can avoid most difficulties. The problems arise mostly when you bend your own rules, become too enmeshed, or are too rejecting.

Mental health professionals generally develop relationships that are more intimate because they are sharing the client's innermost thoughts and feelings. Therefore, when an HCP is involved it is especially important to make no sudden moves in terms of intensity or distancing of the relationship. When an HCP declares rage toward, or love for, the therapist, it is best to rationally deal with it as a therapy issue. I have known therapists to be harassed, stalked and sued when they abruptly terminated therapy with an HCP because problems arose.

When providing advice to family members, keep in mind that they are often in the most difficult position because they cannot really end a relationship with an HCP. Thus, the same principles apply in terms of arm's-length handling of a dispute. Family members can advocate for the HCP, but should not assume responsibility for the HCP's complaint. Family members also have lives to live. They should resist the urge to give in to emotional appeals just to calm the HCP down. In the long run, this often backfires. Family members can provide information and support, but should always encourage the HCP to get professional assistance in handling their high-conflict disputes.

Support workers such as students and volunteers often assist persons identified as victims of crimes, violence and other abuse. These are important roles. However, I have seen misguided cases that were promoted primarily by an over-eager, but untrained, support person. Support workers who apply the same principles of balance and objectivity as other professionals in bonding with HCPs will be more helpful and less stressed.

Dispute Resolvers

Mediators do best when they remain neutral throughout a dispute. By avoiding the appearance of taking sides by bonding too much with one side, mediators can be most helpful to HCPs. While the HCP may demand agreement with his or her point of view, a calm mediator can remain balanced and bonded with both parties. Avoid seeming to agree with the more rational party, although this is tempting. So long as they are in mediation, you need to resist the common temptation to pressure the HCP or the other party to accept a settlement just to get the case done.

Advocates and dispute resolvers are frequently called on to provide counsel to people in business. Managers and administrators often have to handle the high-conflict disputes that arise between employees and customers, and between employees. When managers provide advice in these instances, whether they handle the dispute with both sides together or separated, they should remember that HCPs need to feel that the manager is bonded with them—that the manager respects them and is listening to their concerns. High-conflict personalities are attuned to rejection and judgment, so managers need to show caring for the person while staying neutral and focusing on solutions. Where many managers run into trouble is in personalizing the dispute, and taking one side. The customer is not always right, and the employee is not always right. The most effective managers remain bonded and friendly to all involved, while focusing on what steps to take next.

Judges and arbitrators have to make the tough decisions. They have to favor one party and not the other. From the limited information allowed into evidence, they may not know whether one or both parties is an HCP. They can, however, make decisions while remaining bonded to both sides. Opinions can be delivered with equal eye contact with each party, positive comments can be made about each party, and both parties can be wished well in the future. Even when one party loses or is sentenced, the judge's words can make a difference. With HCPs, the biggest factor in determining whether an unfavorable court decision is accepted or resisted may be the sense of being bonded to a caring and wise decision-maker.

Evaluators and ombudspersons are often in the role of mediating a dispute, but making a recommendation when there is no agreement. The same principles described above apply. However, it is especially important with cases involving HCPs to maintain a sense of objectivity and to avoid reaching conclusions too early. I have seen several cases where psychological evaluators and others were perceived to have reached conclusions too early in a dispute and inadvertently discouraged receiving more extremely important information—information that contradicted their conclusions. By remaining bonded to both parties, those parties will provide the most complete information and they are more likely to accept the outcome as fully evaluated.

When asked to resolve an HCP's dispute, friends and family members will often come to you, as a professional, for advice. If the dispute is between two or more family members, you may wish to counsel the friend to stay out of it and encourage professional help. Alternatively, you can suggest that the friend explain that he or she wants to keep each relationship and would rather assist both sides in negotiating a resolution to the dispute, rather than making a decision for them.

Targets of Blame

It is important for targets to attempt a positive bond with the HCP—or at least to avoid escalating the HCP unnecessarily. (If further controversy is avoided, sometimes HCPs lose interest in the dispute or find a new target.) Targets can do things to minimize the impact of the HCP's negative energy—and sometimes to resolve the dispute. Suggest that targets avoid responding with personal attacks or criticisms of the HCP's intelligence. In some cases, it helps to have a neutral friend or other respected person tell the HCP that the target meant no harm, and that he or she respects the person and would like to discuss ways to resolve the dispute.

Sometimes avoiding any contact with the HCP is best, and other times reaching out to the person is preferable. Consider the possibility of advising the target to apologize for miscommunication or misunderstanding. Since bonding issues are at the core of HCP disputes, apologies can play more of a role in reducing or eliminating the conflict than in ordinary business or financial disputes.

If the target had a prior close relationship with the HCP as a professional, friend or co-worker, he or she may be able to reinforce the prior positive relationship and emphasize that there was no intention to abandon, belittle, dominate or neglect the HCP (although you may want to use other words). Even though the perception of abandonment and so forth may be completely the HCP's own cognitive distortion, sometimes making the effort to clear up this misperception helps the HCP shift back into a positive view of the relationship. While the target may not want to swallow his or her pride and make this extra effort, putting out positive energy in the face of the negative HCP energy may in the long run save significant time, money and emotional distress.

On the other hand, the target can often do very little. The HCP may be fixated on the target as the cause of all the problems, and be totally unaffected by any feedback. In those situations, the target will have to rely on obtaining advocates and dispute resolvers who are able to reasonably assist in resolving the dispute, and who can develop sufficient bonding with the HCP to obtain a long-term resolution.

CONCLUSION

There are many ways to handle bonding. If you pay substantial attention to this issue from the start, you will avoid major problems in the future.

Chapter Eight Summary
Bonding Skills With High-Conflict Personalities

1. Listening to fear and anger (without getting hooked)
2. Being consistent
3. Anticipating crises
4. Adopting an arm's-length bond
5. Validating the person, not the complaint

Advocates: Develop a balanced relationship that is not too close nor too rejecting.

Dispute resolvers: Maintain equal respect and recognition of positive characteristics for both parties, even though your recommendations or decision may require one party to have more consequences or more tasks to do than the other.

Targets of blame: Avoid over-reacting with comments and actions that further escalate the dispute. Avoid making concessions just for the sake of bonding, as they may reinforce the HCP's cognitive distortions that the target is to blame.

Structure

igh-conflict personalities (HPCs) have difficulty regulating their emotions and controlling their behavior. They will often push your boundaries by asking for inappropriate favors, intruding on your time or burdening you with new problems, while resisting taking no for an answer. They are typically preoccupied with their reactions to the latest crisis or with some interpersonal drama. Their goals usually have more to do with looking good to others, or with manipulating relationships, than with long-term planning and problem solving.

As a result they need a great deal of external structure, especially in handling the many tasks (and endless stress) of an ongoing dispute. After addressing bonding concerns, the next step in assisting an HCP in the resolution of his or her dispute is providing structure.

The reason many of these disputes go on for years is a lack of sufficient structure in the HCP's life. High-conflict personalities have a difficult time organizing themselves for letting go, healing loss, and moving on. They usually rely on others to solve interpersonal problems for them. An effective advocate will provide enough structure for the HCP to accomplish many of the tasks in the dispute for themselves, such as compiling documents, doing general research and organizing information.

Skill #1: Setting relationship boundaries, roles and expectations

High-conflict personalities regularly push the boundaries, partly to find out where the limits are and partly to squeeze more out of the relationship. You need to be gentle, but firm, in establishing your boundaries. Avoid bending the rules, especially your own. This only leads to future blow-ups and extra time spent on repairing the relationship. You should know that setting boundaries is appropriate and necessary, even though the HCP may not like it. The HCP may complain, but will generally accept your boundaries as long as you remain in a relationship with him or her. Throughout your relationship you will want to set clear boundaries about your behavior and about the HCP's behavior, similar to the boundaries about your availability for phone calls and crises discussed in the previous chapter on bonding.

Some HCP clients will really push the limits. They may ask you to meet them away from the office, or to develop a social relationship with them. This can lead to many kinds of trouble. First, it will create an expectation that you will focus more and more time on them and their case. Second, the HCP client may feel a sense of intimacy with you which could ultimately trigger intense feelings of love and/or hatred for you—transference from prior intimate and difficult relationships. Some of the worse cases of malpractice start out with a slow erosion of professional boundaries.

Mental health professionals have ethical limitations on their relationships with clients. These limitations disallow "dual relationships." Clients can be reminded of this external rule so that your limit-setting is not seen as a personal rejection, but a standard that controls all therapists.

Frank's Client

Frank used to drive his last client, Peggy, home each week after her psychotherapy session. She lived on his way home, and she had difficulty driving at night. They would have minor chit-chats on these drives. Then one night she confessed to Frank: "I think I have fallen in love with you. I think you feel the same way I do, don't you?"

Frank was shocked by this admission and quickly became emotionally distant. By the time they got to her apartment, he told her that she would have to change therapists. He had not intended for her to misunderstand his generosity in driving her home. Sometimes she asked for a hug before she got out of the car and went up to her apartment—and Frank had always reciprocated. This time, when she asked for the hug, Frank withdrew and refused. "It wouldn't be right," he said. "Ours is a professional relationship, not a friendship."

A few days later, Frank was served with a summons for a lawsuit for malpractice. Apparently, Peggy slit her wrists later that night and was rushed to the hospital after she called police. She was suing Frank for malpractice for causing her such severe emotional distress that she attempted suicide.

Eventually, Frank was found not guilty of malpractice. Most lawsuits against therapists do not result in findings of actual malpractice, but with HCP clients being sued for perceived malpractice (or being sued out of anger) is a serious risk. The best protection is to begin with clear relationship boundaries.

Attorneys are not forbidden to socialize with their clients, but in cases where the client is a potential HCP it is strongly discouraged. In some cases a business opportunity will arise, and attorneys are cautioned to avoid it or to seek consultation from outside counsel regarding the advisability of a business venture with a client.

Mediators are allowed to vary in their boundaries about contact with one or both parties outside of joint mediation sessions. Many mediators do not allow separate contact with the parties, to preserve their neutrality and balance. However, many other mediators do allow separate contact—often called a caucus. This can work so long as everyone is clear about the rules. Separate contacts should be disclosed to the other party, and should not be seen as favoring one or the other in terms of length of time of contact and the setting of the contact (such as by phone or in person).

I have no specific recommendations about separate contacts by mediators. In some cases a separate caucus may help a client understand other points of view, and or help a client consider more options for settling the case. Many business and government mediators use separate caucuses effectively.

However, in family disputes and other heated interpersonal conflicts, separate contacts may be inadvisable because the excluded party may worry about a conspiracy between the mediator and the included party. In particular, with HCPs, separate caucuses may heighten fears (paranoias) that the mediator has taken the other person's side in the dispute. In general, this issue is a matter of the professional's judgment based on his or her assessment of the personalities and nature of the case.

The clearer the initial boundaries, the less likelihood there will be serious conflicts later on. However, you can always set a boundary later if the need for it arises, so long as you do it respectfully, to avoid triggering the HCP's fears of abandonment (Borderline), inferiority (Narcissistic), domination (Antisocial) or neglect (Histrionic).

Gary's Apartment

It is common for an HCP to present you with new, unrelated problems that you are expected to solve. In setting boundaries on the relationship, this also needs to be addressed. Dispute resolution professionals should always get clear about what issues they are responsible for handling, and what issues they are not responsible for. In most cases, there will be a written agreement regarding services to be rendered and fees for those services. In fact, this is an ethical requirement of all professions, and a legal requirement of attorneys and mental health professionals.

In the middle of his divorce, Gary had to move out of his apartment. He called his divorce attorney, Ms. Dewar, in crisis, and asked her if she would sue the apartment owner. In addition, Gary asked if she could help him find another place.

He was so upset—and offended that this could happen to him—that Ms. Dewar reluctantly agreed to meet him in his neighborhood, and to drive him around to look for a new apartment. She decided not to charge him for this assistance. She figured that her moral support and assistance would get him through this crisis more quickly, and then he would be able to pay her for the legal work she had done on his case, which had already exceeded her retainer.

Gary's expectations of the attorney-client relationship with Ms. Dewar escalated rapidly. He told a friend: "I knew my attorney was the best. She's helping me find a new apartment. And she's going to sue my old landlord."

Then an apartment became available when Ms. Dewar was in court and could not meet with the landlord to review the rental agreement for Gary. By then, he expected she would review any legal documents he was asked to sign. He became furious and fired her.

Ms. Dewar would have been better off simply empathizing with Gary's problem and encouraging him to use his own abilities and resources to find an apartment—to set a limit on her attorney-client relationship. Her fee agreement should have stated clearly that she was only responsible for handling his divorce in family court. She would not have been responsible for suing his landlord, for helping him find an apartment or for reviewing his new rental agreement.

It is possible that her fee agreement was limited to his divorce, but that she felt sorry for him or wanted to impress him. These are natural feelings, but in the context of a professional relationship they are inappropriate to act upon. While many attorneys do favors for friends and clients—often in the hope of future business referrals—this is especially unwise with a potential HCP.

As a superior court mediator, I have handled malpractice cases in which clients sued attorneys who allowed the lines to blur between a professional and social relationship. New attorneys are particularly vulnerable to this problem. Structure helps everyone to be clear about the nature and boundaries of the relationship.

Clarifying Expectations and Roles

One of the greatest differences between those with personality disorders and everyone else is exaggerated expectations. High-conflict personality clients may have an extremely grandiose expectation of how their case will turn out. The HCP may anticipate being seen on television or winning a great victory against a despicable public menace. Along with this fantasy will be an enhanced perception of your incredible professional skills. Keep in mind that the HCP usually does not tell you about this fantasy, but simply believes in it.

Alternatively, the client may believe that all professionals are incompetent crooks. At the first sign of minor difficulty in your case, the client may expect total failure and verbally attack you for it—or simply fire you as the attorney, mediator or therapist.

To prepare your client for the normal progression of a legal case, an advocate should predict the range of realistic legal outcomes in advance. For example, if the client is prepared for a loss at a hearing, then even a minor victory can be satisfying. If the client is not prepared, even an insignificant procedural setback can be the basis for a major verbal attack, or being fired.

It is also helpful to predict realistic ups and downs in the professional-client relationship. Suggesting that there will be times when you are not readily available, or when the client may feel critical of your work, makes it easier for both of you to cope. Sometimes it is helpful to predict that the client will feel angry at you, and that this is part of any normal working relationship. Therapists generally do this. In the patient-psychotherapist relationship, it is all grist for the mill of analysis. But many attorneys and mediators pay little attention to these potential relationship issues until after they arise. With potential HCPs it is better, and safer, to plan ahead.

Since you are going to be working together, it is important to clarify what each person's role will be within the professional-client relationship. One of the largest areas of concern will be each person's role in decision making. The client, of course, makes the final decisions about most aspects of a legal case, including whether to accept a settlement or go to court. While an attorney may ethically make decisions about much of the strategy and procedures, with HCPs it is important to share almost every decision. This is because any decision that turns out poorly will be blamed on the attorney if the client did not participate in making it. It is much easier to say "we" misjudged an aspect of the case than to admit that you alone made a decision about which the client is upset.

An easy step to take in this regard is to send drafts of proposed letters to the client for prior review. While this may make the timing awkward and require more planning on your part, it helps the client feel important to the case and more responsible for the outcome.

In mediation, it is advisable to seek mutual agreement on every small step in the process. "It seems like we're ready to move on to the next issue. Would you all agree with that, or am I being premature? What do you all think?"

By putting the responsibility for moving ahead on the parties, no one can later complain that the mediator "rushed me" or "pressured me into this agreement." Since mediation is a voluntary process (with a few exceptions), you do not want to get caught seeming to make the parties do anything. High-conflict personalities are especially sensitive to being told what to do and being forced to do something against their will.

Courts have a difficult time with the expectations of HCPs because they expect a clear-cut procedure like they see on television. High-conflict personalities have exaggerated fantasies about court: that there were be finality; that it won't take long; that you can bring a surprise witness; and many more myths. In reality court can drag on for years, surprise witnesses are rarely allowed and the outcome is often muddy or even the opposite of what you would expect. Subsequent motions or appeals can undo a prior successful decision. Big, clear-cut victories are rare.

In reality, court procedures take a long time, are confusing, boring, inconsistent, frequently delayed and may appear irrational to those who do not know the history. Judges who patiently explain these procedures to the parties help in calming anxiety and reducing conflict. However, there is a limit to how much time the judge has for explanations. It is much better for parties and their attorneys (or other advocates) to research and discuss the realities of court procedures prior to hearing or trial.

Skill #2: Choosing your battles

High-conflict personalities constantly react to minor conflicts and misperceptions in their daily lives. To them many events—especially in legal disputes—are frightening and confusing. One of the greatest gifts you can give HCPs is permission to skip a battle. It is usually a relief, although it may initially be hard for them to understand. There just isn't time, energy or money to fight everything that is wrong in the world. In addition, HCPs generally feel like they have to prove that they are okay at every turn, so it can be helpful to say that this or that issue is not about them, but about something insignificant.

In a serious legal dispute, you cannot really succeed if you are fighting too many battles on too many fronts. You will become too scattered to deal with anything productively—and the emotional tension will become overwhelming. You need to limit your goals and focus your energies. This goes for the advocate as well as for the client. Be a role model of planning, not just reacting.

In many cases, choosing your battles involves clearly and simply explaining the significance of each issue in the larger case, and then jointly choosing issues to fight about. Sometimes settlement on weak or minor issues helps free up time to work on stronger or major issues.

Skill #3: Containing emotions

In family therapy and in mediation, it is common for professionals to open up emotional issues to see where the barriers are in resolving an impasse. Many ordinary interpersonal disputes are simply stuck on hurt feelings, miscommunications, unintended offenses and cultural misunderstandings. Asking how each person feels about a subject can clear the air and resolve the impasse. Once the emotional issues are clarified, the mechanics of the surface issue may be easily resolved. This is one of the most helpful aspects of conjoint family therapy and mediation with both parties present.

With HCPs, however, the opposite approach is better. You generally do not want to intentionally open up emotions. High-conflict personalities have great difficulty managing their emotions and a low tolerance for hearing the emotions of others. It is often best to briefly acknowledge feelings, then focus away from them. This lets the person know that they have been heard, but that probing their feelings is not on the agenda.

This is especially important in mediation cases. When the mediator acknowledges their feelings, they don't need to fight to get attention for these feelings. Once they know that you understand how they feel, their level of tension often reduces without further discussion.

Many of these parties are relieved to avoid focusing on emotions, because they feel so emotionally vulnerable to the other person. In general, in cases with potential HCPs I avoid giving them an opening to vent emotions. This is also my standard approach in divorce mediation because, even though most divorce mediation clients are not HCPs, the emotional issues run so deep that they will rarely be resolved in their lifetimes.

For example: "I understand that you both are feeling frustrated and angry. In particular, Mary seems to have felt ignored and Carl seems to have felt attacked. Recognizing these feelings, I would like to move on to your proposals for how to resolve this dispute. Let me explain how we make proposals in this mediation process. It's a method called brainstorming. Anyone can make a proposal and we don't evaluate it until we have made a full list. Who wants to start with a proposal?"

By getting emotions off the agenda, they are able to focus on true problem solving. Of course, I know that emotions will arise, and I will acknowledge them and again return to problem-solving.

In some cases, the following explanation helps: "From over here where I'm sitting, I can see that you are both hurting and feeling misunderstood. Of course, each of you is feeling that you're the one getting the short end of the stick. That's very common, although you can't see it from where you're sitting. And I know that you each really want the other person to empathize with you right now—but I don't think that's possible in this stressful setting or at this stressful time in your lives. Maybe after this is all resolved you'll be able to tell each other 'Gee, I do understand how upset you were with me. I was being a jerk then and I'm sorry.' But this rarely happens and you shouldn't expect it. Get your support and understanding from your friends and family right now. We all need all the support we can get." Then quickly move on to problem solving.

At this point you may be asking, "But shouldn't I let them vent a little anger?" Dispute resolution professionals hear a lot of anger. Most are trained to ignore it and focus on the unresolved problem underlying the anger. It is true that we often let people vent to us in the privacy of our own offices, when no one else is around to be bothered by it. And with our healthy clients, a little venting does not seem to hurt.

But what about when the other person—the target of the anger—is present in a joint counseling or mediation session? Decades ago, family therapists learned that simply allowing people to yell at each other, or to hit each other with foam bats, did not work. It may have given a brief sense of relief to the upset person, but the recipient of the venting felt so bad that problem-solving could not take place. It is clear today that dispute resolvers should discourage or actively intervene when parties are simply venting anger at each other.

This is especially true with HCPs. For example, most chronic domestic violence abusers are HCPs, and domestic violence treatment programs specifically do not teach venting of anger. Instead, they teach skills for preventing the buildup of anger, for changing the cognitive distortions and for improving communication and problem-solving skills.

In the case of HCPs, it is especially important to prevent the venting of anger in joint sessions because their egos are so fragile. This can include joint negotiation sessions with attorneys, as well as joint mediation sessions. They may not look fragile at all, but remember that HCPs take negative feedback much more personally than most people. They just cannot handle it. They will feel compelled to respond and retaliate in some manner. Therefore, it is best to contain emotional outbursts of anger as much as possible. Be prepared to protect them from themselves. They may thank you for it.

It is also good to avoid venting your own anger at HCPs, even though they may be frustrating and self-sabotaging and you really want to get their attention. In reality, venting your frustration at your client will backfire, as the HCP client will feel the need to convince you that you are wrong to criticize them. They will respond with verbal counter-attacks, firing you or even—in extreme cases—stalking or assaulting you.

Skill #4: Focusing on tasks

Since focusing on emotions is usually discouraged with HCPs, the solution is to focus them on tasks. High-conflict personalities generally have escalated anxiety and heightened energy, so it is not enough to tell them what not to do. Instead, you need to give them something else to do. Focusing on tasks may be difficult for them in some cases, so a lot of repetition by the professional may be necessary. In other cases, the client may be eager to have something to do and will volunteer for more and more tasks. In either case, this helps the client focus their energy and feel good about their contribution toward resolving the dispute.

Attorneys can assign tasks to their HCP client (actually all clients benefit by this) such as gathering documents, doing some research and preparing notes for declarations or other necessary documents. With HCPs, however, you should make sure to mention that you cannot guarantee you will use every piece of information they provide, but that you will use as much as is appropriate when the proper time comes. Many clients can be helpful by providing you with this assistance; it is not just a technique for handling difficult clients.

In many of my mediations, I have also found that the best response to emotional venting is to focus on clear-cut tasks, as the following example demonstrates.

Fran and Jim's Furniture

In a heated divorce mediation, Fran consistently tried to move the discussion to Jim's alleged financial irresponsibility—even when that was not the issue we were working on—and Jim was easily triggered to respond. We were working on dividing up the furniture, which is rarely a problem in my divorce mediations because the parties are usually able to divide those items on their own.

Fran: "Jim, I can't believe that you're getting away with wasting all our money on your cars. What did we need all of those old cars for anyway? None of them really run."

Me: "Forgive me if I'm wrong, but I believe you both had decided to focus on dividing up the furniture now, is that correct?"

Jim: "That's right. I don't think it's fair that Fran gets to keep changing the subject. Can't you control her any better than that?"

Me: "So then, do you both agree that we're focusing on the furniture for now. Fran?"

Fran: "Oh, okay."

Me: "Jim?"

Jim: "Yeah."

Me: "Okay, let's look at these lists you both made up."

Fran: "His list is so offensive. I can't even look at it. Can you believe that he put the dresser I got from my grandmother on the list? After all the money he wasted on his cars?"

Me: "Let's stay focused here. One approach some people use is to make a joint list together, with four columns for the wife's separate property, the husband's separate property, and for community property that's being assigned to each of you. What do you think? That way we don't have to fight over which list we're using."

Jim: "Sounds good to me."

Fran: "Of course it would. Look how he agrees with you, Bill. Are you on his side?"

Me: "I'm not on any side. That's just one approach that some people have used. I can give you some other suggestions if you want. Or do you have another suggestion for how we should proceed?"

Fran: "No. Let's just do the four columns. And my grandmother's dresser goes in mine. Right, Jim?"

Jim: "Yeah. Sure. I never said it wouldn't."

Me: "Great. An agreement. What's the next item we should put on our list?"

And on and on. Eventually, all of the furniture was divided. By focusing on a piece of paper that they both helped generate, they developed a routine and eventually reached agreement on all issues. Incidentally, I generally consider it an error for the mediator to make just one suggestion, as I did in the example above. When you do that, the party who does not like it identifies the mediator with the suggestion. It is better to make more than one suggestion, so that the rejection of a suggestion does not mean rejecting the credibility of the mediator. In the above case, I backed out of it successfully. Part of the beauty of mediation is that you can make corrections as you go along.

For mental health professionals involved in legal disputes, it helps to have the client work on getting some of the relevant legal documents. Assigning this task to the client may help him or her feel more in control. However, make sure the client is not leaving out any information you really need to know. For example, if you are counseling the child of a divorcing couple, make sure to get the consent of both parents. If one parent claims to have the sole right to sign up a child for counseling, make sure to get a copy of the most recent court order on this issue.

When a mental health professional is performing a court-ordered evaluation, it helps the client to feel that he or she is participating by obtaining letters and other useful information that may help in the case. Otherwise, the client feels like a passive victim of a legal process beyond control or influence.

Skill #5: Managing the enablers

Cases involving HCPs often involve one or more enablers: family members, friends or others who want to have direct contact with the dispute resolution professional to control the case or to help. At first, this may seem to be a nuisance to the professional and a drain on your time. However, the wise professional will develop a relationship with family members who indicate they want to be involved. When a client with a personality disorder is involved, family members can be very helpful, or they can sabotage your hard work. Establishing a positive relationship with a potentially sabotaging relative may help resolve the dispute.

Since personality disorders begin to develop in early childhood, family members have been dealing with the HCP's behavior most of their lives. Therefore, they can provide a wealth of information about the person's life history and patterns. They may also provide helpful insights into how to manage the HCP.

In some cases, family members have responded to the HCP's behavior by confronting and fighting with the HCP. However, you will not meet many of these family members, as they generally want to avoid the HCP. More common are the families in which everyone has learned to "walk on eggshells" around the HCP. In these cases, family members act much like the family members of an alcoholic, making excuses and cleaning up the social messes. These co-dependents have learned to cope by adapting their own behavior, rather than by confronting the HCP. Over a period of twenty or more years, this pattern can become quite ingrained throughout the entire family.

In some families, other family members also have personality disorders. However, other family members can be part of the problem even if they don't have a personality disorder. They may sabotage your best effort in many subtle ways, just as the HCP does. Generally, the best approach with family members is to involve them in positive tasks. Just as with clients, you can ask family members to gather information, to propose lists of people or resources to investigate, and to provide you with suggestions for arguments and insights. Use as much of their information as you can. Working with family members means they are less likely to be working against you.

If family members have come to your office with the HCP or contacted you separately, it means that they want to be involved. One of the most helpful things they can provide is information. That includes information about your client, information about the case brought to you by the client, and information about the other parties to the case. Family members are often helpful in providing some background on the problems that have escalated into a legal dispute.

With the permission of your client, interview each family member who wants to be involved. Your client can be present or not, depending on his or her wishes. Remember, you do not want to take steps that alienate your client, but instead develop a sense of a team working together to solve legal problems.

Be as open-ended as possible during the interview, so that you gather the most accurate, independent perspective on the case. To get familiar with the case, you can use the same general questions you asked your client. Asking the why, when and how questions may fill in some of the gaps in your understanding.

Further, family members may tend to corroborate or contradict information provided by your client, which may be helpful in deciding how to proceed with the case. If you have some excellent witnesses among family members, you may be more willing to litigate than if they contradict your client—in which case you may want to negotiate a settlement as quickly and quietly as possible.

Family members may also have resources helpful to the case. These can include funds, technical skills, important friends and free time. Since they want to help, feel free to use their services, but be careful to remain in control of the case.

If your client has a HCP, family members may be quite skilled at getting the HCP's attention, steering the HCP into constructive action, and convincing the HCP to accept the opinion of others when necessary.

If you are headed to court, family members may be helpful in keeping the client cooperative, on schedule, reasonably dressed and out of trouble. If you are negotiating a settlement, family members may be helpful in getting your client to accept the legal and/or financial realities. Remember, HCPs believe adamantly in their cases, even though there may be no legal basis for them. Family members may be able to persuade the client to accept a reasonable settlement, even though the client feels that it is a failure, or giving in to the enemy, or a devastating setback, or totally unfair. Given the HCP's cognitive distortions, it is common for a reasonable settlement to feel unreasonable to the HCP.

Keep in mind the all-or-nothing thinking of an HCP. If you alone give the client bad news, and appear alone in your perspective, the HCP may single you out as the new enemy. When family members share in the process of delivering bad news, or directing the client into productive activities, the HCP will be less likely to cast you in a negative role.

I have described the positive roles family members can play in managing your client. You are fortunate if this occurs. In many cases, the problem is the opposite. There is a higher incidence of personality disorders in families where one member has a personality disorder. These cases can be extremely difficult, but usually can still be managed.

Assessing for HCPs in family members should, by now, be fairly easy. Remember to look for rigid thinking, impulsive or other troublesome behavior, intense emotions and excessive demands for attention. You can use the same methods to structure the relationship and counsel the family members as you would for clients, as described in this book.

Remember how important it is to bond with HCPs from the start. At the same time, remember the importance of setting limits and keeping expectations within reason. These suggestions apply to bonding and structuring with the enablers as well.

Sometimes, family members can be a greater problem than the client. In these cases, feel free to use the client in helping you manage the family members. This may mean excluding them from the office and refusing to take their calls. In these instances, always make it clear that it is because of the confidential professional-client relationship. Sometimes, a brief interview with the family member and the client can set boundaries in the case. (If a client brings a family member to the first interview, I usually leave it up to the client whether to include them—it tells me a lot. But this may also dilute or eliminate the confidentiality of the meeting.)

You, as the professional, are in charge of the case—so long as you are so employed. If you have accepted the case, case management must be on your terms. Cooperation is essential, and everyone involved must respect your professional expertise. It is essential that the client make all major decisions. Even though the ethical rules may allow you, as the professional, to make various strategic decisions, when an HCP is involved you must include him or her in any potentially important decision. Otherwise, you run the risk of the client's wrath and a possible malpractice claim against you.

However, you must also be cognizant of the roles of family members in the client's decision-making process. Strong family members may sabotage your case, or indirectly harm your client, if they are not on board with major decisions. Therefore, you will need to clarify with your client what decision-making role—if any—family members should have.

Confidentiality is another great concern. With HCPs, family members often have fewer emotional and informational boundaries. Everyone may know everyone else's thoughts, feelings and behavior on an intimate level—or at least think they do. You must clarify with your client how you will handle issues of confidentiality. It is most helpful from the start to inform family members that you have a confidential relationship with the client, and that there may be things you cannot share with them.

If a family member is paying your fees, it is especially important to clarify that this person will not necessarily be included in the confidential talks you have with the client. However, since you should develop a comfortable relationship with the financial sponsor, you may regularly want to ask your client if you can share certain pieces of information. Sharing otherwise confidential information may help the financial sponsor feel important and included. Just be clear with your client which information, if any, you may share.

Boundaries concerning your time are also important with family members. If the client easily gets into trouble and rarely worries about it, family members are probably the key worriers. To relieve their anxieties they may constantly contact you for direction or to give you advice. Sometimes setting them up with a good counselor may be helpful. However, you must be able to work closely with this counselor so they are not giving conflicting advice or information about how to handle the case.

Different professionals have different styles and comfort levels with managing family members. You should develop boundaries that feel comfortable and that work for you. You will not be effective in handling your client or the legal issues unless you are comfortable occasionally listening to family members, and occasionally telling them no. Ultimately, the way you handle the family members may determine the overall success of your case—and whether you are fully paid.

SPECIFIC CONCERNS FOR SPECIFIC ROLES

Advocates

Attorneys are usually more concerned about structuring their own work on the case, rather than structuring their clients. With potential HCP clients, however, it is often helpful to give them something to do, especially after they contact you with problems or crises. Tasks help lower anxiety, and they actually help get the work done. High-conflict personalities are more likely than other clients to (unconsciously or purposefully) omit important pieces of information. The more they gather documents, make lists and do research, the more their knowledge helps the case. Sharing this structuring process may help you discuss the objective realities of the case later, if you decide that their claims are not likely to succeed in court.

In many cases the attorney is representing a target of blame, rather than an HCP. Targets also tend to be quite anxious, because they are being charged with greatly exaggerated or false claims, which at the beginning of the case may be given great credence by legal professionals and the court. A well-organized target can give you key documents, notes on the HCP's past activities and behavior, and insights into where useful evidence may be located. Targets need lots of reassurance, so boundaries and tasks will still be helpful, even though many targets are not HCPs.

Mental health professionals can do a great service to their clients (HCPs or targets) by giving them homework about their dispute between sessions, such as writing about possible cognitive distortions, beliefs about court, beliefs about the other party and the role of the dispute in the context of their life goals.

In your advice to family members, you should make sure that they are not doing too much of the work on the case and enabling the HCP (or target) to do too little. In many cases, parents or spouses make phone calls and even schedule appointments when the HCP (or target) should be doing this work. Remember that self-esteem and skills-building often come from accomplishing tasks that were at first difficult or overwhelming.

Support persons, students and volunteers like to be useful and often like to do tasks. Just as with family members, they often assume that the person (HCP or target) is not able to do much for themselves or their case. Make sure that they are not working harder than the HCP.

Dispute Resolvers

Mediators are generally careful to set boundaries and expectations at the beginning of the mediation process. You must be confident in the process and able to protect the process from pressure to bend the rules, which is common with HCPs. It is important to control the venting of emotions, which may work with reasonable people but usually quickly backfires with HCPs. Redirecting into tasks—especially joint, cooperative tasks such as generating ideas and reviewing lists—is often a relief to parties who cannot stop themselves from focusing on emotions. In a high-conflict dispute, avoid asking how the parties "feel" about different ideas; instead ask what they "think" about them.

Managers and administrators are in a good position to give the parties tasks to help resolve the dispute. It is important for you, as the professional, to help managers and administrators understand that gathering more information will often lead to a resolution. Help them discourage focusing on how each party feels, and instead focus on solutions. In workplace disputes, the parties often have the most information about what can and cannot work. Managers must pay attention to disgruntled customers or clients, and ask them to gather information and propose solutions. This often helps them feel like everyone is on the same team. The manager should tell the HCP client what tasks are going to be done—this often reassures the HCP that they are being taken seriously and that things will improve.

Judges and arbitrators are skilled at doing all the work of deciding a dispute. However, in ongoing cases with several hearings, it may reduce the level of conflict if you expect both parties to work on reducing the number of issues or submitting joint statements on the disputed issues. Having the parties collaborate on even minor tasks (with the help of their attorneys or other advocates, and not necessarily in the same room) can reduce the emotional conflict and force the parties to re-focus on solutions rather than just problems. This can be positioned as, "The court requires us to submit this joint statement of the issues and proposed solutions."

Evaluators and ombudspersons are often asked to solve everything by the institutions that appointed them as well as by the HCP and their targets. They are under a great deal of pressure to fix things beyond their control. With HCPs, it is important to keep expectations about your role realistic, otherwise they quickly go to your superiors to complain and to find the "real" source of power. Involving them in the solution with tasks, information and proposals sometimes helps reduce the tension and refocuses their energy in a constructive direction. Meeting with family members or others who have joined in a dispute is a good idea, so that they too can be given constructive tasks to do, rather than putting all of their energy into escalating the conflict.

Family members who are asked to resolve an HCP's dispute can use the same principles described in this chapter, although it may be harder because they are considered family and expected to tolerate more than professionals. In reality, one family member can say no to other family members who are asking too much of them. Family members can offer to help, but they should put the burden of gathering information and proposing solutions on those involved in the dispute. They should avoid taking sides (because that never ends) and they should share the role of advocate or dispute resolver with other family members so they do not get overwhelmed on their own. They should be careful not to raise expectations about their assistance too high, so that they will not become a new target of blame later on if things do not work out well.

Targets of Blame

It is difficult for targets to structure an HCP when they are being attacked and blamed. However, if they have any contact at all, they should try to keep it consistent, avoid raising expectations, and focus on tasks rather than emotions. Targets may be required to collaborate on solving the problem, in which case they should try to have neutral persons present to keep things calm and to witness any improper behavior. This protects both parties. Targets should choose their battles, so that they are not fighting about everything. A small concession on a minor issue may help them save their strength for what really matters.

Certainly, targets should cooperate with advocates and dispute resolvers in doing all requested tasks. A higher level of cooperation may ultimately demonstrate to everyone that is it the HCP who is difficult and escalating the conflict, not the target. Sometimes targets become obsessive about details—relevant and irrelevant—in trying to be helpful and proving their innocence. However, they should ask you, as the advocate or dispute resolver, what kinds of information you want. Finally, targets should structure some fun and/or support time to help get through the demands of the dispute.

CONCLUSION

By providing the structure that one or more parties may lack in a legal dispute, you may have a less-prolonged case and a more positive outcome. High-conflict personalities and their negative advocates often encourage the escalation of disputes (sometimes unconsciously, sometimes on purpose), not to resolve the dispute, but rather to have an emotional outlet and an opportunity to blame others and validate their cognitive distortions. Resist the urge to respond emotionally to each allegation and insult. You will reduce your own stress and possibly reduce the costs of a dispute by adding as much structure as you can.

Chapter Nine Summary
Structuring Skills with High-Conflict Personalities

1. Setting relationship boundaries, roles and expectations
2. Choosing your battles
3. Containing emotions
4. Focusing on tasks
5. Managing the enablers

Advocates: Acknowledge the emotions of the client (whether an HCP or a target), then focus on tasks they can do. This may require a lot of gentle repetition. Avoid escalating the dispute with emotional attacks or by raising unrealistic expectations.

Dispute resolvers: Be firm about containing emotions and focusing on solutions. Limit the expressions of anger and the allegations. Give the parties tasks that require them to contribute to the solution of the problem. Limit venting.

Targets of blame: Show that you are cooperative in being solution-focused. Be helpful in providing verifiable information. Do not hold back on providing your analysis of the real dispute and focus your energy on obtaining information and witnesses in support of the truth. Avoid preoccupation with irrelevant misbehaviors and unimportant details.

Reality Testing

"*Mr. Vandenburgh will see right through you now.*"

Most of those with high-conflict personalities (HCPs) can only tolerate one view of reality—their own. To them, their feelings become facts. They will try to persuade you of the truth of their one reality, and they will escalate their emotions until you agree with them. Rather than recognizing that everyone has a different view of reality and that a successful society requires peaceful co-existence, they will see your point of view as a personal betrayal or a dangerous threat.

Cognitive Distortions

Mental health researchers have identified ten common cognitive distortions that everyone experiences from time to time. The following list of cognitive distortions is paraphrased from *Feeling Good: The New Mood Therapy*, a 1980 book written by David Burns:

1. **All-or-nothing thinking**—seeing things in absolutes, when in reality little is absolute
2. **Emotional reasoning**—assuming facts from how you feel (I feel stupid, therefore I am)
3. **Personalization**—taking personally unrelated events, or events beyond your control
4. **Shoulds**—living by a set of rules that are unachievable and illogical
5. **Mental filter**—picking out a single negative detail and dwelling on it
6. **Fortune telling**—believing that you know the outcome of events, when you cannot
7. **Labeling**—eliminating the realities of life with broad, negative terms (dummy, failure)
8. **Mind-reading**—believing that you know what other people are thinking, intending or doing
9. **Minimizing the positive, maximizing the negative**—distorting reality to fit internal biases
10. **Overgeneralization**—drawing sweeping conclusions from minor or rare events

Cognitive distortions involve a negative, self-sabotaging, inaccurate view of the world. As we grow up these distortions, which are based on our life experiences and our interpretation of those experiences, become imbedded in our thinking. As adults reacting to daily life, these negative thoughts can occur automatically. However, most people suspect that their cognition is becoming distorted and seek more information to verify this. (Am I over-reacting? Is it really as bad as it feels? I'll get another opinion.) With more information, most people are able to correct their cognitive distortions.

Unfortunately, HCPs believe their cognitive distortions are true. They do not absorb new information. Because they cannot see the distortions that are causing the difficulties in their lives, they live in a highly distressed state of internal conflict. Instead of seeking more realistic information, they fight off contradictory information and seek to convince others that their cognitive distortions are true. They try to persuade others to adopt their distorted reality.

Since few people readily agree with their distorted thinking, HCPs escalate their emotions, trying even harder to obtain agreement with their distorted reality. It seems as though people with HCPs have permanently recorded, and are constantly replaying, the negative comments and experiences of their lives. These have become their cognitive distortions. Those with personality disorders are bombarded constantly with automatic negative thoughts based on these cognitive distortions.

Cognitive distortions are like computer viruses. On the surface, you cannot tell that the virus carries misinformation that can be highly destructive if acted upon. Most people have programs that regularly sweep for viruses and to eliminate them. But HCPs cannot even see that a "virus" (cognitive distortion) exists in their thinking.

Because cognitive distortions are not immediately obvious to the person who has the thoughts, the distortions can cause them to seriously misbehave if they believe in them. Betty Broderick, Susan Smith and many others committed outrageous murders based on their extreme cognitive distortions. They were not able to recognize that their thinking was distorted.

The following five skills are often helpful in dealing with reality testing for HCPs.

Skill #1: Maintaining a healthy skepticism (keeping an open mind)

From my observations over the last three decades, more high-conflict disputes are unnecessarily escalated by the lack of healthy skepticism than for any other reason. Many advocates, dispute resolvers and even targets of blame accept the misinformation of HCPs as truth. This is why so many high-conflict disputes start out backward in the courts (blaming an innocent target for minor, absurd or non-existent events based on cognitive distortions) and take such a long time to resolve—it is because the burden is on the target to prove that the initial decision was wrong. Of course, the HCP becomes desperately defensive about his or her perceptions, and vigorously defends the cognitive distortions. The apparent equality of the two different points of view (HCP and target) push the dispute higher and higher.

The HCP produces escalating emotions and increasingly dramatic emotional facts (which are false but require thorough legal examination), while the target becomes motivated to produce more and more true, factual information. As each true fact gets trumped by another emotional fact, then each emotional fact gets trumped by a true fact, the case spirals upward.

All of this can be avoided by maintaining a healthy skepticism. In a legal dispute—or in any dispute—questions should be asked from the start. Is that really true? What evidence do you have for that? Claims that seem to require immediate action often receive a blanket presumption: "We better be safe and award the restraining order." Or, "We better be safe and change custody." Yet it is often the power of these emergency, unquestioned "to be safe" orders that fans the flames and escalates the conflict—and the use of the court's time over the next several months or years—when a little more fact-finding at the start without presumptions would separate the true from the false.

More reality testing of the initial claim, based on a higher level of skepticism, would be better before granting emergency temporary orders. Temporary restraining orders, residence eviction orders, change of custody orders, control of funds and similar orders are commonly brought by HCPs because of their cognitive distortions—and at the beginning of the case in a hearing which only lasts a few minutes they often win. Then it may be months or years before a full hearing or trial, which often leads to the conclusion that the initial order was based on inaccurate information. Some courts are trying to deal with this, but most courts have much further to go.

Therapists, attorneys, family members and the courts are all gullible at times. This is especially true when a likeable, but upset, person is making dramatic claims that appear to need immediate action. As human beings, the natural tendency is to help. Therapists, judges and the majority of attorneys are sincere people who like to help others. However, as professionals we could be more wary than we are. I like to approach each claim as equally likely to be true or not true. This helps keep me from jumping to conclusions.

With a mental health background, these cases seem clearer to me in terms of interpersonal dynamics than to many others. More training for all professionals—and more skepticism for family members—would go a long way toward reducing the escalation of some of these unnecessarily high-conflict disputes.

Recognizing personality types helps us, as professionals, recognize the type of cognitive distortions occurring in the generation of false emotional facts. If the "facts" weigh heavily on the theme of "he abandoned me," I suspect it may be a Borderline misperceiving the situation, or getting revenge. If the "facts" lean toward "she's trying to control me," I consider that I may be dealing with an Antisocial who feels dominated and is over-compensating by trying to dominate the other person. In these cases, the advocates and dispute resolvers need to ask detailed questions right away, before the HCP develops a cover story and begins building credibility with more and more emotional facts.

"How did he abandon you? Tell me in detail." Or, "How is she controlling you? Is that really control?"

By asking these questions, you can get a better idea if the case is constructed out of cognitive distortions or reality. Even if the party was abandoned or controlled, it does not mean that there is an emergency. By focusing immediately on detailed facts, the emotional facts often fall apart and the true facts come into sharper focus. In this way, the dispute can be better controlled, never escalating into a high-conflict case or even going to court.

From the start, advocates and dispute resolvers need to be far more skeptical with HCPs. As the case progresses, they must still maintain this healthy skepticism. It is tempting to assume that we have enough facts to reach a clear conclusion, but we never have all the facts. In high-conflict disputes, I think it is best to never be more than ninety-five per cent certain that anything is as we think it is.

In some cases, the most important facts come out much later and may contradict everything we previously thought. If we do not let in this new information, we ourselves are essentially operating on cognitive distortions. Yet it is hard to accept that we were wrong or misled. It is not uncommon for cases to end based on inaccurate information—or remain incorrect for a long time—because advocates and dispute resolvers were unwilling to accept new information. It is best to examine each new piece of contradictory information and weigh its ability to more accurately explain the case.

A common danger in high-conflict disputes is for dispute resolvers to become rigid advocates for their decisions after they have made up their minds. Psychologists have studied the difficulties they have in changing their minds after making a determination. Yet they believe that this openness is important.

It also helps the parties to know that advocates and dispute resolvers can admit that they will never know exactly what happened. Otherwise, they lose credibility with the parties, who know much more about the dispute. Lecturing someone with certainty about that person's private life is always a risky venture. A decision can be made, and action taken, while still keeping an open mind—forever.

Skill #2: Recognizing cognitive distortions

Five of the most common cognitive distortions in high-conflict disputes, and their dynamics in court cases, are:

1. Emotional reasoning

Emotional reasoning occurs when someone feels that something is true, and therefore believes it is actually a fact. For that person, it becomes an emotional fact. For example, in a divorce case a wife felt that her husband cut off the utilities and telephone when he moved out. In fact, the husband had informed her that he would no longer pay the utilities and phone bill after he started paying child and spousal support. The wife was particularly sensitive to feeling abandoned, and would get tearful about the concept that the husband had cut off the utilities and phone service. In fact, he was able to use utility and phone bills to show that he had kept paying them until a month after support payments began.

Because she *felt* abandoned, she believed that she actually was abandoned. Her emotions became emotional facts. Unfortunately, in a court of law the husband had to prove that he had not in fact cut off the utilities and phone. Much of what occurs in hotly contested interpersonal disputes in court today involves similar cognitive distortions giving the appearance of factual conflicts.

2. Minimization

It is common for those who commit domestic violence, child abuse, sexual abuse and many other forms of misconduct to minimize what they have done. In their own minds, the perpetrators of such behavior have not caused any harm. Instead, they believe that they have had an insignificant effect on the victims of their misconduct.

In court, many people in interpersonal disputes minimize their own behavior and exaggerate the other party's behavior. In fact, many of these disputes are over behavior that is similarly inappropriate, but does not rise to the level that requires court intervention. We see this especially in divorce cases.

On the other hand, while a true victim of another's misconduct may in fact need court intervention, legal professionals may minimize the problem by simply viewing the perpetrator as a difficult, but harmless person. This area requires careful, discriminating assessment, rather than quick and easy assumptions that are often wrong.

3. Exaggeration

The opposite of minimization is exaggeration or maximization, or what some people call "catastrophizing." Many cases in court include catastrophizing. For example, a husband went to court to get a restraining order against his ex-wife because she sent him angry faxes and emails using four-letter words. He was seeking a court order requiring the wife to communicate respectfully with him by phone, instead of using these forms of correspondence, to discuss parenting of the children.

At court, it came out that the husband had left at least one angry voice-mail message for the wife in which he also used a four-letter word. The husband had minimized his own behavior, and maximized or exaggerated the wife's behavior. The result was that the court ordered them not to communicate by phone, fax or email, but instead to use a correspondence book to be delivered to each other at visitation exchanges. This is not at all what the husband wanted. He wanted the court to order her to talk nicely with him because he wanted more, not less, contact with his ex-wife. He truly couldn't see that he was minimizing his own behavior and exaggerating hers.

4. Personalization

This distortion occurs when someone takes personally an event that has little or nothing to do with him. For example, a person driving in traffic may become upset when another car cuts in front. The HCP may feel offended that the other driver had the nerve to get in his space. He may feel the need to take revenge by using certain gestures or using threatening vehicular behavior. The other driver, however, may have simply not noticed the HCP's car when changing lanes. Personalization is especially common with Narcissistic personalities, because they feel so easily injured by other people's benign behavior.

Mental health professionals treat cognitive distortions with self-training techniques to help the individual reality-test their own "automatic negative thoughts." Such thoughts happen to all of us—they simply pop into our heads. However, HCPs have them constantly and are more likely to believe these distortions absolutely, rather than to routinely consider them inaccurate.

5. Projection

Projection is the term for a psychological concept that goes on unconsciously. People with this cognitive distortion experience an emotion, but for one psychological reason or another it is so disturbing that they cannot consciously acknowledge it. However, at one level they intensely feel the emotion, so they must do something with it. What they appear to do is to project the emotion (or characteristic) onto someone else, just as a movie projector throws an image onto a screen across the room.

Mental health professionals describe projection as the unconscious process of seeing in others what is really going on inside oneself. For example, a woman may feel angry at someone she loves, but not feel safe to get angry because she is so dependent on that person. Someone with a personality disorder related to childhood abandonment may project that anger outward, believing the other person is angry. The HCP may then engage in clinging behavior, which actually pushes the person she loves away. As a result, the HCP may feel the abandonment she so feared—thereby re-enacting the conflicts of her childhood rather than changing her own dysfunctional behavior.

Another HCP may feel sexually frustrated, but be unaware of this feeling. Instead, the HCP may get angry at his partner and believe she is having an affair. Then the HCP may beat up his partner out of jealousy and fear, when the real issue was the projection of his frustration and anger onto her. This is a common scenario in domestic violence cases, which often involve HCPs.

Since HCPs cannot see their own role in interpersonal problems, they must blame the other person for whatever problems exist. In some cases, HCPs are not aware that the person is actually acting appropriately or only slightly inappropriately, because they feel so strongly that the other person is to blame. In other cases, HCPs may know the other person is not guilty of their allegations, but they are so angry about the relationship that they feel justified in harming the other person anyway.

This tendency to blame others often leads HCPs to seek assistance in building a case against the other party. They often include family members and friends in these appeals for assistance, and may eventually involve attorneys, mediators or therapists. The intensity of the HCP's concerns can easily persuade legal professionals, and even the courts, that the allegations are true. This may be the case even when the opposite situation—that the HCP was the perpetrator and the other person was the victim of the HCP's projections and unwarranted blame—is actually true.

It is fascinating to see how many legal disputes include a HCP projecting his or her own behavior onto an innocent party. I have seen this in many domestic violence cases. The victim of the abuse is accused of doing what the perpetrator is actually doing.

For example, an aggressive man may accuse a passive woman of aggressive behavior. In one case, a man claimed that a woman threw cans of food and pots and pans at him in the kitchen. Ultimately, it was revealed that the man was throwing things at the woman. Nevertheless, with true projection this man may actually come to believe that the woman was doing it to him—that he was not in fact throwing these objects. However, in some cases the person doing the projecting is simply telling a lie.

Skill #3: Suspecting lying

Lying is a difficult issue for the courts. The structure of the court process appears to encourage lying more than it discovers lying. Even though declarations are made under penalty of perjury, and testimony is given after being sworn to tell "the truth and nothing but the truth," in reality there is little enforcement for perjury. Instead, decision-makers simply focus on the substance of the case, and do not mete out special penalties for lying. For example, in most criminal trials the defendant takes a "not guilty" position. The jury decides who to believe. At the outcome of the case, the defendant is found guilty or not guilty, but is rarely held accountable for lying.

There is a great problem in determining lying with HCPs. In many cases they believe they are telling the truth when in fact what they are saying is such a distortion of the truth that it is completely false. With HCPs, it may simply be a case of cognitive distortion. There are, however, cases where people knowingly lie. As an advocate, I have found that challenging their statements with true information in the office, before the case goes to court, may help reduce conflict. If they know that their statements will backfire in court and reflect poorly on them, they may back off from pursuing inappropriate action.

Confronting lies with true information is one of the most effective tools in handling high-conflict opponents in court. In fact, it often helps bring the party into negotiations and leads to an out-of-court settlement. When people ask me how they can explain a HCP to a judge or a jury, I suggest obtaining substantial evidence of lying behavior. This behavior is common for HCPs, and exposing it helps reduce their desire to litigate. As well, exposing any lie helps reduce the credibility of the HCP's other statements.

For example, at a court hearing over custody, a father argued that the parenting evaluator had not stated that the son expressed a wish to live with his mother. At the same hearing, the mother stated that the parenting evaluator did, in fact, say that the boy wanted to live with her. At that point in the process, the judge said "Then we shall hear from the parenting evaluator."

The parenting evaluator worked for Family Court Services and happened to be in the building. Within 20 minutes the evaluator was in the courtroom, testifying, "Yes, I did say the boy wanted to live with his mother." The father's claim that the evaluator had not made this statement was exposed. He immediately lost his credibility with the court, and the judge found in the mother's favor.

Skill #4: Learning the legal realities (and eliminating the fantasies)

So many high-conflict disputes include one or two parties who have a fantasy view of the law. They may be expecting their "day in court," or perhaps they are expecting a total vindication or validation. But the law is rarely so simple.

It is important that both parties get objective legal information early in the case. The attorney they have hired may simply be telling them what they want to hear. For example, I have seen many family court cases in which two attorneys provide opposite information on key issues, such as spousal support. One attorney may say that spousal support will be generous and long-lasting. The other attorney may predict no spousal support at all. Not knowing the legal standard for people in similar circumstances, the client could spend months or years and tens of thousands of dollars pursuing these beliefs. Once the fantasy has burst, realistically learning the law would cut short many high-conflict disputes.

Most high-conflict disputes I have seen at the trial level include one or more parties with a personality disorder, or severe personality disorder traits. They seem to be the only people who believe that the courts have a clear-cut process, and that absolute victory is possible. In reality court is often unpredictable, frequently delayed, and does not go as anyone planned or expected.

Skill #5: Finding evidence by personality type

High-conflict personalities operate in rigid patterns of behavior. They are often predictable in terms of the trail of evidence they leave during the course of their lives.

Borderline—As stated throughout this book, those with Borderline Personality Disorder are preoccupied with fears of abandonment, intense anger and frequent mood swings. Many "vexatious litigants" are actually Borderlines who are easily enraged at interpersonal events. "Hell hath no fury like a [Borderline] scorned."

For example, a Borderline woman may sue a doctor or lawyer because the professional did not respond quickly enough to her crisis call. Anther example is the Borderline man who has a history of domestic violence in relationships.

In looking for evidence when a client appears to be Borderline, it helps to see if there is a history of legal actions with the same pattern of behavior. High-conflict personalities experience enduring patterns of behavior from early in their lives, so it is likely that a history exists out there somewhere. Anyone who has been in prior relationships with a Borderline, who may have information about domestic violence or other incidents of interpersonal anger, may be a source.

This is especially helpful for cases in which the HCP refuses to negotiate, and insists on going to court. In many cases, this aggressive and adversarial behavior has been repeated many times. As the saying goes, those who live in glass houses shouldn't throw stones. Ironically, HCPs generally live in glass houses but because of the psychological principles of distortion, projection and outright lying, they believe their own lives will not be examined. If you have to go to court, historical information may be quite helpful.

Narcissists–Narcissists have a lifetime history of offending people, because they show so much disrespect and exhibit such demeaning behavior. When NPs feel that they are the target of a narcissistic injury, they may sue again. For that reason, a good place to start is a search of prior lawsuits. It may be productive to look for a history of this behavior in prior interpersonal and employment contexts. However, be prepared to run into brick walls, because those from the past may not want to deal with the Narcissist ever again.

Antisocial–Antisocials are the most rewarding in terms of finding a history. Antisocials are social rule-breakers, even of the smallest rules. Some psychologists recommend looking for even minor traffic offenses. As we saw with the case of Mr. Gossage in Chapter One, possible Antisocial personalities may have a history of traffic tickets that have never been paid, and minor violations for which the person has not attended a hearing.

An interesting case example from my files includes a father who went to court about visitation. The mother (who I represented) had concerns about the father driving drunk and endangering the children. In their meeting with the parenting evaluator, the father stated that he did not have a problem with alcohol, and that he had been alcohol-free for at least a year. In addition, he stated that he had been to a treatment program for alcoholism and that his counselor could verify that.

The parenting evaluator asked if he ever had any drunk driving arrests, which the father denied. The parenting evaluator then obtained a form signed by the father allowing the parenting evaluator to speak to the alcohol treatment counselor.

Having sensed that he had an Antisocial personality, I decided to investigate his traffic record. Not surprisingly, the father had two drunk driving arrests—one of them a month before they met with the parenting evaluator—and he had a trial just one month after the meeting in which he lied to the counselor. He had completely misrepresented his history. In addition, the father told his alcohol treatment counselor that he would not allow him to release any information to the parenting evaluator, and he revoked his Release of Information authorization to the parenting evaluator.

Needless to say, after all of the above information was provided to the parenting evaluator, a much more structured visitation arrangement was recommended.

You may wonder why such a person would lie about information I could so easily discover. Once again we go back to the old saying, "People who live in glass houses shouldn't throw stones." People with these personality disorders can't seem to reflect on their own behavior. They truly do not recognize that they are living in a glass house.

The main idea here is that in dealing with a personality disorder or maladaptive traits, you need to look inside their glass house. While this may sound aggressive and unsympathetic, we do the HCP no good when we allow them to continue to throw stones. As in the tough-love approaches to treating alcoholics and addicts, if HCPs insist on going to court they need to be confronted with their own behavior, and the courts need to be informed of the truth.

Histrionic–Histrionics have similar histories to the personalities described above. It is not uncommon for them to fabricate dramatic information. Therefore, researching their dramatic stories may produce some powerful contradictions.

In many cases, the Histrionic person has not lied or fabricated, but simply burned out those before them. In dealing with such persons, talking to those who have gone before will lend insight into how to deal with them in the future. While this may or may not reveal evidence that can be used in court, it may reveal personality-based behavior that may be helpful in forcing the person to negotiate, or in otherwise resolving the dispute out of court.

CONCLUSION

Reality testing is a key issue for HCPs. Using the skills outlined in this chapter may be crucial to resolving the dispute. When disputes are eventually resolved, it is usually due to sufficient reality testing. Allowing parties to go to court without testing their facts and fantasies does a disservice to the party, to the court and to society.

Chapter Ten Summary
Reality-Testing Skills with High-Conflict Personalities

1. Maintaining a healthy skepticism (keeping an open mind)
2. Recognizing cognitive distortions
3. Suspecting lying
4. Learning the legal realities (and eliminating the fantasies)
5. Finding evidence by personality type

Advocates: Avoid agreeing with the content of the person's complaint before investigating it. Jointly examine the facts and gather evidence with an open mind. Admit that we will never know everything and that we all sometimes make mistakes of perception.

Dispute resolvers: Be aware of emotional facts and peripheral persuasion. High-conflict personalities are often more convincing about false information than a target will be about the truth. When dramatic allegations are raised ask, "Is that really true?"

Targets of blame: Be assertive about searching for evidence and presenting it to dispute resolvers. Do not hold back on negative, but true, information about your accuser. Check for your own cognitive distortions.

Consequences

"If it please the Court, my client would like to let it be known he has already learned his lesson and is very, very sorry indeed."

P eople with personality disorders have enduring patterns of behavior. It takes strong consequences to change them. Well-intentioned lectures and routine negative feedback about their dysfunctional daily lives have no lasting impact on their behavior.

Consequences need to be logical and directly connected to solving the problem. If the problem is chronically abusive behavior, part of the consequence should be a requirement to change that behavior, as well as further consequences if the abusive behavior happens again. This is the principle of diversion programs for drug-related crimes and domestic violence.

If the problem is related to misperceptions and false allegations, psychological treatment and legal or financial consequences if it happens again are required. Of course, if the problem involves repeated dangerous behavior (such as murder or rape), a sentence of life in prison without parole may be needed because the behavior is enduring in the person's personality. However, most of today's legal disputes involve two or more people who will remain in society. Society needs them to resolve their own problems so they can avoid repeating their high-conflict behavior and consuming social resources.

Just as consequences motivate alcoholics and addicts into recovery, HCPs need strong and structured consequences. A program of change—not just a promise or order to change—is necessary to produce real and lasting new behaviors. To help these changes take places, such a program usually includes repeated small consequences. Only when a person takes responsibility for changing his or her own thinking and behavior will any meaningful resolution of the dispute occur. In some cases one person's misbehavior is driving the legal dispute, while in other cases both parties may need consequences before the dispute can be resolved.

Skill #1: Mandating cognitive-behavioral counseling

Cognitive and behavioral methods that have been widely used in mental health treatment over the past two decades are practical and effective in long-term change for those with (and without) personality disorders and traits. Requiring such counseling may be the best thing you ever do for your client in a high-conflict legal dispute.

Cognitive methods refer to changing the way we think. I was trained in the 1980s to treat depressed and anxious clients with the cognitive therapy techniques developed by Aaron Beck and David Burns. I found their worksheets and techniques extremely helpful—not only for my clients, but also for myself when I became stuck on issues in my personal or professional life.

Cognitive therapy focuses on challenging our own automatic negative thoughts and cognitive distortions. The great benefit of cognitive methods is that they empower the individual to help himself or herself with handy methods which can be applied anywhere, at any time. As I described in the previous chapter, common cognitive distortions in legal disputes include emotional reasoning, all-or-nothing thinking, minimization, maximization, and personalization.

Since those with personality disorders do not reflect on their own behavior, litigation is an opportunity to attack and blame the other party. Perhaps attorneys and the courts could require a counseling step before the court allows a high-conflict dispute to be heard, just as mediation is becoming a required step.

Even one counseling session with a properly trained therapist could be helpful. There could be a focus on examining motivations in going to court, examining fantasies about what to expect, and exploring alternatives for handling emotions (especially fear and anger). The courts could require specific lessons to be learned and issues to be resolved.

For example, many people who go to court for personality-based reasons share the same core cognitive distortions. Prior to going to court they could be required to address these distortions in counseling. This would help to focus on the legal issues and to screen out the personality-based cognitive distortions.

NEGATIVE THOUGHTS	NEW POSITIVE THOUGHTS
It's all someone else's fault.	It's usually everyone's fault to some degree. One person may bear more responsibility, but you are fully responsible for your life and your part (however small) in this dispute.
There is only one point of view—mine!	There are always two or more points of view, and we can reasonably differ.
I deserve my day in court.	Court is not what we see on TV. It can be boring and dissatisfying. It's not about you, but about a narrow legal issue. It would be better to have "your day" with support persons or a therapist.
There is only one solution - mine!	There are usually several solutions. By creating more solutions, you may be able to save money and both sides may be able to "win" something.
I will be vindicated in my beliefs.	Even if you win, you will rarely feel totally satisfied. The horrible statements made about both parties, the narrow basis of the decisions, and the cost to everyone involved are rarely worth the minor vindication you might receive—especially after several years.

I've explained this process of challenging cognitive distortions so that you can see how beneficial it can be to anyone involved in a court case. It may be especially helpful for reducing defensiveness and frustration in high-conflict personalities, which is often what is actually driving the legal dispute. Some of the conflict comes from their own thoughts, not from the other person's behavior.

Many high-conflict cases are driven by the constant negative thoughts that HCPs have, the feeling that they have to prove something to someone else just to feel okay about themselves. That feeling will not change in court—in fact, it usually gets triggered and escalates during the court process. Instead, it is more easily dealt with in counseling with methods such as cognitive therapy.

Behavioral methods refer to changing the way we behave. For example, drug treatment programs and domestic violence treatment programs use behavioral methods to help individuals manage and redirect their own impulses. They teach methods of avoiding situations where one's behavior may get out of control—like staying out of bars or predictable angry confrontations. They teach methods of recognizing warning signs leading to out-of-control behavior, and they teach healthy methods of managing and releasing stress. They also teach relapse prevention, to avoid the build-up that comes before a relapse into old dysfunctional behavior.

Misbehavior is the focus of legal disputes. In cases where there is chronic misbehavior, it is common to seek a court order punishing this misbehavior. If you know of a program that would be helpful for treatment of such misbehavior, focus on that in the legal case. Maybe there can be an agreement that the person will enroll in that program, which will avoid the necessity of an embarrassing trial and the risk of being court-ordered into treatment.

The true goal in a case of serious misbehavior is behavior change. Most prisoners eventually get out, but most guilty parties in civil disputes never go to jail. It is in everyone's best interests that the individual make actual changes in his or her ongoing behavior. This requires a program of change. This is the most appropriate consequence for inappropriate behavior.

Counseling is a broad term covering a wide range of services. However, while it is increasingly common for courts to order counseling, there needs to be a specific explanation of the treatment method and treatment objectives.

I recommend cognitive-behavioral counseling, with identified issues and specific treatment goals. From my experience, I recommend that therapists take a more active and questioning role in supportive therapy with HCPs by asking questions like, "Is that really true?" or, "What is your part in all of this?"

It is easy, but not helpful, for mental health professionals to become focused on supporting the client's court-related negative thinking and projections without even realizing it. It is easy to go on for months and months empathizing with a client's anger toward an abusive spouse without some corroboration that it is really true.

In therapy, being a victim is a comfortable role to play. It just doesn't help one make changes. Even true victims need to make changes, otherwise they will repeat the pattern in new situations with new people.

I have seen many cases in which one party is stuck in the anger stage of the Five-Stage Grief Process described by Elizabeth Kubler-Ross in her classic book *On Death and Dying*. Anger is just one of the stages on the way to acceptance. If a person is stuck in the anger stage, he or she will not heal and recover from the loss that triggered the grief process. This loss may be a divorce, loss of a job, loss of money or some other loss.

In court, all the anger gets directed outward. The person may lose track of the need to also feel sad, and to receive empathy from others. Instead, the parties get caught up in feeling angry and having people agree with their anger, rather than in nurturing their sadness as well. People with personality disorders have an inability to move through the grieving process on their own. They need a lot of re-direction. Re-direction enables them to focus on their own feelings of vulnerability and sadness while forming new bonds. Court allows them to stay stuck.

With true spousal abuse, for example, the victim is better served by focusing on grieving and on making personal cognitive and behavioral changes, rather than just venting and getting support for remaining an angry or helpless victim. That is why I recommend that counseling be very specific for HCPs—especially to assist them in reflecting on their own thoughts, feelings and behavior. Understandably, this is extremely difficult for them to do, because one of the key problems of their personalities is an inability to reflect on their own behavior, and an inability to grieve. They need help learning how to address these essential human needs.

Specific treatment goals might include:

- Moving through the five stages of the grief process
- Learning to tolerate different points of view
- Identifying common cognitive distortions in thinking
- Identifying and avoiding relapse situations triggering anger
- Learning to regulate intense emotions
- Learning to control violent impulses

Specific treatment methods that would be generally appropriate:

- Individual counseling for the grief process
- Counseling for identifying and challenging cognitive distortions
- Classes for learning anger management
- Classes for tolerating different viewpoints
- Group therapy for learning skills for regulating emotions
- Group therapy for true victims of abuse
- Batterer's group therapy for controlling violent impulses
- Drug treatment program for controlling drug use impulses

Treatments not recommended include individual therapy for alcohol or drug addiction. Experience has shown that addicts cannot change without the input of other similarly addicted people. That's why Alcoholics Anonymous is so effective and individual therapy is not. As well, individual therapy of any type doesn't work for treating Antisocial personalities. They will simply con the therapist, and never change themselves. Antisocials need to be in a group of others with similar behavior problems to help confront their own denial. Also not recommended is individual therapy that only empathizes with a client's complaints of being a victim, without corroborating the truth of the complaint and without helping the client make personal changes. Clients will avoid dealing with their own role in their life problems, and be doomed to repeat them.

In short, cognitive and behavioral counseling is an appropriate consequence for anyone involved in a high-conflict legal dispute. Even if the person is a true victim of another's misbehavior, that person needs to explore how he or she got into the situation, and what life choices can be made to avoid such situations in the future. This applies to most people going through a high-conflict divorce, regardless of how badly the other person may have acted.

"I am ordering you to participate in six months of individual or group counseling with a qualified mental health professional. You are to address your own thinking and behavior; learn to identify self-sabotaging thoughts and behaviors; learn skills for changing those thoughts and behaviors; and be able to describe how the other people in this dispute may feel and think."

The above judicial order could be very helpful in a protracted divorce, in an interpersonal injury case or in an extended dispute between neighbors. However, it does not have to be a court order. It could be a family requirement for a particularly upset member of the family who is headed for court, or it could be a requirement by an attorney with a client in a high-conflict dispute, even if it is not primarily that client's fault. It may help him or her cope and limit the damage of the legal dispute.

Skill #2: Considering court action

In our society we expect the courts to deliver the strongest consequences for misbehavior: large fines, jail time or even the death penalty. Simply the threat of going to court is sufficient in many cases to get someone's attention and motivate them to change—or refrain from—certain behaviors.

Unfortunately, this threat can be abused. Often it is HCPs who say, "I'll see you in court" as a bullying tactic. This is because HCPs are more likely to use extremes for problem solving, and they have more of a fantasy of using court as vindication or validation. It is important to know that it is unethical for an attorney to threaten someone with a lawsuit.

On the other hand, once you are involved in a lawsuit it is helpful to know that those with HCP disorders or traits are usually preoccupied with their public image. You can threaten them with exposure of certain information, with requests for large fines, or even with jail time. They do not like to have their non-public image come out, and they do not like to have to pay extra money for misbehaving. An effective technique is to threaten to seek monetary consequences, and to threaten to expose delicate information—as long as this is true. Even though the court may not make the orders you are requesting, the threat of it will often get the HCP to act more appropriately, at least for the duration of the trial.

As an attorney in an active case, I may threaten to expose lies in their statements that I can prove are false. I may send the threat in a letter or court declaration, along with the suggestion that we settle this out of court.

Filing a counter suit is common in legal cases. High-conflict personalities truly do not see that your claim is as strong, or stronger, as the one they are claiming against you. Because HCPs often throw stones without realizing that they live in glass houses, it helps to threaten them with exposure of their areas of vulnerability. They may agree to settle or drop their lawsuit. However, in many cases they do not.

Filing a request for sanctions may be appropriate. Even though the courts don't like to give sanctions, I have found that requesting sanctions often inspires more appropriate behavior. Even if the court does not order sanctions, the threat makes it clear that I will not tolerate the unnecessarily litigious behavior of the other party. It keeps them on their toes. I may get the sanctions next time, so they are usually more cautious in the future.

People say it's not good to threaten consequences that you can't enforce. However, HCPs take the threat seriously because it challenges their shaky self-image. They don't want to risk that you will expose a weakness. If you put damaging, but truthful, information before the court they will angrily deny it—but they will also know that you are not going to enable them to remain unexposed.

I have had to do this in many family court cases where I suggested we settle out of court. After the other party—usually an HCP—insists on going to court with exaggerations, absurd claims or false allegations, I do not hold back in exposing the HCPs true history and contradictory statements. Many of my clients are co-dependents who have been walking on eggshells around an HCP for years. If we have to go to court, it is no time to keep secrets and "protect" the HCP from information that gets to the truth.

I have represented clients—both men and women—who were physically abused for years, but who refused to allow me to disclose the truth of this history of abuse. Since the court never heard the full truth, the other party—the abuser—gained confidence in making up stories that sounded plausible. The result has been that my clients were blamed for behavior they did not do, they lost time with children when they were the better parent, and they even lost out on financial issues they should have won.

Without the threat of exposure and possible court consequences, HCPs escalate their stories in court with confidence that they won't be found out. I believe that you have to be as aggressive as the HCP in presenting the full story, however ugly. Of course, this is a last resort. But if they won't settle (and they often don't) the whole story comes out along with the consequences—court consequences.

Skill #3: Obtaining court sanctions

While many people would like to see HCPs put in jail for their aggressive and often abusive use of the court system, this happens only extremely rarely. I think the courts feel that jail time isn't worth pursuing in interpersonal disputes. Even lying is not punished by sending people to jail.

Likewise, many people ask about filing for contempt of court orders, since HCPs violate court orders so often. This is also not realistic. Since contempt of court is essentially a criminal action, even if heard in a family court, judges do not like to deal with it. It requires stricter courtroom procedures, and is potentially punishable by up to five days in jail (in California) for each violation of a court order.

However, sanctions exist under all areas of the law. Sanctions usually involve an order for one party to pay the other party's attorney fees as a consequence of litigation misbehavior. While attorney fees are not easy to get, it is usually a procedurally easy request. It can be for any amount of money. With sanctions, even a small amount of money can have a powerful impact.

In California, Family Code Section 271 states as follows:

...the court may base an award of attorney's fees and costs on the extent to which the conduct of each party or attorney furthers or frustrates the policy of the law to promote settlement of litigation and, where possible, to reduce the cost of litigation by encouraging cooperation between the parties and attorneys.

I have sought and received sanctions, although rarely. I don't seek sanctions unless it is a true case of misconduct. Otherwise, I would lose credibility with the court and the opposing attorney. The question is usually the extent of the misconduct (does it really merit sanctions?) and the actions of the other party (did they engage in any misconduct which may cancel out sanctions?).

In some cases, sanctions stop the escalation of the case. For example, Karen Smith in Chapter Six was sanctioned $500 for her request for child and spousal support arrears, when there were no arrears. Mr. Persistent in Chapter Seven was eventually sanctioned $2,000 for repeatedly bringing hearings to court for a change of child custody. At the end of the previous hearing, the judge had commented on the attorney's Points and Authorities regarding Antisocial personality: "I read the papers on Antisocial personality, but I don't see that it has any relevance here."

At the time, the mother's attorney had replied: "It's just that such a personality won't respond to lectures, and nothing is likely to change without strong consequences. But thank you for reading it."

A year later, at the following hearing, the judge imposed sanctions. Perhaps he had re-read the Points and Authorities and reconsidered the idea of consequences rather than another lecture. After he imposed the sanctions, the case remained out of court longer than ever before.

Skill #4: Crafting orders with future consequences

High-conflict personalities view a court order as invalid if it doesn't fit within their one view of reality. If the judge doesn't agree with the HCP's position, the judge must be wrong. If the judge imposed punishment, the judge must be mean and ignorant. To an HCP, the idea that he or she is wrong is inconceivable.

Following the court's orders may feel like an intrusion to the HCP, and an insult. The HCP will do everything in his or her power to avoid following the court's orders. But if there are court consequences, the HCP will have to be careful. The result is that the HCP will only violate the court order in ways in which it can be argued that he or she is following the court order—so that there will be no punishment or other consequence.

Antisocials are particularly skilled at—and often obsessed with—manipulating this fine line. If they view the court order as a victory for the other party they will feel dominated. This will cause them to feel like they have to violate the order to maintain their sense of identity as a person who is in control. The net result of all this is that court orders regarding possible HCPs must be written very specifically, and they must have very specific consequences. The future consequences can be monetary fines, as in the case of Mr. Persistent, or the consequence can be a reduction in parenting contact. In very rare cases, the consequence can be jail or prison.

It is especially helpful, I think, to ask the HCP parties involved what the consequence should be in the event of future misconduct. At first they will deny that they would ever violate the court orders, although they know they intend to violate them. If they deny any risk of violation, simply ask them what they think the penalty should be. If they participate in determining the consequences, they are much more likely to accept the order and not need the consequences.

I have done this in divorce mediations involving an addict or an alcoholic. I have helped the parties spell out in detail what will happen with regard to custody and visitation if a parent has a drug or alcohol relapse. There are different consequences for a brief "therapeutic" relapse and for an ongoing relapse. With everyone participating in creating the consequences, we rarely need to implement them.

Skill #5: Terminating the relationship

Many advocates quickly burn out trying to help those with HCPs. When they realize how odd or how difficult the HCP is, they want to escape as soon as possible. In a sense, they decide that a logical consequence of the HCP's bad behavior is to end the relationship. But be careful!

There is much danger in the temptation to cut off the relationship abruptly. High-conflict personalities are in a constant bonding crisis. If you cut them off, you will be treated as those before you were treated. Some HCPs will become verbally attacking, and some will follow you or even assault you. We know from many news headlines that terminating employees needs to be done carefully. This is also true for advocate-client relationships.

First, it may not be necessary to terminate the relationship. You can set limits, and then let the client know that terminating the relationship is a possibility if there are problems in the future. Most HCPs will try to behave—at least for a short period of time—because you are one of their strongest advocates and they don't want to lose you. However, they need to know what your rules are, or they will feel surprised and betrayed if you seem to have unfairly rejected them. After briefly working with them in court and seeing how they handled prior relationships, you will have a good idea about how they handle losses. Did they verbally attack their prior advocates? Did they follow them, or assault them? Did they sue them? Get ready, because it could be your turn next.

If you have to terminate the relationship, make sure you are ready before you do it. Have your paperwork in order, in case you get subpoenaed. Have a termination conversation that is empathetic and blames the termination on something other than the client's personality. You may truly be too busy to handle the case, or the law may make the case difficult. Just try to avoid a direct criticism of the person because they are really delicate, even though they may appear to be just the opposite. Also, be firm: don't leave the door open to vague contact in the future, unless you can handle it. Connect with the advocate to whom they may be transferred. Don't leave them stranded, ignoring their calls. An ignored HCP client is a client getting ready to sue.

It is not uncommon for an HCP client to suddenly want to terminate the relationship with you. Avoid resisting this sudden rejection—it's probably a blessing in disguise. Tell the HCP that it's fine, that you want the best for him or her. Don't try to convince the HCP not to leave. Simply agree that a fresh start is for the best.

Once you are at this point, avoid apologizing for anything big. If things did not go well between the two of you, best to blame it on external circumstances rather than to blame yourself and make a major apology. The risk of such apologies is that the client will come to believe that you did do something wrong, and that the outcome (if they don't like it) is all your fault. Don't give this impression, because it's usually not true. Remember, they tend to hear what they want to hear, and blame is easy for them.

On the other hand, social etiquette apologies (sorry I was late) are fine, and they may even be helpful to making the client think that you are sensitive to how she or he must feel. If circumstances warrant, sometimes giving a small fee reduction helps ease the emotions involved in a termination with an angry, disappointed HCP client. Your sensitivity now may save you a lot of difficulty later on. Take the time to handle this situation well.

CONCLUSION

With HCPs, consequences are necessary and complicated. This is an area where therapists and mediators have little power, but they can be instrumental in designing the consequences. Attorneys and courts, however, have a great deal of potential power in obtaining and enforcing consequences. The more information shared between the professions in this regard, the more effectively consequences can be used. This is one of the most exciting things about the collaboration of the different professions in legal disputes: rather than just punishing HCPs and seeing their dysfunctional behavior repeated, we can actually help people change for the better.

Chapter Eleven Summary
Consequences Skills with High-Conflict Personalities

1. Mandating cognitive-behavioral counseling
2. Considering court action
3. Obtaining court sanctions
4. Crafting orders with future consequences
5. Terminating the relationship

Advocates: Family and professionals can require counseling as part of their ongoing relationship. If the HCP will not get counseling, then you will have to work much, much harder. This is true whether your client is an HCP or a target.

Dispute resolvers: You can recommend or order counseling, but be clear on whether individual or group programs are best for a specific party. Avoid lectures, unless you have a strong bond with the client. Threaten and use financial consequences to produce real change. Detailed orders and followup are necessary with HCPs.

Targets of blame: Propose specific orders or agreements for behavior change. Research alternative treatments, counseling professionals and outcomes. Explain to advocates and dispute resolvers the likelihood of behavior change. Consequences should fit the HCP.

A United Approach

"It's time to stop blaming everything on the Tartars, Mr. Ragner."

C ongratulations! You now know more than the vast majority of your colleagues (advocates and dispute resolvers) about how to resolve the disputes of high-conflict personalities (HCPs). Yet you will find that it is still difficult to manage HCPs and to achieve long-term resolution of their conflicts. With negative advocates, unaware dispute resolvers and an increasing number of HCPs, the task is bigger than any one individual can fully handle. The more professionals who understand and agree on how to manage HCPs, the better it is for everyone—including HCPs.

It only takes one person to validate the cognitive distortions of an HCP—to become a negative advocate. With validation, the HCP will stay locked in battle and become preoccupied with blaming a target, rather than with changing his or her own behavior. This is especially true if the HCP has several negative advocates and unaware dispute resolvers in his or her camp.

But there is growing awareness of personality disorders in legal disputes. The situation is similar to that of the widespread denial of the effects of alcoholism and drug addiction several decades ago. For many years business, government, educational institutions, families and courts denied the social significance and cost of substance abuse. Now, there is a fairly united social approach to treating addictions and to helping individuals into recovery, rather than enabling them to stay sick or simply punishing them.

This same positive approach to the handling of personality disorders in high-conflict disputes is just beginning to occur. It is just a matter of time and education at all levels of society.

Educational Approach

The first step in facilitating a united approach is to resist the natural urge to be adversarial, adopting instead an educational approach. Admittedly, it may seem like the negative advocates and unaware dispute resolvers are being incredibly naive or intentionally harmful. However, they may have been trained to ignore issues such as personality, as is the case with most attorneys; they may be sincere but misled, as happens to many therapists, mediators and judges; or they may have HCPs of their own, which means they cannot hear your feedback.

To elevate the level of awareness about personality disorders in your area, you may wish to bring in an experienced professional, such as a mental health professional who has been trained in personality disorders or frequently works on court or institutional disputes (in business, government, education, health care and so on). Ideally, such a person can become a primary educator in your area.

If you cannot find such a trained person, as a positive advocate or dispute resolver you can still attempt to give a different perspective. The key educational messages (a brief summary of this book) are as follows:

1. One or more HCPs are driving the behavior in the dispute, rather than the surface issues.

2. Emotions and emotional facts are highly unreliable sources of information.

3. Ordinary reasoning and argument will not resolve the dispute nor cause meaningful change.

4. Meaningful change involves identifying and correcting the cognitive distortions of the HCP, and all others involved, in a constructive manner and providing consequences for the HCP's misconduct.

5. Only a united approach will be effective, as the more negative advocates there are, the more the HCP will resist or avoid changing and resolving the dispute.

COLLABORATIVE ASSESSMENT AND CASE MANAGEMENT

Accurately understanding a dispute involving an HCP requires the information and brain power of everyone involved. The exchange of information to examine cognitive distortions, screen out inaccurate emotional facts and control rumors is extremely important. To cover up their private, negative persona and behavior, HCPs invest substantial energy in presenting a public "false self" which appears very positive.

In dealing with mental disorders and substance abuse, many hospitals and treatment programs use a team meeting, collaborative assessment approach. Treatment professionals know that there will be cognitive distortions and strong denial of problems, and that different staff will see different behavior. By meeting together as a team, they are able to obtain the most information and correct the most misinformation.

Research shows that groups of many people (such as juries) are more effective at catching errors and misinformation than one person, or even two or three people. The more, the better. Interestingly, in many mental health and substance abuse programs, the patient is invited to be part of the assessment of their problem, and part of the treatment planning process. The final assessment of the problem by the professionals may or may not agree with the patient's view, but doing it with the patient's input makes it more accurate and encourages the patient's buy-in to the treatment plan.

Procedurally, legal disputes are handled in an adversarial court process with many limitations on information exchange (objections, exclusions of evidence), separate decision-makers (often a single expert such as a psychologist or accountant, and a single judge), and dueling advocates who try to minimize the disclosure of information deemed harmful to their client and maximize information seen as harmful to the other side. When applied to HCPs, such a process regularly fails to provide meaningful information with which to make a useful assessment.

Interestingly, Collaborative Law and Collaborative Divorce™ have grown rapidly over the past decade as more effective approaches to resolving legal disputes—and more satisfying to professionals. I personally became involved in this approach after writing the first edition of this book, and I have found it to be particularly effective in potentially high-conflict cases for the same reasons I described above. By working as a team, the case is understood and handled with much more appropriate sensitivity than in the adversarial process of court. Yet, at this time, collaboration is a voluntary process and many of those HCPs who would most benefit from it have no interest in collaborating with those they see as their "enemies."

SHARED PLAN FOR CHANGE

When dispute resolvers recognize one HCP in a dispute, they are faced with a dilemma: focus on that person as the problem or try to get the parties to equally share responsibility for the problem. Mediators, judges, evaluators, ombudspersons and even family members constantly struggle with this issue.

I recommend the approach used in substance abuse treatment programs involving family members, namely that each person has a role to play in the solution—whether they are equally creating the problems is not an issue. By sharing responsibility for the solution, defensiveness is reduced and the treatment fits the diagnosis of each person's problem. Everybody gets better.

A co-dependent in a relationship with an addict or HCP may need to work on becoming more assertive, recognizing his or her own cognitive distortions, and taking more responsibility for life decisions. An HCP may have more serious behaviors to change, but each person has a role in resolving the dispute and improving themselves. This avoids the fight over who has the problem and replaces it with personal growth for everyone.

UNITED MESSAGE

Over the years, many family members and individual therapists have found that they were unable to motivate an alcoholic or addict into recovery with only their own repeated feedback. Instead, they learned that it usually takes many people with a united message. Seventy years ago Alcoholics Anonymous became one of the most effective group treatments for alcoholism, and that program has been successfully applied to many other problems.

The concept of an intervention was developed as a united approach for motivating entry into alcohol and drug treatment programs—an approach that may be appropriate for HCPs. In an intervention, all the significant people in a person's life gather together to give the person a specific, united message such as: "Go into this treatment program today, or we will all immediately remove our support from you."

Betty Ford is an excellent example of someone who went through an intervention that included her husband, President Gerald Ford. Hearing the same message from all of her close family members and associates, she went into a treatment program for her addictions. Today, she runs one of the country's most respected treatment programs at the Betty Ford Center.

In legal disputes involving HCPs, the message is generally not united (negative advocates can still be found after a court or administrative decision); it is not specific (negative behavior often gets general lectures but no plan for change); and it is not immediate (court cases regularly take months or years before a final decision). Perhaps these characteristics do not matter with criminals who will spend the rest of their lives in prison. But the majority of criminal cases and all civil disputes involve people who will remain in society. Since HCPs are increasing in number we must collectively start addressing this problem by providing a united message for behavioral improvement, rather than a message of social tolerance for the self-sabotaging and often destructive behavior of HCPs.

CONCLUSION

The issue of HCPs is a growing and costly problem at all levels of our society. If we work together in a united approach, we can help most HCPs, and protect our society from the rest. Families, friends and professionals can learn to stop enabling HCPs and focus their intense emotions on acceptance and personal growth. By collaborating and getting training on personality disorders, courts and professionals can motivate parties to truly resolve their disputes, rather than escalating their problems based on cognitive distortions.

Can we afford to ignore this growing problem? The difficulties driving high-conflict personalities will never be resolved in court. Properly addressed, the problems of HCPs can be reduced, our courts will be less crowded, and society will save substantially in the long run—in terms of time, money and emotional peace.

■

APPENDIX A
Potential Indicators of High-Conflict Personalities

1. Long history of relationship conflicts
2. History of abuse in childhood or disrupted early-childhood relationships
3. Views relationships as inherently adversarial
4. Inability to accept and heal loss
5. Lack of insight into own behavior
6. Denial of responsibility in contributing to conflicts
7. Perpetual self-identification as a victim
8. Projection of own problems onto others
9. Preoccupation with analyzing and blaming others
10. Intense emotions over-rule thinking
11. All-or-nothing thinking
12. High level of mistrust or paranoia
13. Denial of responsibility for resolving conflicts
14. Persistent drive to control others
15. High level of aggressive energy
16. Persistent drive to be center of attention
17. Difficulty connecting present actions to future consequences
18. Avoidance of mental health treatment
19. Defensive about any feedback
20. Unconscious distortions and delusions
21. Conscious lying and fabrication of events
22. Expects legal process to provide revenge and/or vindication
23. Inappropriately involves others in disputes (children, neighbors, co-workers)
24. Views friends and family as either allies or enemies
25. Triggers confusion and conflict among professionals

APPENDIX B
Key Skills For Handling High-Conflict Personalities

- **Bonding**

    Skill #1: Listening to fear and anger (without getting hooked)
    Skill #2: Being consistent
    Skill #3: Anticipating crises
    Skill #4: Adopting an arm's length bond
    Skill #5: Validating the person, not the complaint

- **Structure**

    Skill #1: Setting relationship boundaries, roles and expectations
    Skill #2: Choosing your battles
    Skill #3: Containing emotions
    Skill #4: Focusing on tasks
    Skill #5: Managing the enablers

- **Reality Testing**

    Skill #1: Maintaining a healthy skepticism (keeping an open mind)
    Skill #2: Recognizing cognitive distortions
    Skill #3: Suspecting lying
    Skill #4: Learning the legal realities (and eliminating the fantasies)
    Skill #5: Finding evidence by personality type

- **Consequences**

    Skill #1: Mandating cognitive-behavioral counseling
    Skill #2: Considering court action
    Skill #3: Obtaining court sanctions
    Skill #4: Crafting orders with future consequences
    Skill #5: Terminating the relationship

APPENDIX C
Common Issues of High-Conflict Clients For Attorneys and Staff

- Extremes of behavior
- Difficult relationships
- Preoccupied with own issues
- Chronically adversarial and blaming
- Views everyone as an enemy or an ally
- Rigid, similar responses to wide range of events
- Lying and/or distorting events
- Can be extremely appealing and charming
- Life-long problems
- Takes little or no responsibility for their problems
- Family members often protect them from consequences
- Legal problems are common

BORDERLINE PERSONALITY DISORDER

Common signs:

- Dramatic mood swings
- Impulsive, risk-taking and self-destructive behaviors
- Sudden and intense anger even at benign events
- Sometimes: suicidal, delusional, chemically dependent and violent

Common relationship issues with attorneys/staff:

- Preoccupation with fears of abandonment
- Unstable relationships, with extremes of idealization and devaluation
- Manipulative, attractive and seductive
- Pushing the limits
- Splitting attorney/staff against each other

Common coping methods:

- Consistent and reassuring contact with attorney
- Provide structure and limits to relationship
- Allow brief venting
- Empathize with their frustrations
- Avoid criticism and anger
- Educate and include when appropriate

NARCISSISTIC PERSONALITY DISORDER

Common signs:

- Preoccupied with himself or herself
- Arrogant, wants excessive admiration
- Manipulative, exploitative of others
- Lacks empathy
- Sometimes easily hurt and enraged, chemically dependent and violent

Common relationship issues with attorneys/staff:

- Manipulative, attractive and seductive
- Expects special treatment, exceptions to the rules
- Devalues and criticizes attorney
- Frequent suggestions and demands

Common coping methods:

- Reassuring their egos
- Provide structure and limits to relationship
- Allow brief venting
- Empathize with their frustrations
- Avoid direct criticism and anger
- Educate and include when appropriate
- Explain how it could be worse

ANTISOCIAL PERSONALITY DISORDER

Common signs:

- Repeatedly breaks major rules of society
- Repeatedly cons and deceives others
- Irritable and aggressive
- Cold, lack of empathy, lack of remorse, violent

Common relationship issues with attorneys/staff:

- Manipulative, attractive and seductive
- Reckless, continually creating new problems
- Tricks and challenges attorney
- Impulsive and uncooperative with planning
- Projection of their own thinking or behavior onto attorney
- Irresponsible, fails to honor financial obligations

Common coping methods:

- Remain skeptical and cautious
- Get help from family members
- Provide structure and limits to relationship
- Allow brief venting
- Empathize with their frustrations
- Educate about consequences of their behaviors

THE ENABLERS
(Some Family, Friends and Professionals)

Common characteristics:

- Compulsive efforts to protect difficult client
- Anger and frustration with difficult client
- Frequent threats to withdraw from helping client
- May abandon client
- May have own personality disorder

Common relationship issues with attorneys/staff:

- Desire to be close friends with attorney
- Efforts to direct and control the legal case
- Efforts to explain and justify client's behavior
- Obsessive need to talk to relieve guilt and anxiety about client

Common coping methods:

- Provide structure and limits to relationship
- Allow brief venting
- Empathize with their frustrations
- Avoid criticism and anger
- Educate and include when appropriate

APPENDIX D
Identifying and Managing High-Conflict Personalities

Borderline	Narcissistic	Antisocial	Histrionic
Unconscious Drive			
Fear of being abandoned	Fear of being inferior	Fear of being dominated	Fear of being neglected
Constant Over-Compensating Behaviors			
Frequent anger, manipulation, efforts to control others	Self-absorbed, bragging, shows disdain for others	Dominating, manipulating, controlling, deceiving	Attention-seeking, drama, emotionalism
Bonding			
Reassurance, arms-length, consistency, avoid excessive flattery	Recognize strengths, avoid confronting weaknesses	Be wary of false charm and false allegations about others	Empathy with person, not dramatics
Structure			
Provide security with clear relationship boundaries	Provide tasks, use strengths, share credit for successes	Avoid doing favors, focus on goals and good behavior	Keep focusing on tasks, encourage use of own skills
Reality Testing			
Avoid great expectations, avoid jumping to conclusions	Reduce expectations of easy success and need to be special	Expect lying, corroborate information, see consequences	Find out about real abilities, encourage self-sufficiency
Consequences (restraining orders; possible jail time)			
Skills training in regulating emotions, penalties for false statements	Cognitive therapy, penalties for false statements	Group program for abusers, penalties for false statements	Cognitive therapy, penalties for false statements

APPENDIX E

Handout for new clients:

Before You Go To Family Court

Make sure you have realistic expectations: In family court, the judge will never really know what is going on in your case. The family court's job is to decide narrow legal issues based on limited permissible evidence. Hearings are mostly short and to the point. In real life, family court is not like most court cases on television or the movies—or even the news. Trials are rare, as most cases are resolved by hearings and/or settlement by agreement of the parties—often with the help of knowledgeable attorneys.

Do not expect validation or vindication: The judge does not decide your character as a person—or who has been "all good" or "all bad." In family court, it is assumed that both parties have contributed to the breakup of the family and that it is not a matter of "fault," but of "irreconcilable differences." Finding fault is against the principles of family court. Instead, family courts focus on problem solving. If the court finds that someone has acted improperly, then the focus is on what should be done now—such as modifying custody, visitation, support, property division, issuing restraining orders and, in rare cases, sanctions. Rather than punishment and blame, the court prefers to order drug treatment, domestic violence programs, individual counseling and parenting classes.

Avoid emotional reasoning: When we are upset our perceptions can be distorted temporarily or permanently. Our emotions may cause us to jump to conclusions, view things as "all or nothing," take innocent things personally, fill in "facts" that are not really true, unknowingly project our own behavior onto others, and unconsciously "split" people into absolute enemies and unrealistic allies. This happens at times to everyone, so check out your perceptions with others to make sure they have not been distorted by the emotional trauma of the divorce and related events. Many cases get stuck in court for years fighting over who was lying, when instead it was emotional reasoning which could have been avoided from the start.

Provide the court with useful information: The judge does not know your family or your issues, except for the information that is properly submitted to the court. Make sure to provide important information, even if it is embarrassing. The court cannot sense the behavior of each party. If you have an abusive spouse, the court needs sufficient information to make helpful decisions. If you hold back on important information, it may appear that abusive incidents never occurred and that you are exaggerating or making knowingly false statements. If you are accused of actions you did not take, the court will not know this information is inaccurate or false unless you inform the court.

Be careful about unverifiable information: The accuracy of the information you provide to the court is very important. Based solely on what you say in declarations or testimony in court, the judge may make serious orders regarding the other party, yourself, your children and your finances. If it later turns out that you made false or reckless statements—even if you were well-intentioned—there may be negative consequences, such as sanctions (financial penalties), loss of custody or restricted contact with your children.

Try to settle your case out of court: Today there are many alternatives to going to court which can be used at any time in your case, including Divorce Mediation, Collaborative Divorce, negotiated agreements with attorneys, and settlement conferences assisted by a temporary settlement judge. The expense for each of these is much less than for court hearings and prolonged disputes. You have nothing to lose, and you can still go to court afterward if you do not reach a full agreement. By trying an out-of-court settlement, you can limit animosity and protect your children from the tension of having parents in long, drawn-out court battles.

William Eddy 5/05

REFERENCES

"Annals of Finance: Marisa and Jeff," Calvin Trillin, The New Yorker, 2000.

Beck, A. and Freeman, A. *Cognitive Therapy of Personality Disorders*. New York, NY: The Guilford Press, 1990.

Bockian, N. *New Hope for People With Borderline Personality Disorder*. Roseville, CA: Prima Publishing, 2002.

Bramson, R. *Coping With Difficult People*. New York, NY: Dell Publishing, 1981.

Burns, D. *Feeling Good: The New Mood Therapy*. 1980.

Cavailoa, A. and Lavender, N. *Toxic Coworkers: How to Deal With Dysfunctional People on the Job*. Oakland, CA: New Harbinger, 2000.

Ceci, S. and Bruck, M. *Jeopardy in the Courtroom*. Washington, DC: American Psychological Association, 1995.

American Psychiatric Association: *Diagnostic and Statistical Manual of Mental Disorders*, Fourth Edition. Washington, DC, American Psychiatric Association, 1994.

American Psychiatric Association: *Diagnostic and Statistical Manual of Mental Disorders*, Fourth Edition, Text Revision. Washington, DC, American Psychiatric Association, 2000.

Dutton, D. *The Abusive Personality: Violence and Control in Intimate Relationships*. New York, NY: The Guilford Press, 1998.

Eddy, W. *Splitting: Protecting Yourself While Divorcing a Borderline or Narcissist*. Milwaukee, WI: Eggshells Press, 2004

Feinberg, R. and Greene, J. *The Intractable Client: Guidelines for Working With Personality Disorders in Family Law*. Family and Conciliation Courts Review 35: 351-365.

Fisher, R. and Ury, W. *Getting to Yes: Negotiating Agreement Without Giving In*. New York, NY: Penguin Books, 1981.

Ford, C. *Lies! Lies!! Lies!!! The Psychology of Deceit*. Washington, DC: American Psychiatric Association, 1996.

Johnston, J. and Campbell, L. *Impasses of Divorce: The Dynamics and Resolution of Family Conflict*. New York, NY: Simon & Schuster, 1988.

Kreisman, J. and Straus, H. *I Hate You – Don't Leave Me: Understanding the Borderline Personality*. New York, NY: Avon Books, 1989.

Lawson, C. *Understanding the Borderline Mother: Helping Her Children Transcend the Intense, Unpredictable, and Volatile Relationship*. Northvale, NJ: Jason Aronson, 2002.

Lewicki, R. et al. *Negotiation*. Boston, MA: Richard Irwin, Inc., 1994.

Linehan, M. *Cognitive-Behavioral Treatment of Borderline Personality Disorder*. New York, NY: The Guilford Press, 1993.

Mason, P. and Kreger, R. *Stop Walking on Eggshells: Taking Your Life Back When Someone You Care About Has Borderline Personality Disorder*. Oakland, CA: New Harbinger, 1998.

Markam, U. *How to Deal With Difficult People*. London, UK: Harper Collins, 1993.

McKay, M. et al. *When Anger Hurts: Quieting the Storm Within*. Oakland, CA: New Harbinger, 1989.

Millon, T. *Disorders of Personality: DSM-IV and Beyond*. New York, NY: Wiley & Sons, 1996.

Ney, T. *True and False Allegations of Child Sexual Abuse: Assessment and Case Management*. New York, NY: Brunner/Mazel, 1995.

Portnoy, S. *The Family Lawyer's Guide to Building Successful Client Relationships*. Chicago, IL: American Bar Association, 2000.

Rieke, R. and Stutman, R. *Communication in Legal Advocacy*. Columbia, SC: University of South Carolina Press, 1990.

Schreier, L. *Emotional Intelligence and Mediation Training*. Conflict Resolution Quarterly 20: 99-119.

Young, J. *Cognitive Therapy for Personality Disorders: A Schema-Focused Approach*. Sarasota, FL: Professional Resource Press, 1994.

ABOUT THE AUTHOR

William A. ("Bill") Eddy is Senior Family Mediator at the National Conflict Resolution Center in San Diego, California. He is a Certified Family Law Specialist in California with twelve years' experience representing clients in family court, and a Licensed Clinical Social Worker with twelve years' experience providing therapy to children, adults, couples and families in psychiatric hospitals and outpatient clinics.

He has taught Negotiation and Mediation at the University of San Diego School of Law, and he provides seminars on mental health issues for attorneys, judges and mediators, and seminars on law and ethics for mental health professionals. His articles have appeared in national law and counseling journals. He is the author of several books, including *SPLITTING: Protecting Yourself While Divorcing a Borderline or Narcissist* (Eggshells Press, 2004). Bill has become an international speaker and consultant on the subject of high-conflict personalities, providing seminars to attorneys, mediators, collaborative law professionals, judges, ombudspersons and others.

He obtained his law degree in 1992 from the University of San Diego, a Master of Social Work degree in 1981 from San Diego State University, and a Bachelors degree in Psychology in 1970 from Case Western Reserve University. He began his career as a youth social worker in a changing neighborhood in New York City and first became involved in mediation in 1975 in San Diego. He considers conflict resolution the theme of his varied career.